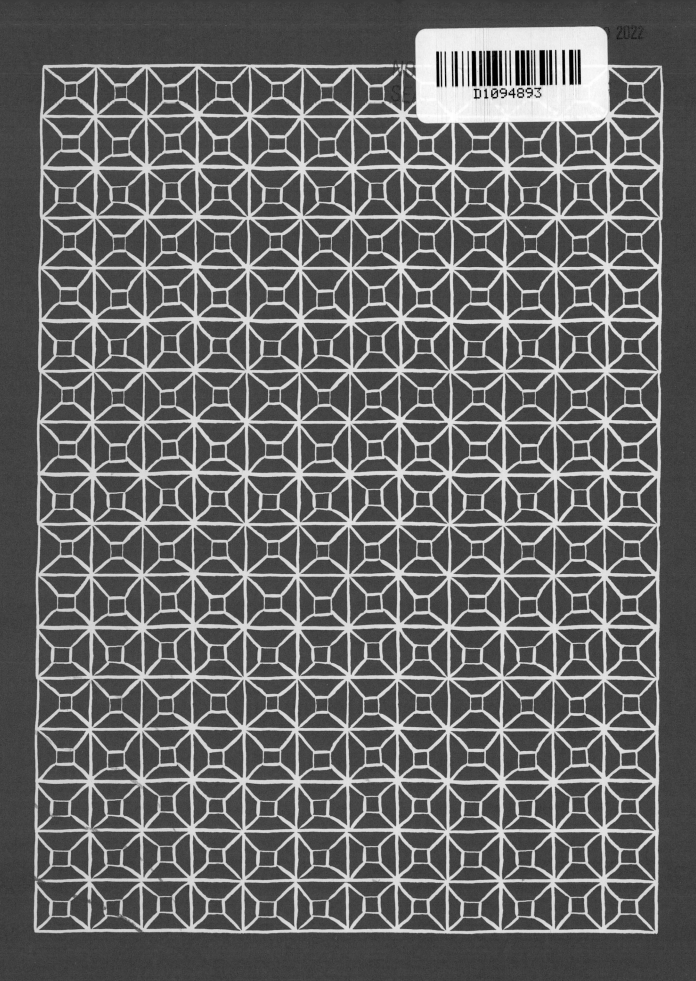

MAN IN FURS

FROM DIVINE PUNISHMENT
TO PUNISHMENT DIVINE

CATHERINE SAUVAT

•

ANNE SIMON

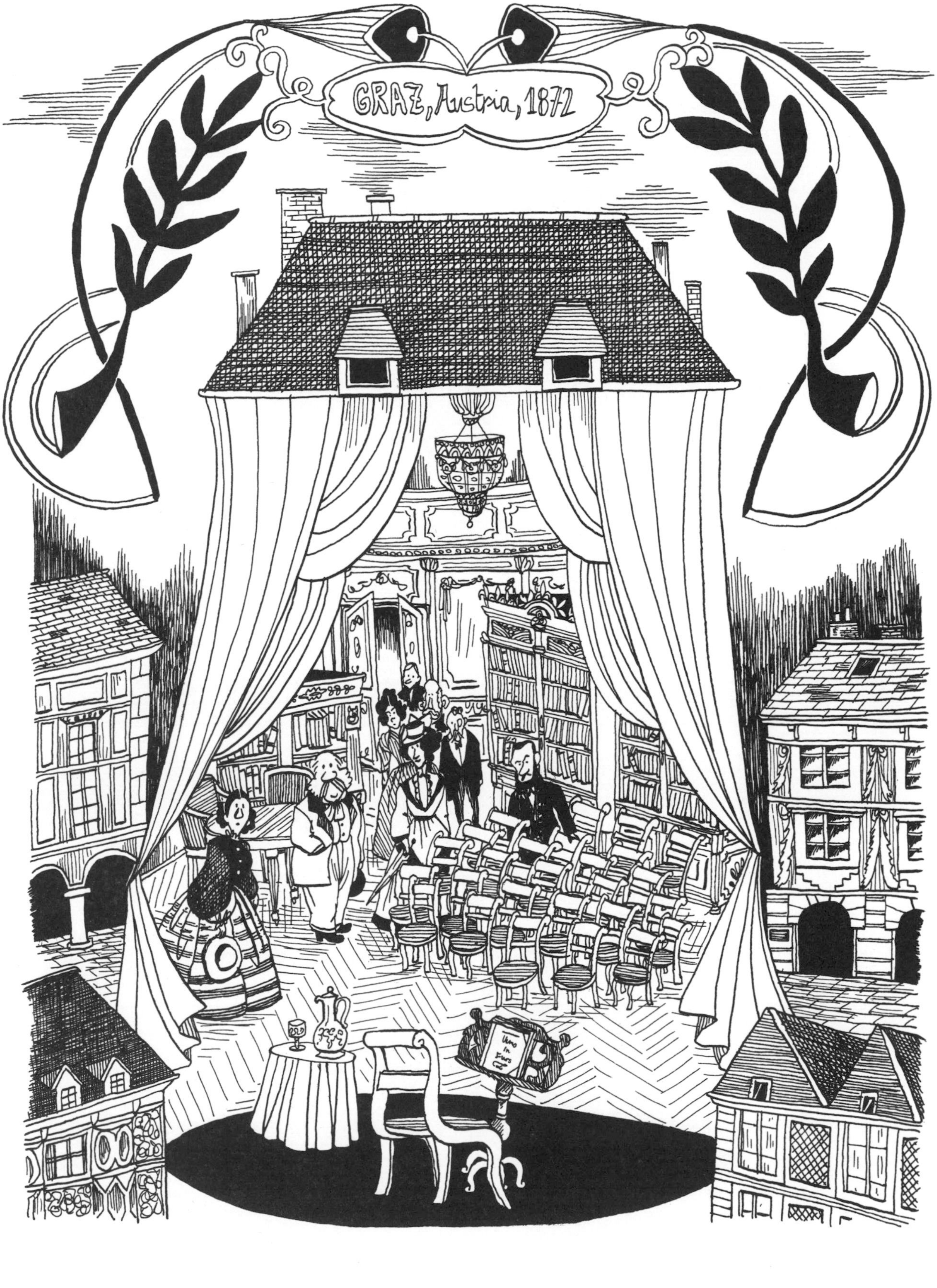
GRAZ, Austria, 1872

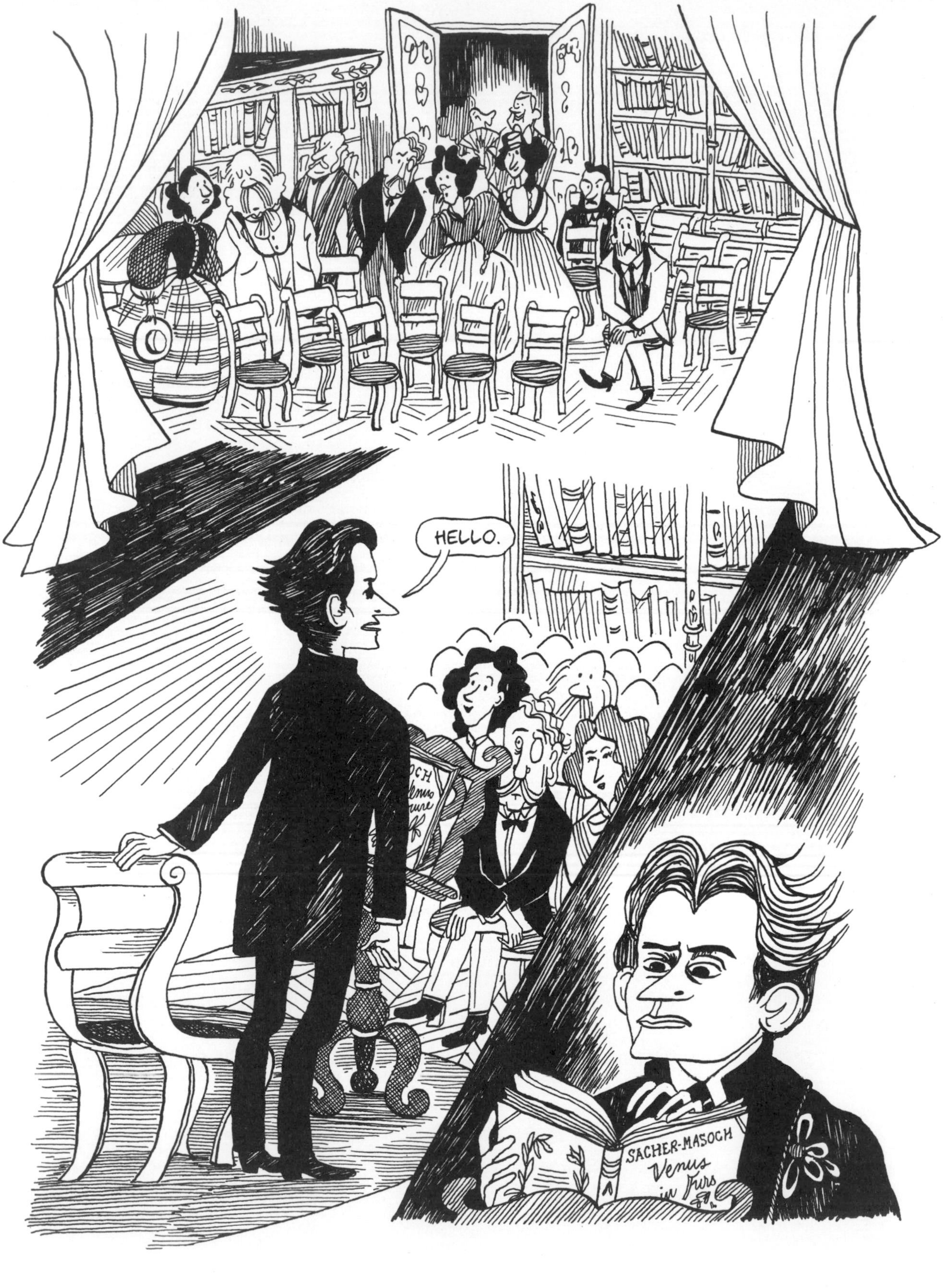
HELLO.
SACHER-MASOCH
Venus
in Furs

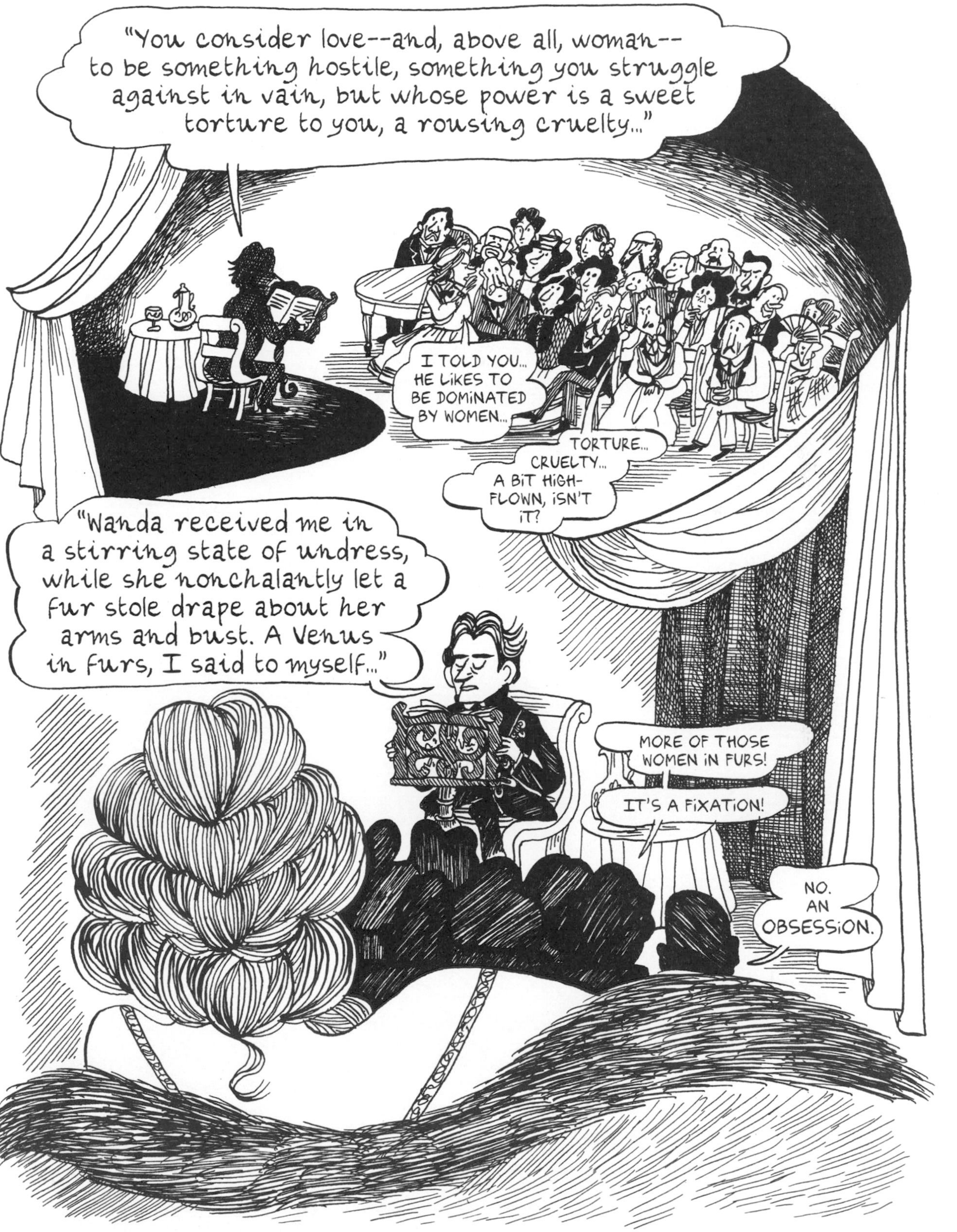
"You consider love--and, above all, woman--to be something hostile, something you struggle against in vain, but whose power is a sweet torture to you, a rousing cruelty..."
I TOLD YOU... HE LIKES TO BE DOMINATED BY WOMEN...
TORTURE... CRUELTY... A BIT HIGH-FLOWN, ISN'T IT?
"Wanda received me in a stirring state of undress, while she nonchalantly let a fur stole drape about her arms and bust. A Venus in furs, I said to myself..."
MORE OF THOSE WOMEN IN FURS!
IT'S A FIXATION!
NO. AN OBSESSION.

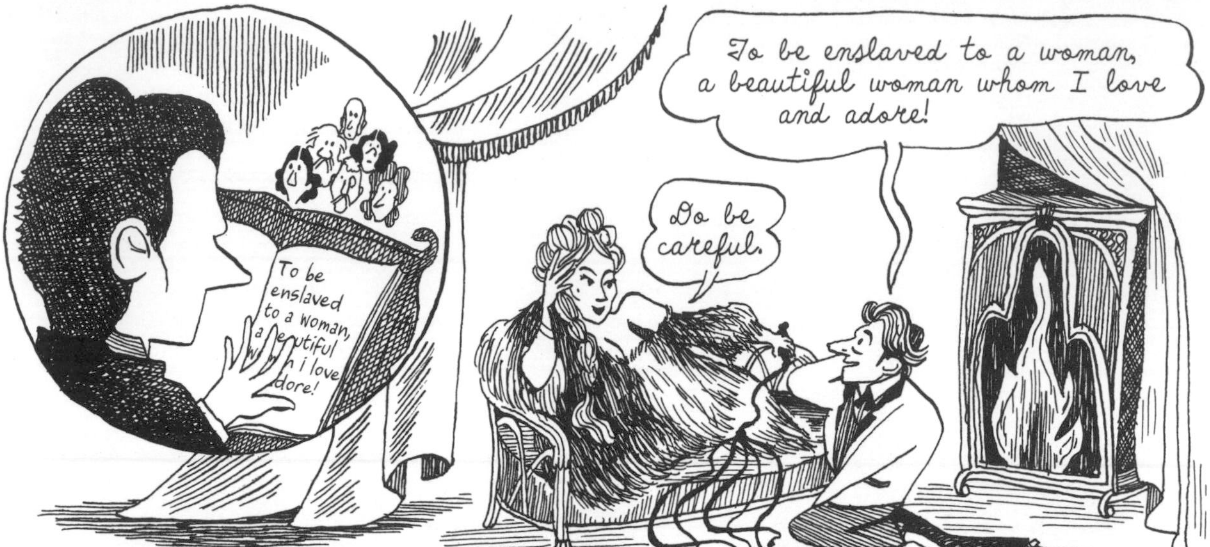
To be enslaved to a woman, a beautiful woman whom I love and adore!
Do be careful.

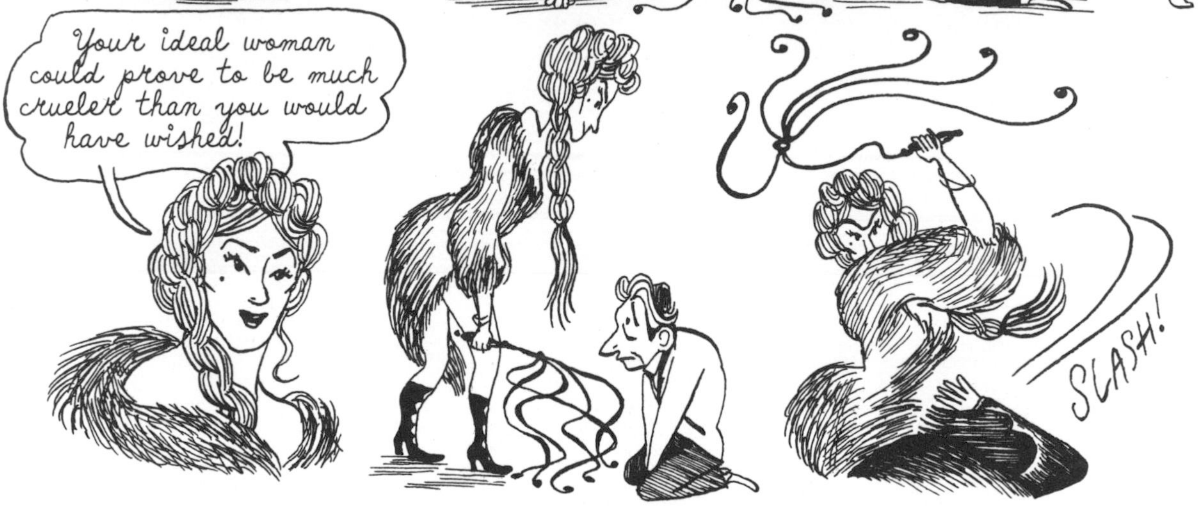
Your ideal woman could prove to be much crueler than you would have wished!
SLASH!

"I relished my suffering, for it came from the woman I adored, the woman for whom I was ready to give my life at any moment."

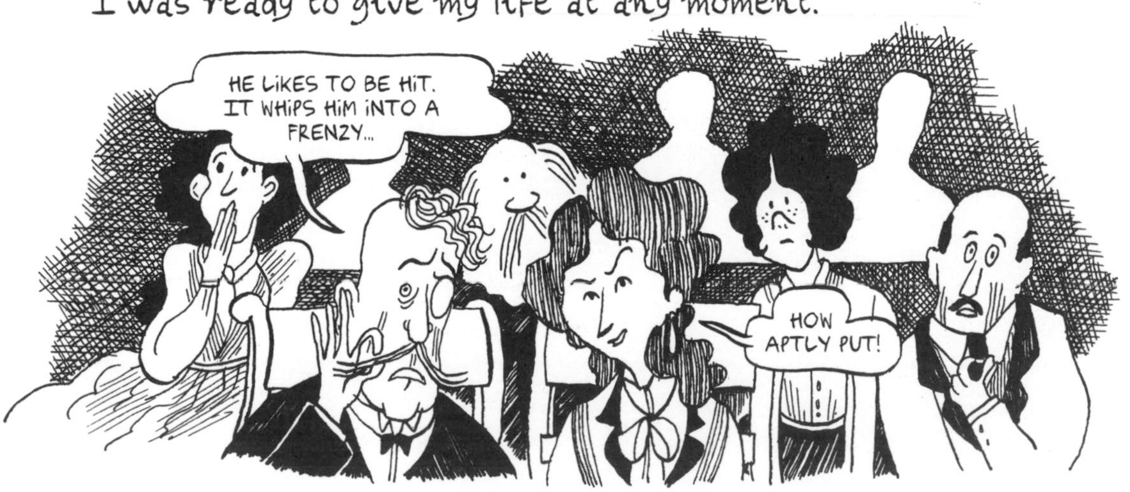
HE LIKES TO BE HIT. IT WHIPS HIM INTO A FRENZY...
HOW APTLY PUT!

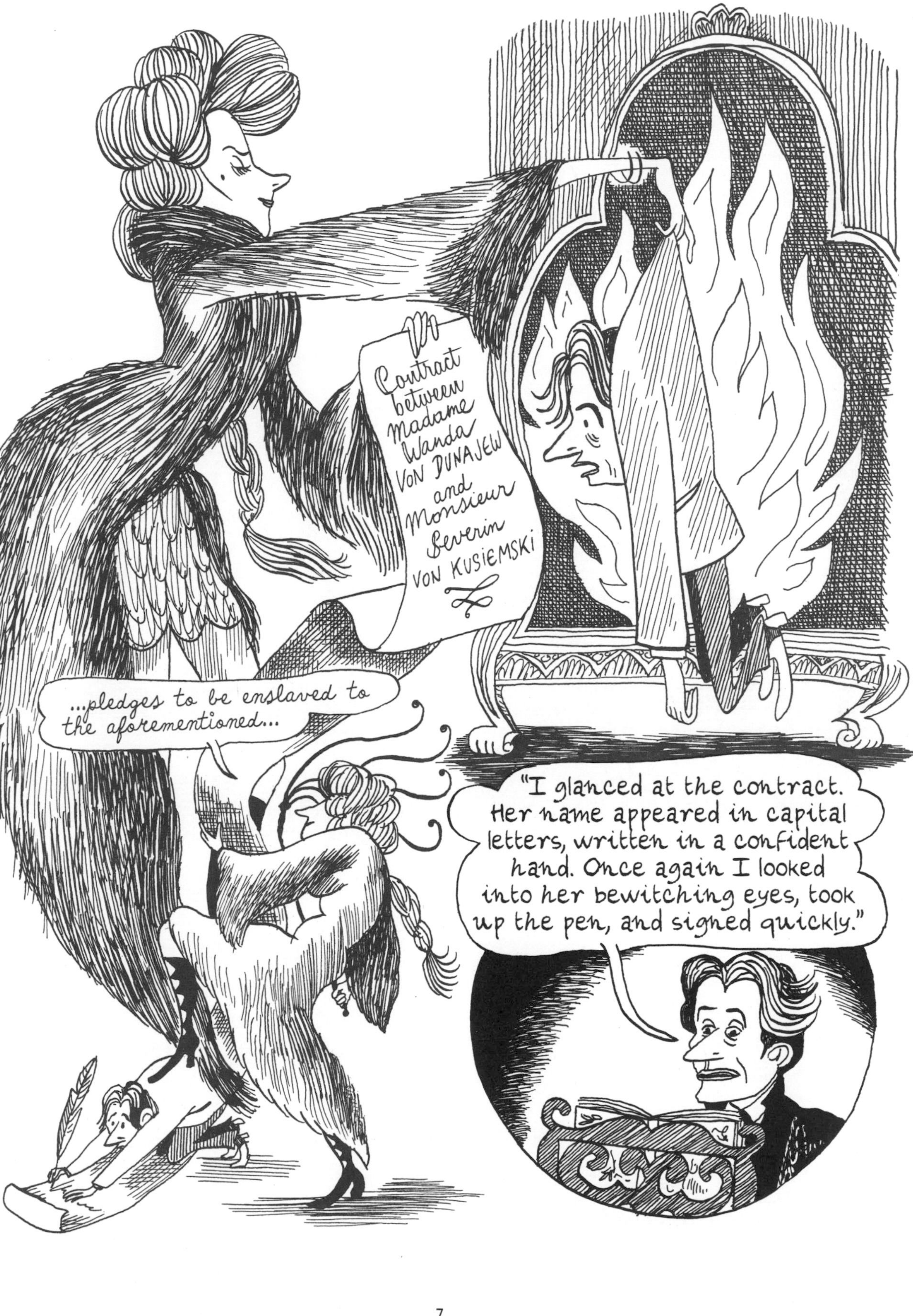
Contract between Madame Wanda VON DUNAJEW and Monsieur Severin VON KUSIEMSKI
...pledges to be enslaved to the aforementioned...
"I glanced at the contract. Her name appeared in capital letters, written in a confident hand. Once again I looked into her bewitching eyes, took up the pen, and signed quickly."

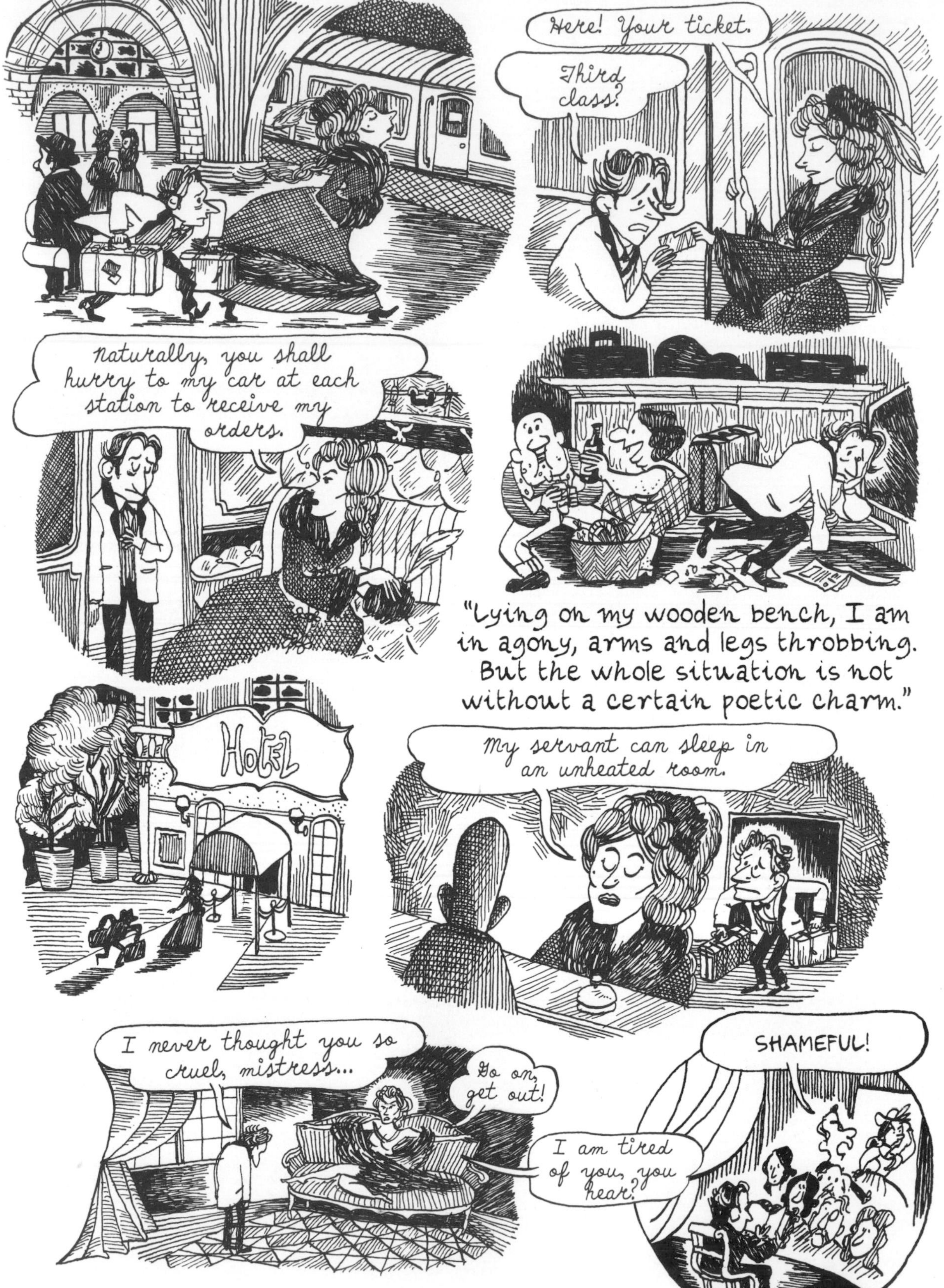
Here! Your ticket.
Third class?
naturally, you shall hurry to my car at each station to receive my orders.
"Lying on my wooden bench, I am in agony, arms and legs throbbing. But the whole situation is not without a certain poetic charm."
HOTEL
My servant can sleep in an unheated room.
I never thought you so cruel, mistress...
Go on, get out!
I am tired of you, you hear?
SHAMEFUL!

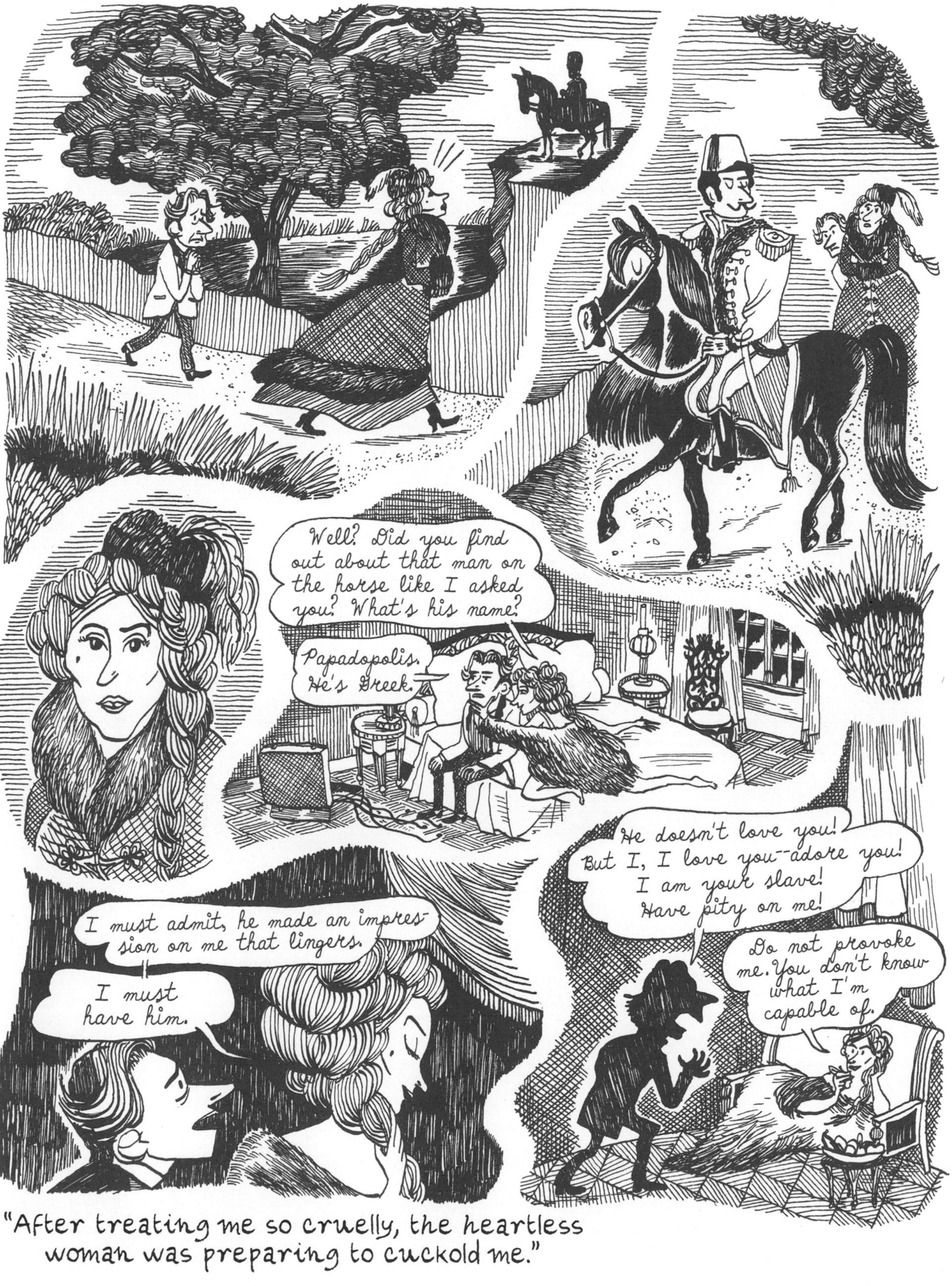
Well? Did you find out about that man on the horse like I asked you? What's his name?
Papadopolis. He's Greek.
I must admit, he made an impression on me that lingers.
I must have him.
He doesn't love you! But I, I love you--adore you! I am your slave! Have pity on me!
Do not provoke me. You don't know what I'm capable of.

"After treating me so cruelly, the heartless woman was preparing to cuckold me."

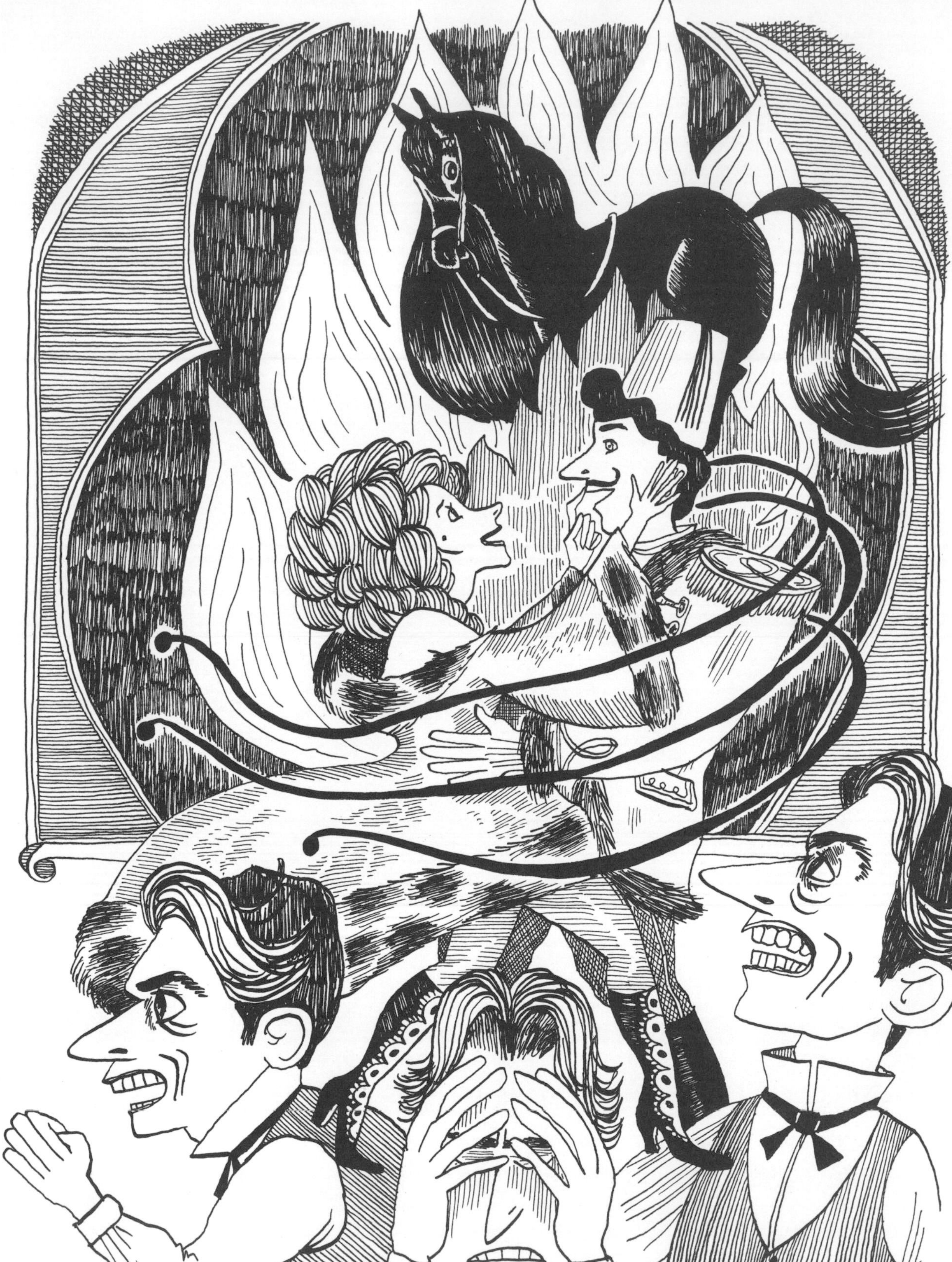

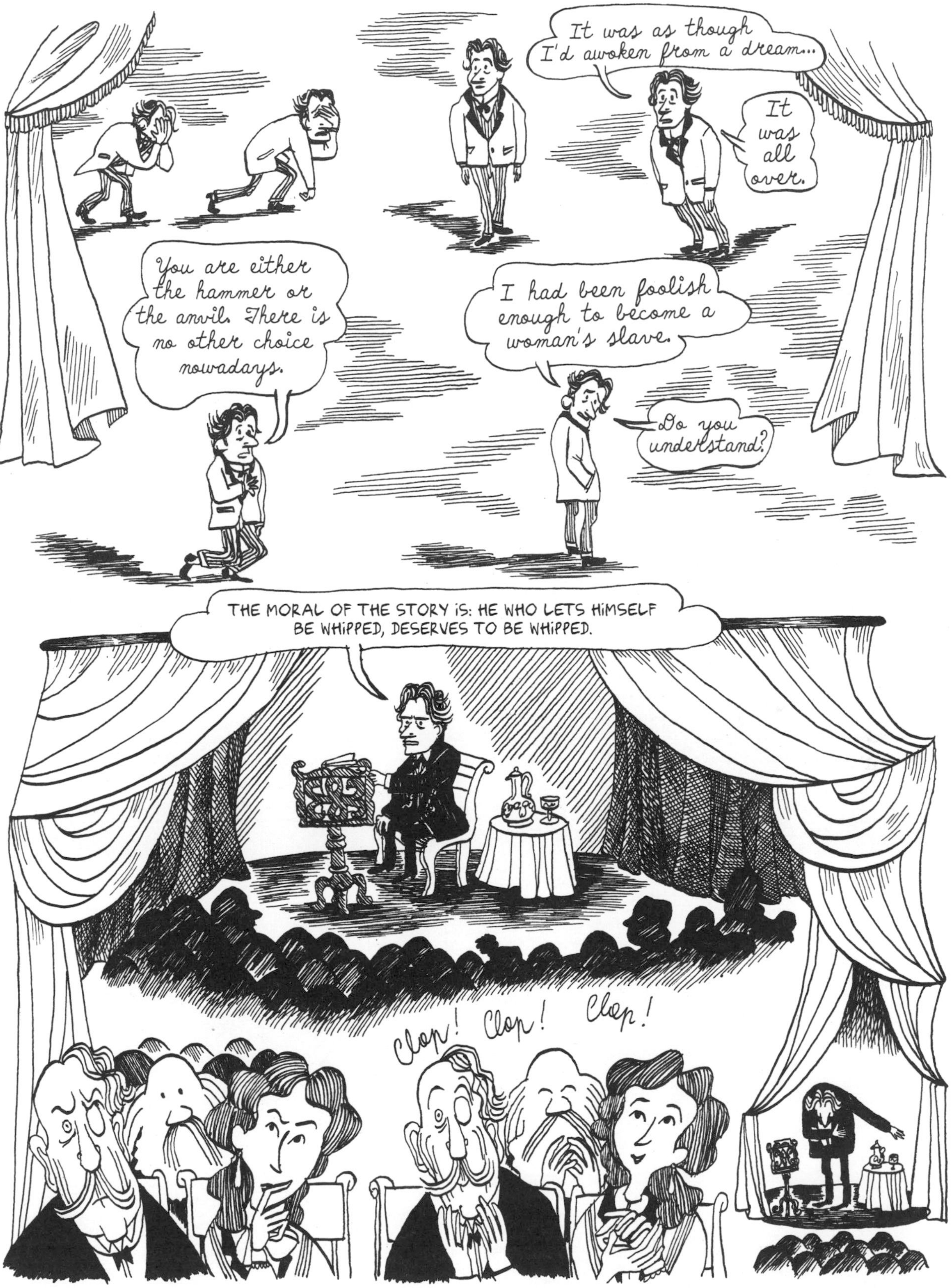
It was as though I'd awoken from a dream...
It was all over.
You are either the hammer or the anvil. There is no other choice nowadays.
I had been foolish enough to become a woman's slave.
Do you understand?
THE MORAL OF THE STORY IS: HE WHO LETS HIMSELF BE WHIPPED, DESERVES TO BE WHIPPED.
Clap! Clap! Clap!

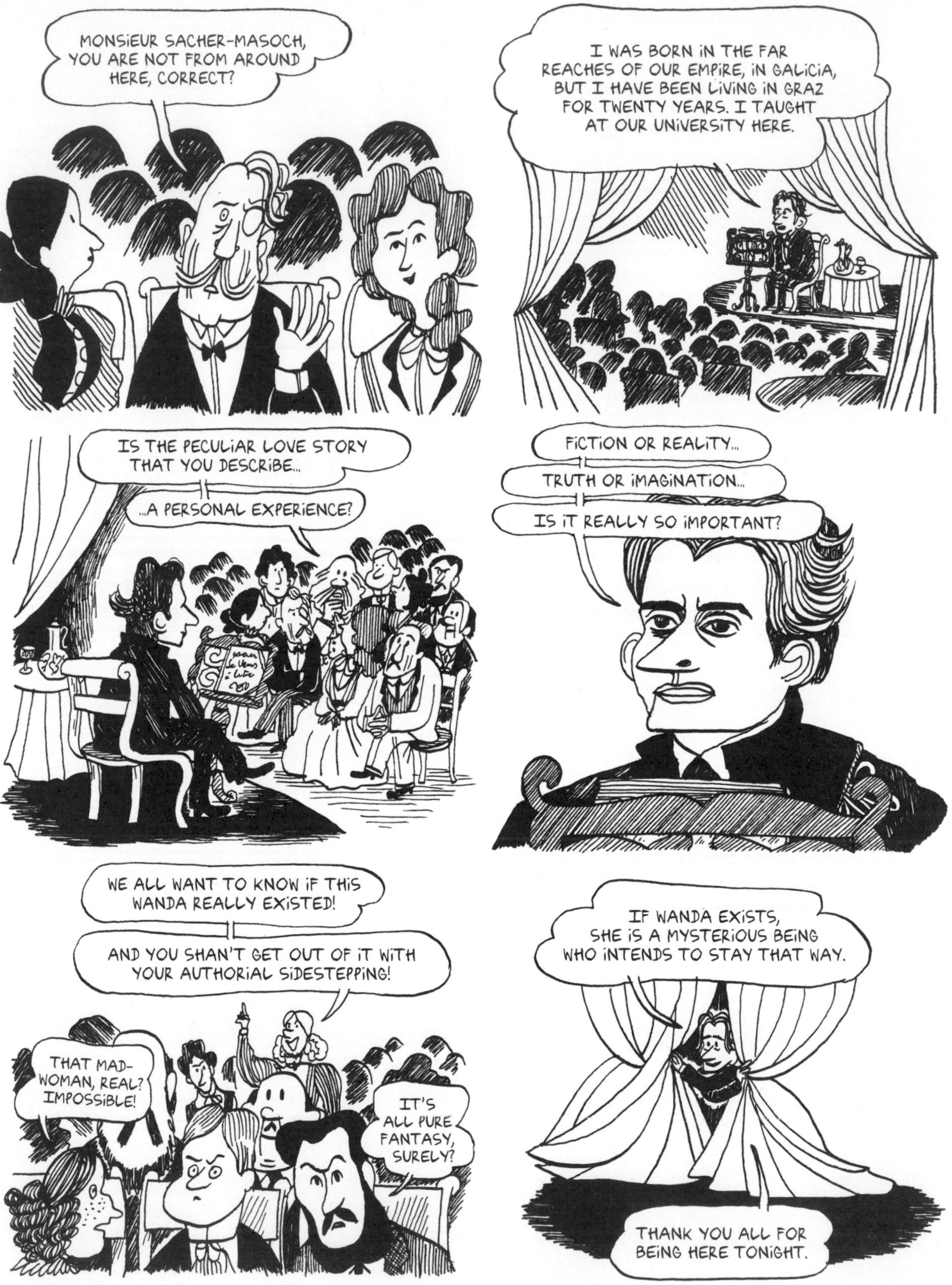
MONSIEUR SACHER-MASOCH, YOU ARE NOT FROM AROUND HERE, CORRECT?
I WAS BORN IN THE FAR REACHES OF OUR EMPIRE, IN GALICIA, BUT I HAVE BEEN LIVING IN GRAZ FOR TWENTY YEARS. I TAUGHT AT OUR UNIVERSITY HERE.
IS THE PECULIAR LOVE STORY THAT YOU DESCRIBE...
...A PERSONAL EXPERIENCE?
FICTION OR REALITY...
TRUTH OR IMAGINATION...
IS IT REALLY SO IMPORTANT?
WE ALL WANT TO KNOW IF THIS WANDA REALLY EXISTED!
AND YOU SHAN'T GET OUT OF IT WITH YOUR AUTHORIAL SIDESTEPPING!
THAT MAD-WOMAN, REAL? IMPOSSIBLE!
IT'S ALL PURE FANTASY, SURELY?
IF WANDA EXISTS, SHE IS A MYSTERIOUS BEING WHO INTENDS TO STAY THAT WAY.
THANK YOU ALL FOR BEING HERE TONIGHT.

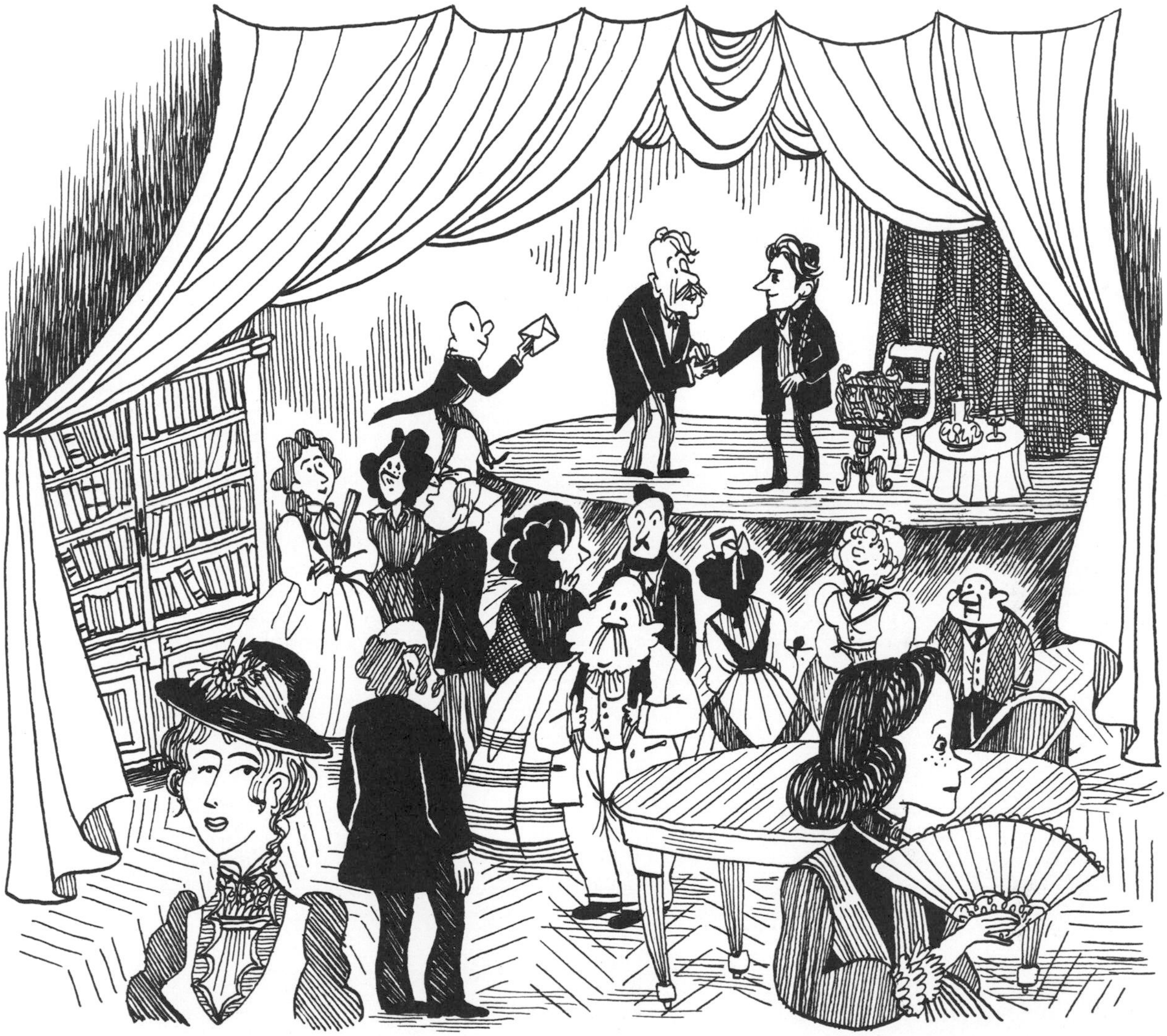

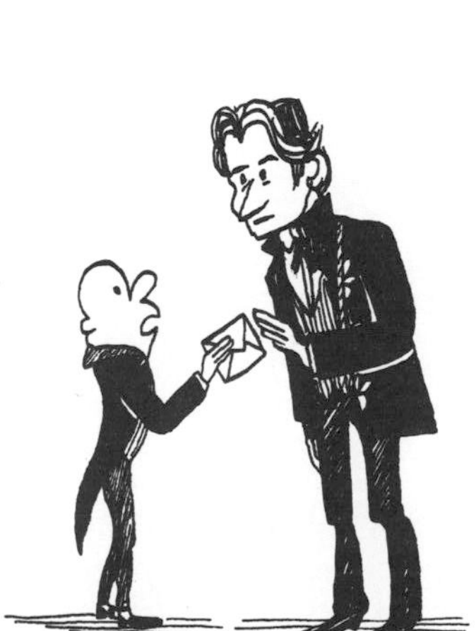

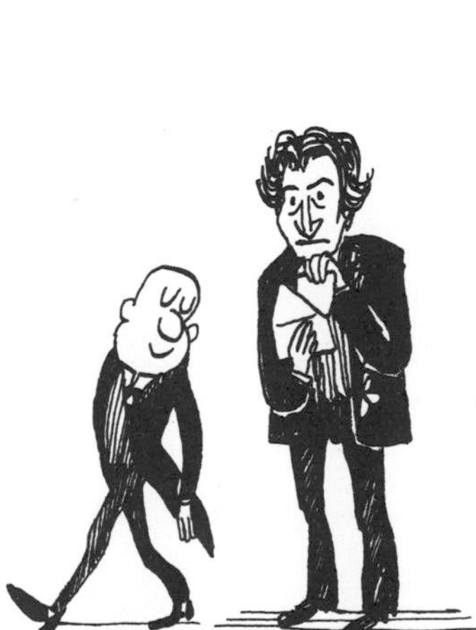

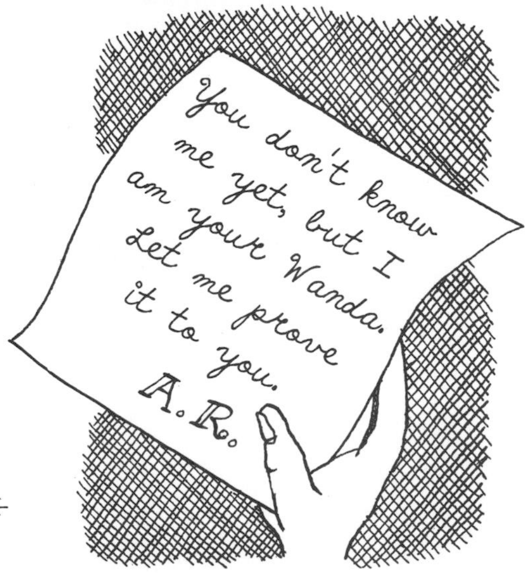
You don't know me yet, but I am your Wanda. Let me prove it to you.
A. R.

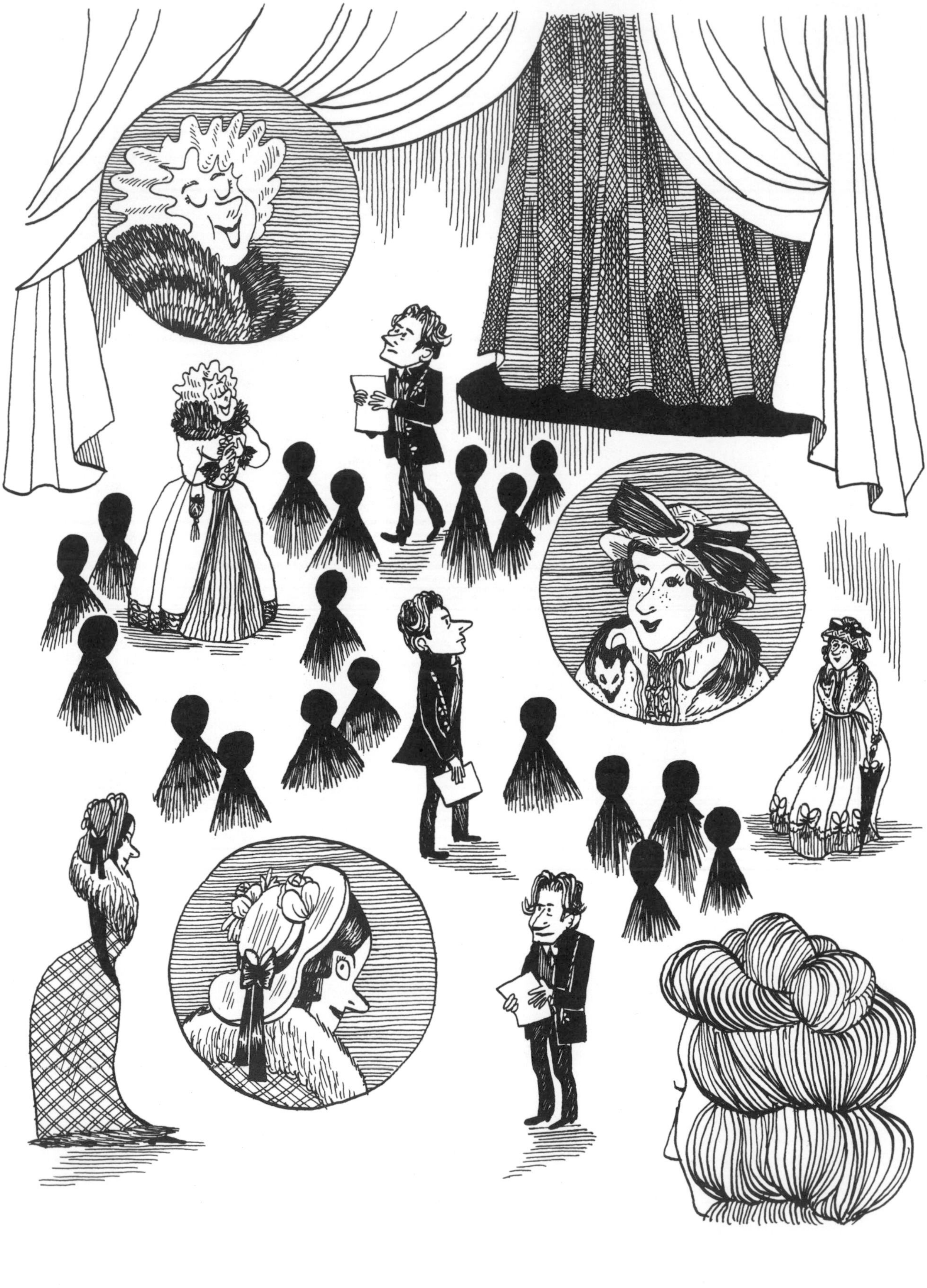

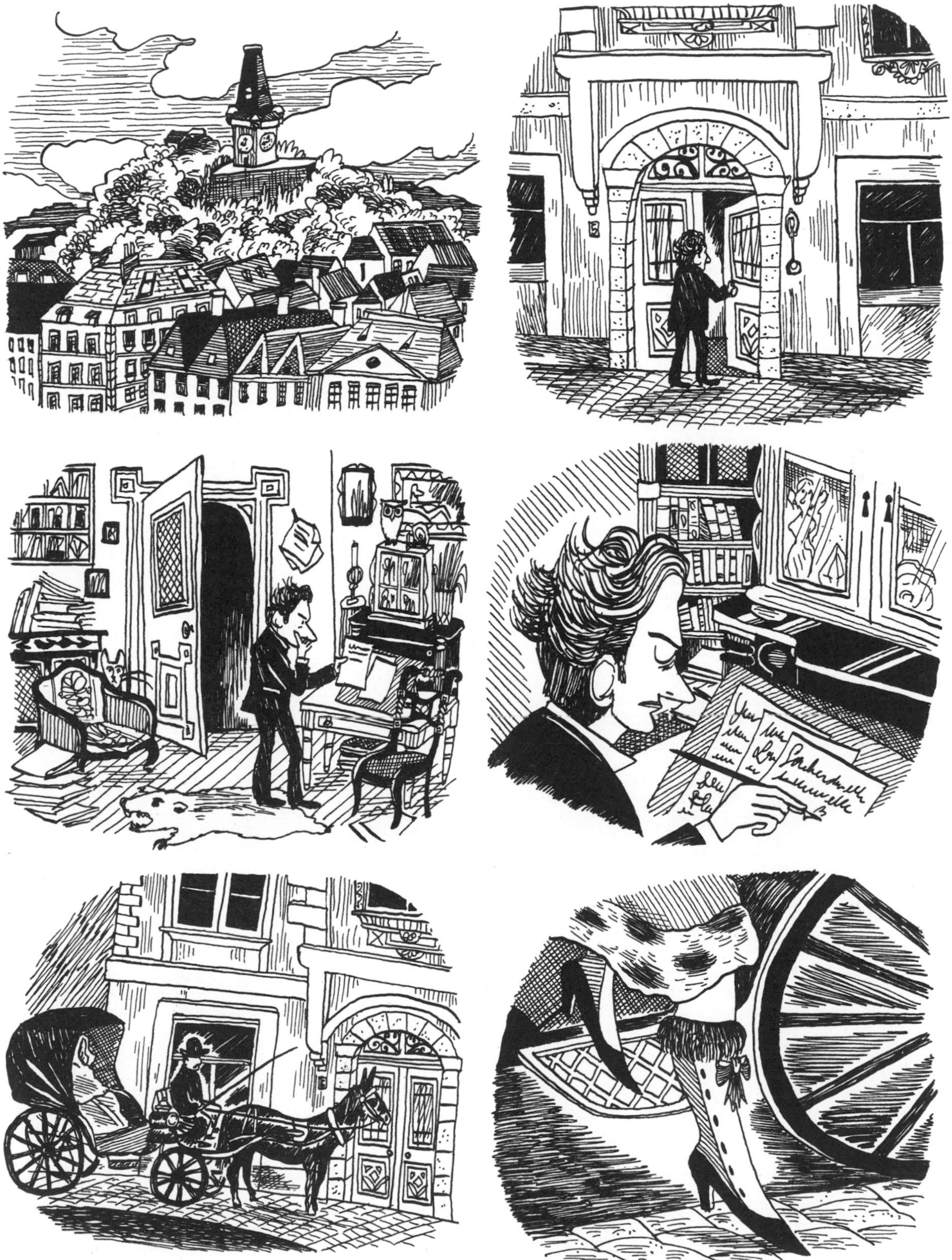

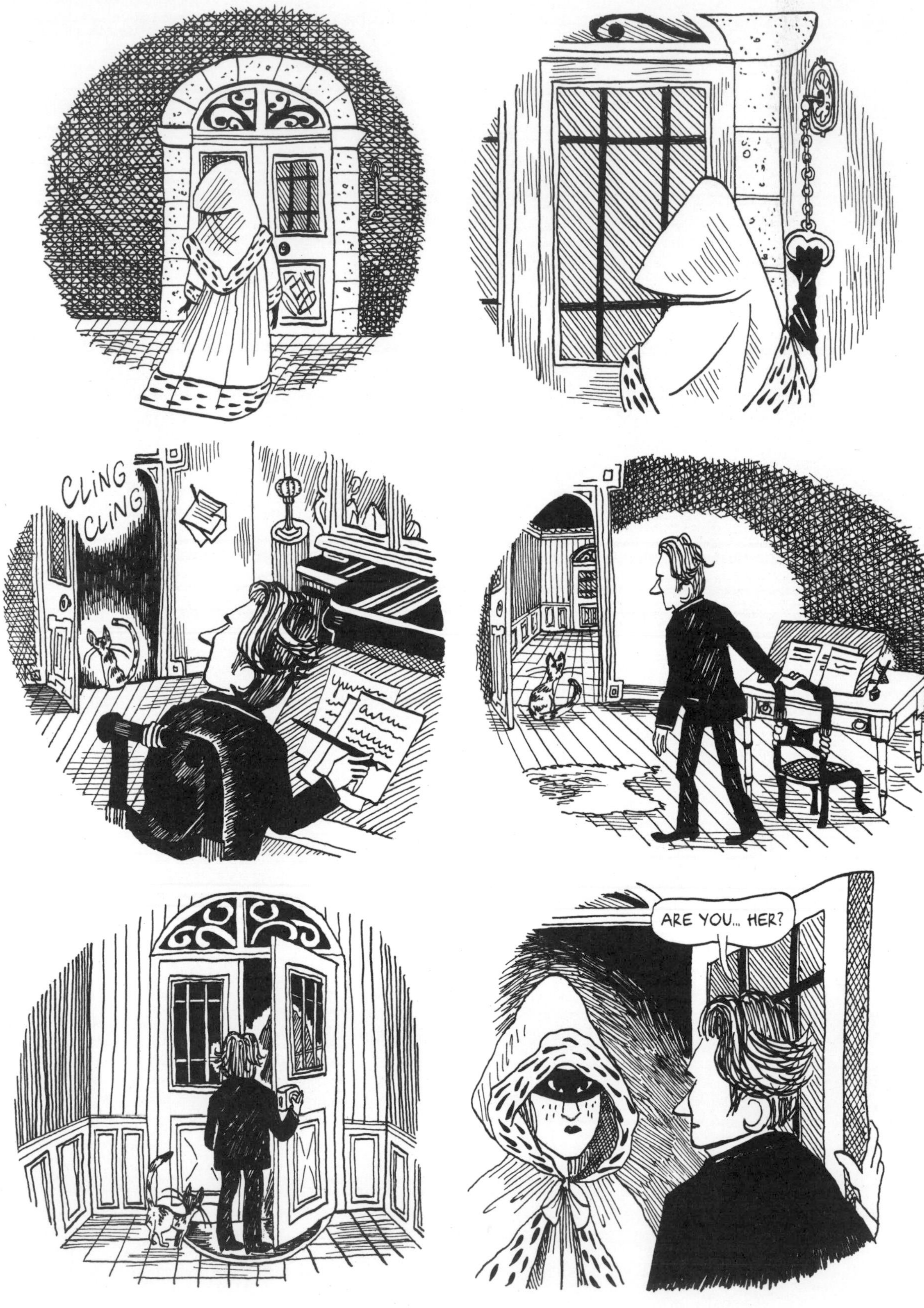
CLING
CLING
ARE YOU... HER?

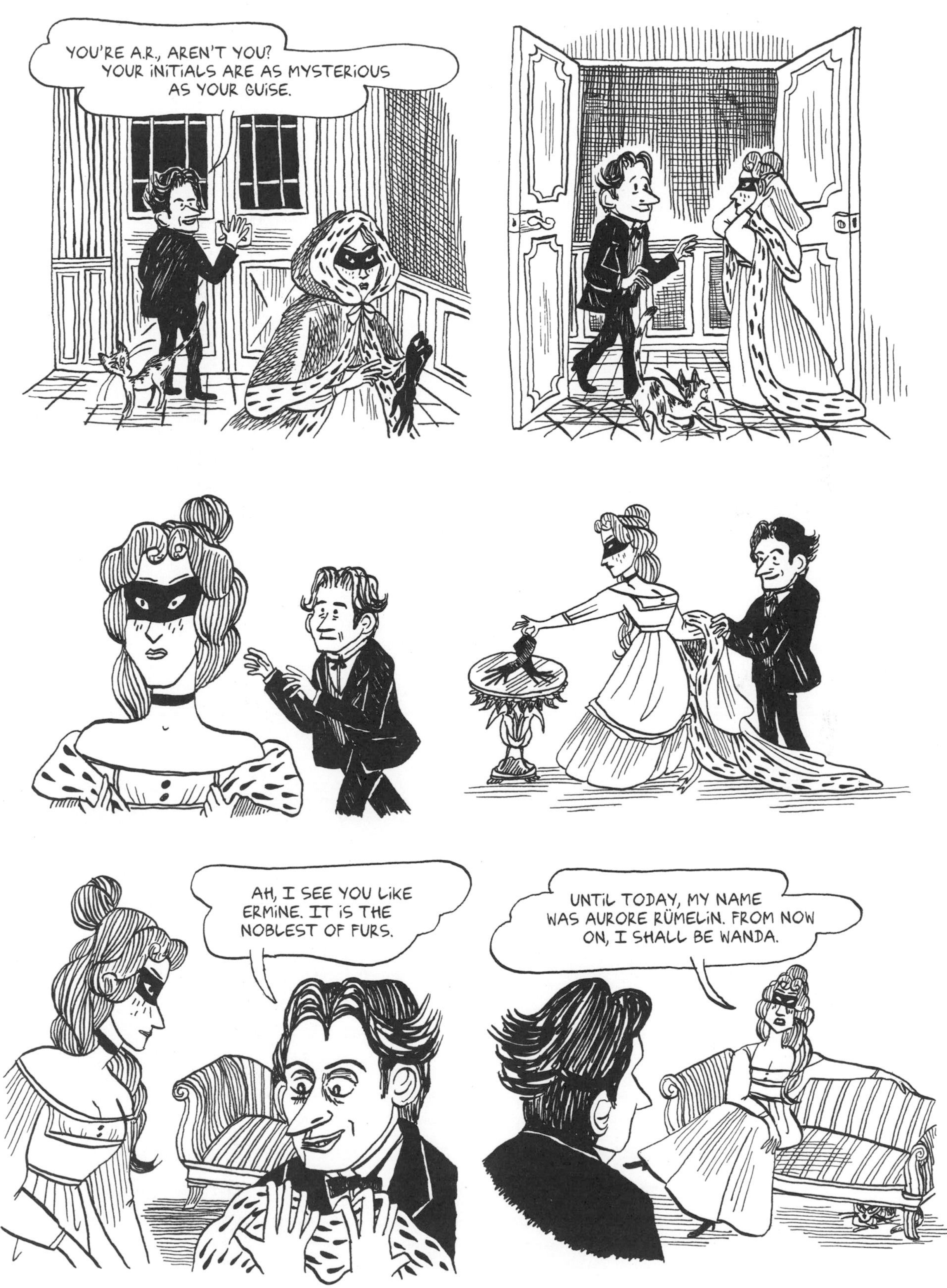
YOU'RE A.R., AREN'T YOU? YOUR INITIALS ARE AS MYSTERIOUS AS YOUR GUISE.
AH, I SEE YOU LIKE ERMINE. IT IS THE NOBLEST OF FURS.
UNTIL TODAY, MY NAME WAS AURORE RÜMELIN. FROM NOW ON, I SHALL BE WANDA.

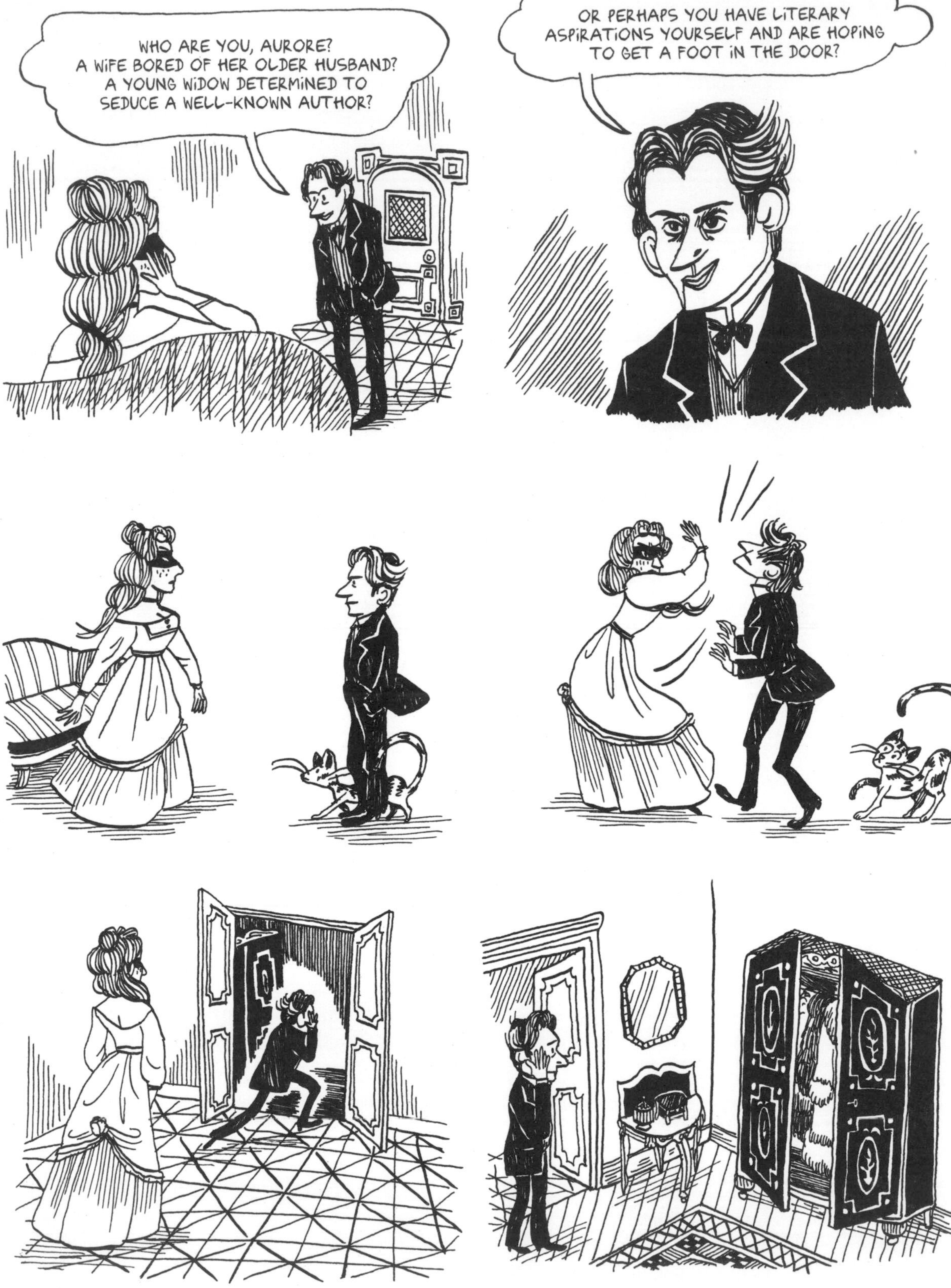
WHO ARE YOU, AURORE? A WIFE BORED OF HER OLDER HUSBAND? A YOUNG WIDOW DETERMINED TO SEDUCE A WELL-KNOWN AUTHOR?
OR PERHAPS YOU HAVE LITERARY ASPIRATIONS YOURSELF AND ARE HOPING TO GET A FOOT IN THE DOOR?

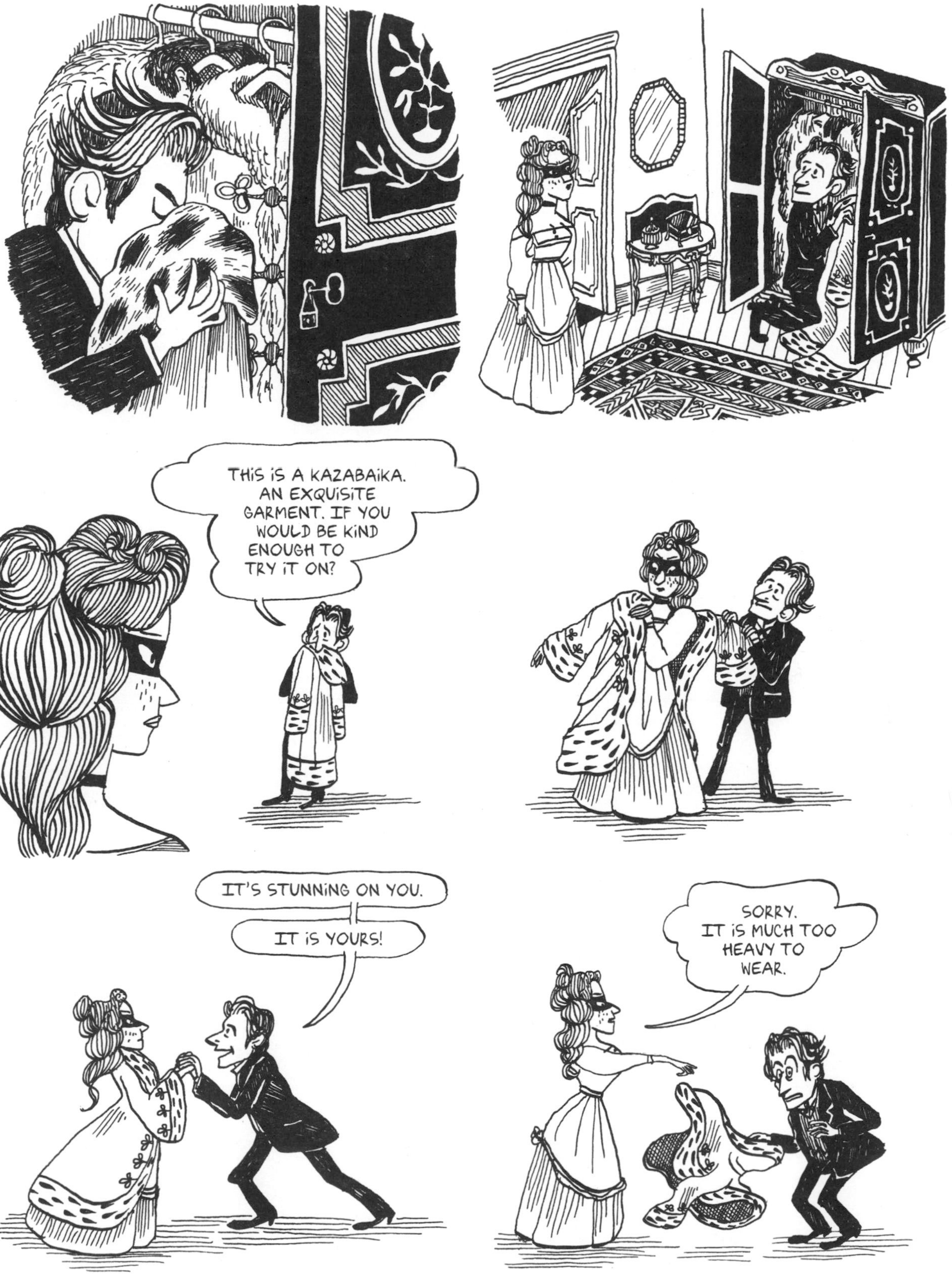
THIS iS A KAZABAIKA. AN EXQUiSiTE GARMENT. IF YOU WOULD BE KiND ENOUGH TO TRY iT ON?
IT'S STUNNiNG ON YOU.
IT iS YOURS!
SORRY. IT iS MUCH TOO HEAVY TO WEAR.

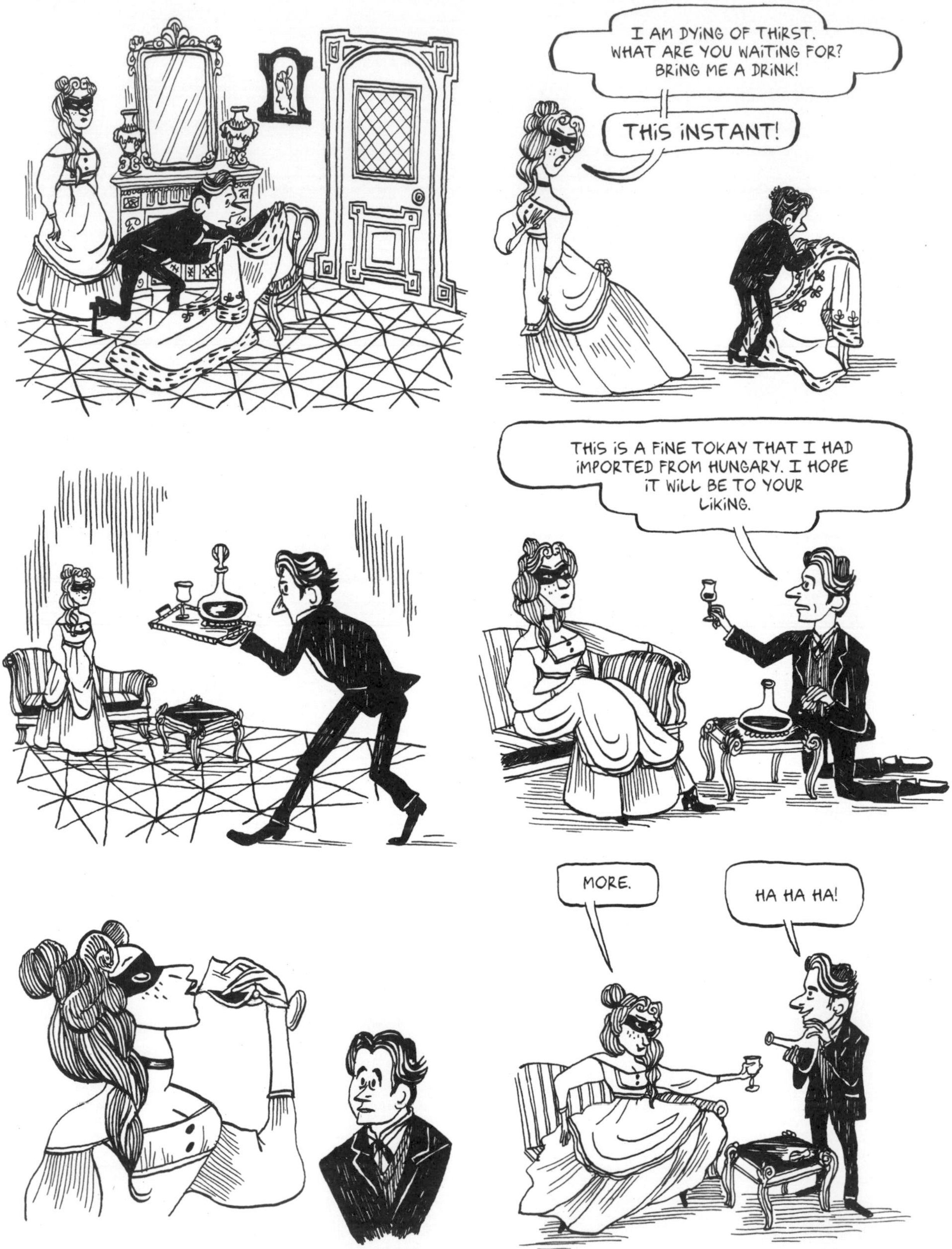
I AM DYING OF THIRST. WHAT ARE YOU WAITING FOR? BRING ME A DRINK!
THIS INSTANT!
THIS IS A FINE TOKAY THAT I HAD IMPORTED FROM HUNGARY. I HOPE IT WILL BE TO YOUR LIKING.
MORE.
HA HA HA!

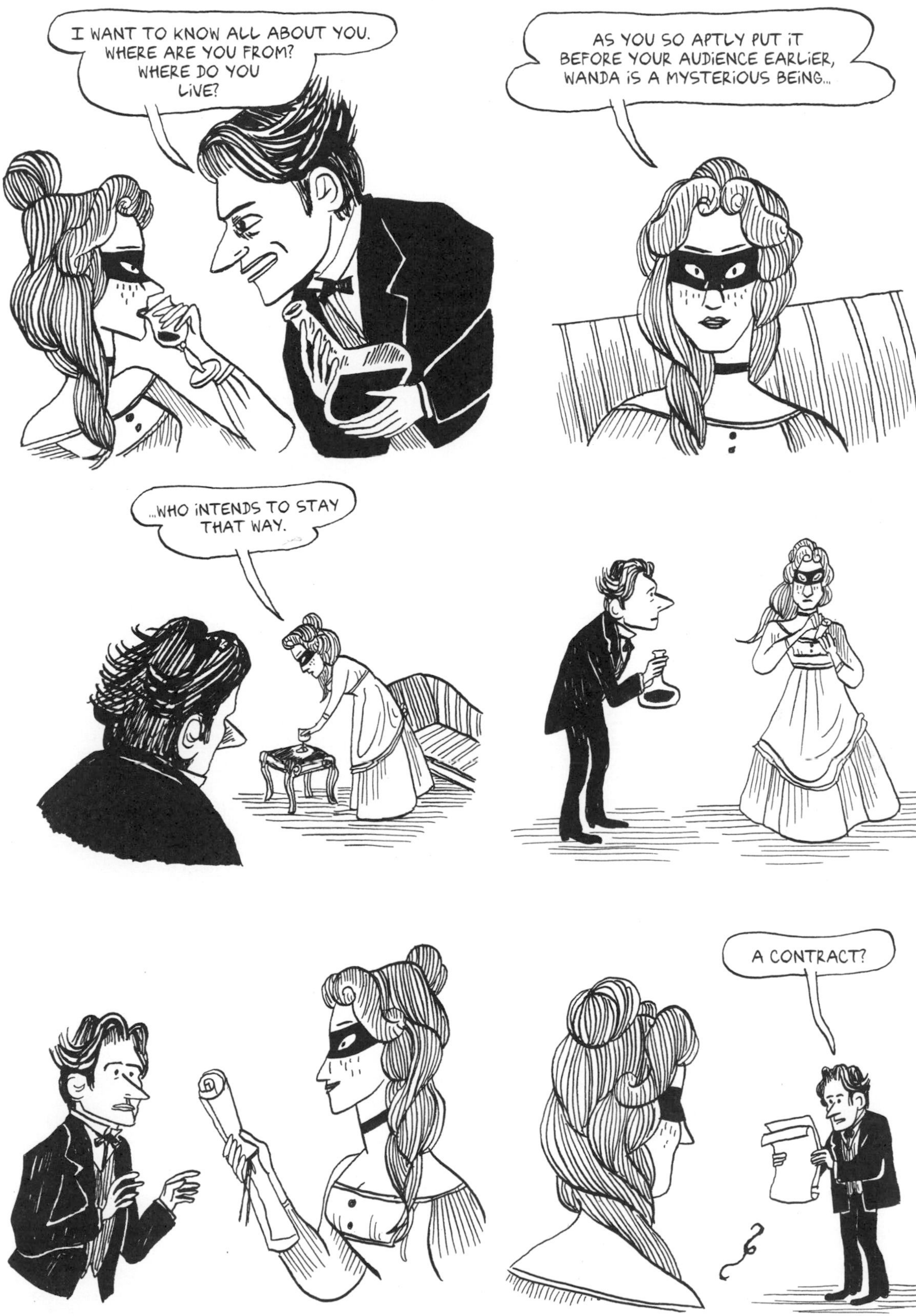
I WANT TO KNOW ALL ABOUT YOU. WHERE ARE YOU FROM? WHERE DO YOU LIVE?
AS YOU SO APTLY PUT IT BEFORE YOUR AUDIENCE EARLIER, WANDA IS A MYSTERIOUS BEING...
...WHO INTENDS TO STAY THAT WAY.
A CONTRACT?

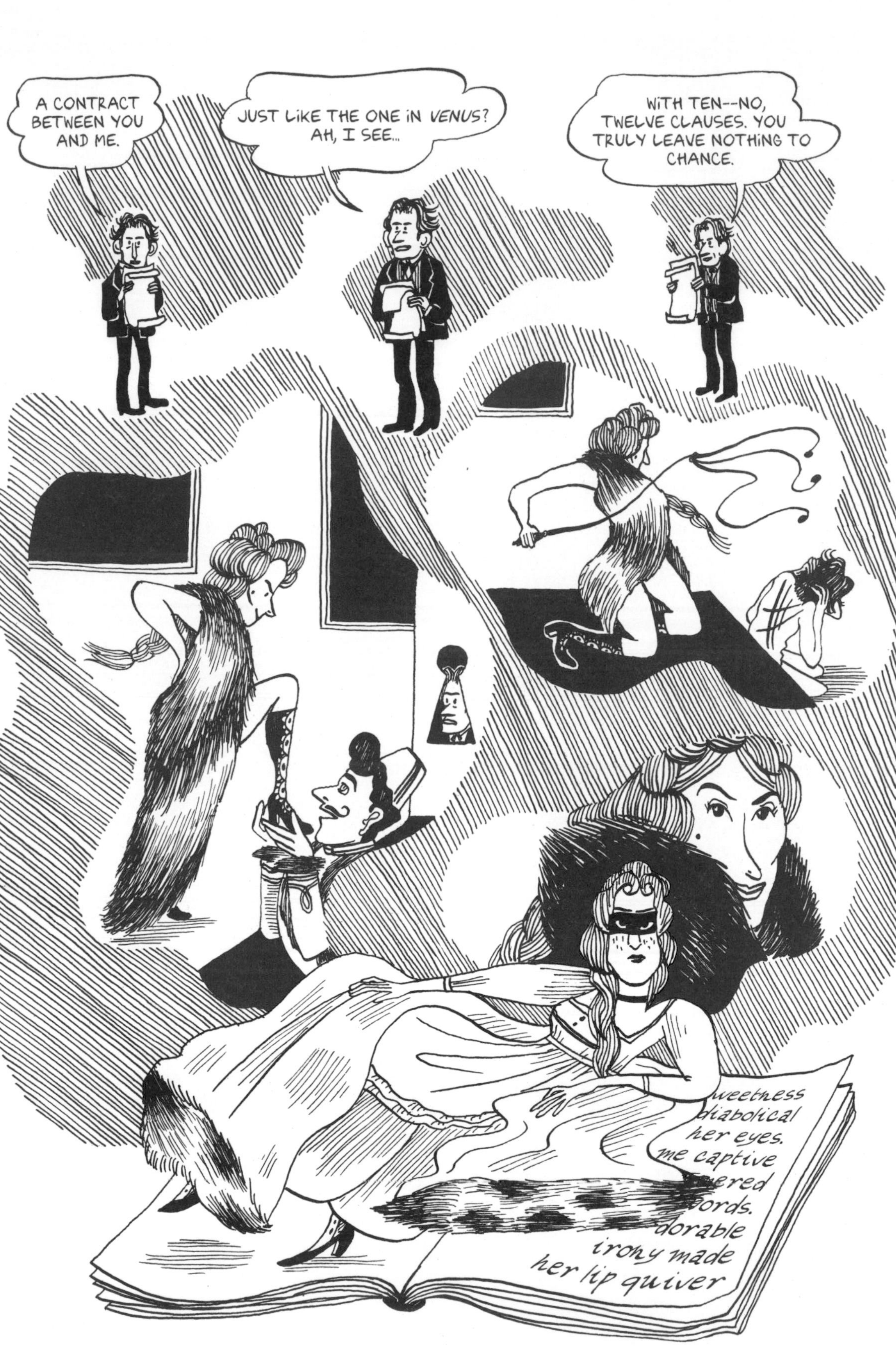
A CONTRACT BETWEEN YOU AND ME.
JUST LIKE THE ONE IN *VENUS*? AH, I SEE...
WITH TEN--NO, TWELVE CLAUSES. YOU TRULY LEAVE NOTHING TO CHANCE.
weetness
diabolical
her eyes.
me captive
ered
ords.
dorable
irony made
her lip quiver

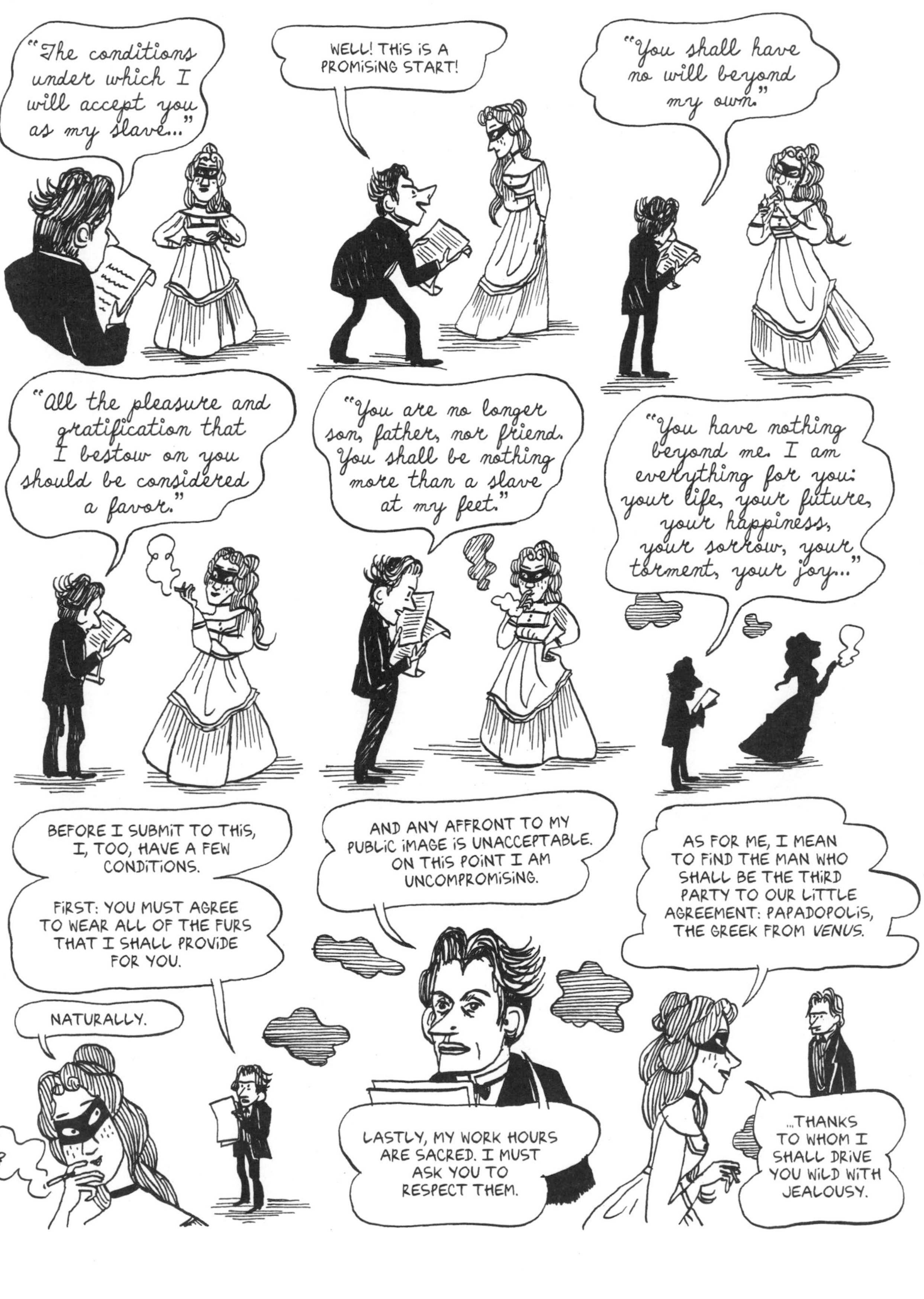
"The conditions under which I will accept you as my slave..."
WELL! THIS IS A PROMISING START!
"You shall have no will beyond my own."
"All the pleasure and gratification that I bestow on you should be considered a favor."
"You are no longer son, father, nor friend. You shall be nothing more than a slave at my feet."
"You have nothing beyond me. I am everything for you: your life, your future, your happiness, your sorrow, your torment, your joy..."
BEFORE I SUBMIT TO THIS, I, TOO, HAVE A FEW CONDITIONS.
FIRST: YOU MUST AGREE TO WEAR ALL OF THE FURS THAT I SHALL PROVIDE FOR YOU.
NATURALLY.
AND ANY AFFRONT TO MY PUBLIC IMAGE IS UNACCEPTABLE. ON THIS POINT I AM UNCOMPROMISING.
LASTLY, MY WORK HOURS ARE SACRED. I MUST ASK YOU TO RESPECT THEM.
AS FOR ME, I MEAN TO FIND THE MAN WHO SHALL BE THE THIRD PARTY TO OUR LITTLE AGREEMENT: PAPADOPOLIS, THE GREEK FROM VENUS.
...THANKS TO WHOM I SHALL DRIVE YOU WILD WITH JEALOUSY.

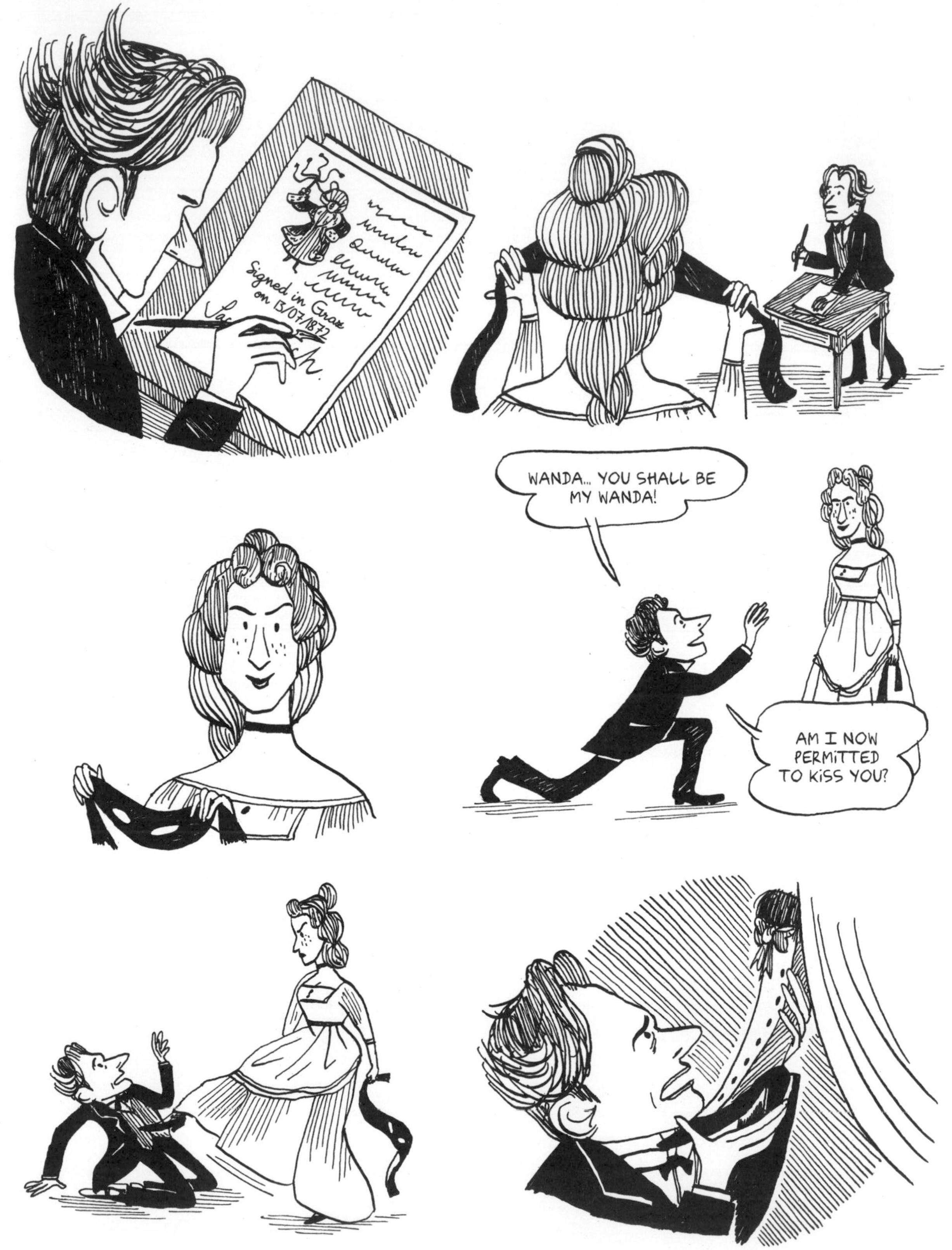
Signed in Graz
on 13/07/1872
WANDA... YOU SHALL BE MY WANDA!
AM I NOW PERMITTED TO KiSS YOU?

One year later, Leopold von Sacher-Masoch and Wanda were married in Graz. Now living as husband and wife, the author is still publishing novels and plays. The couple's daily life continues to be inspired by *Venus in Furs*.

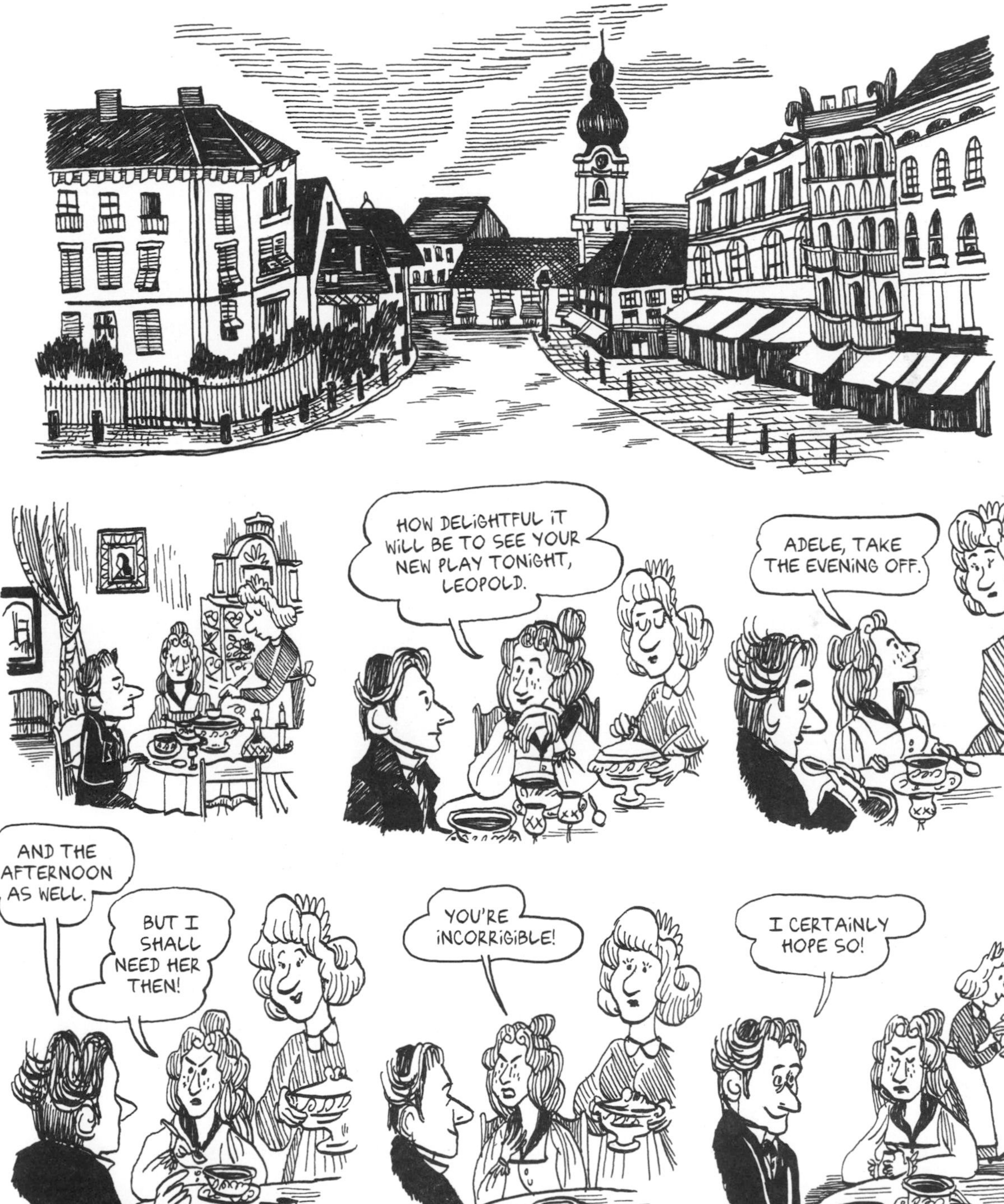
HOW DELIGHTFUL IT WILL BE TO SEE YOUR NEW PLAY TONIGHT, LEOPOLD.
ADELE, TAKE THE EVENING OFF.
AND THE AFTERNOON AS WELL.
BUT I SHALL NEED HER THEN!
YOU'RE INCORRIGIBLE!
I CERTAINLY HOPE SO!

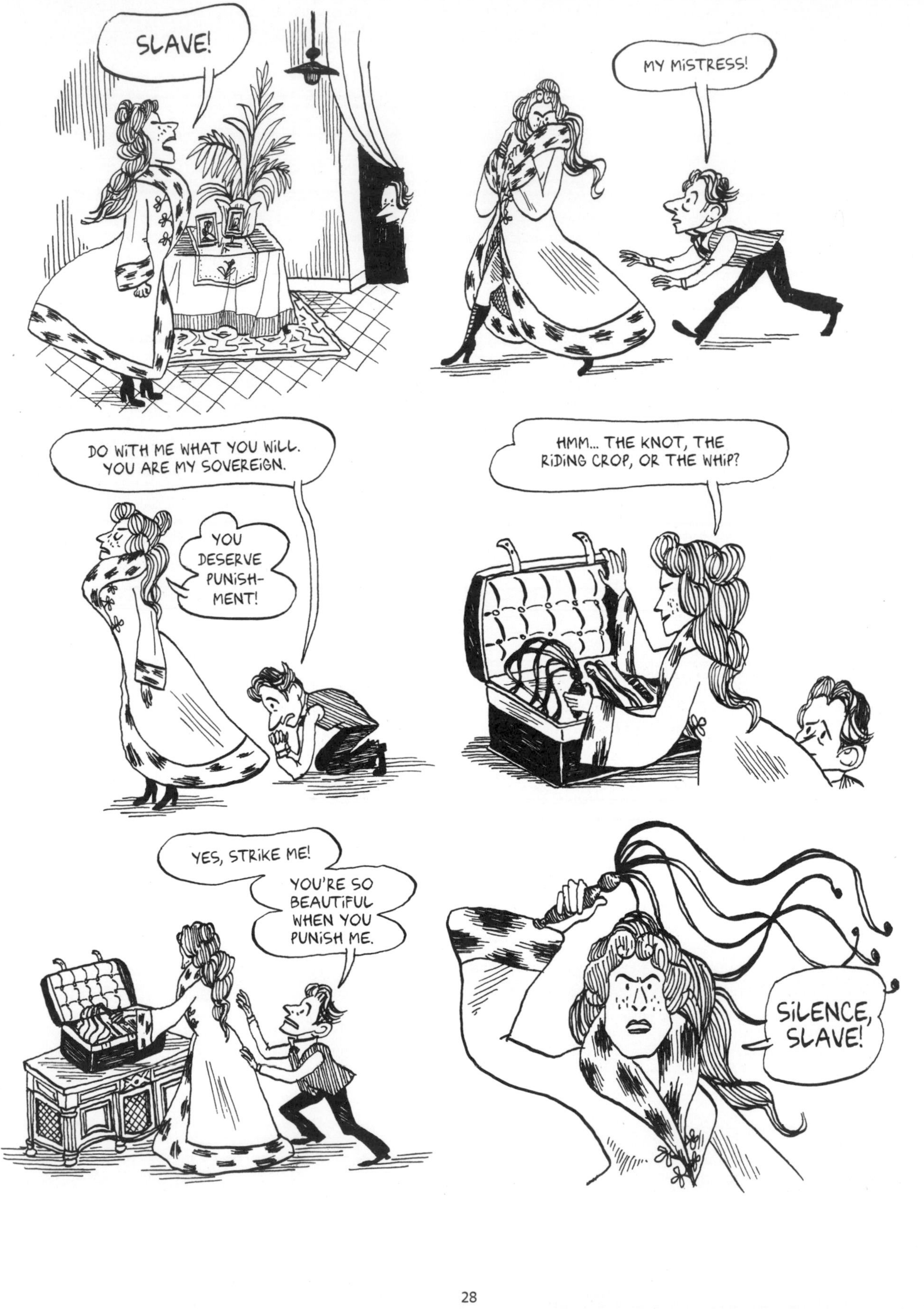
SLAVE!
MY MISTRESS!
DO WITH ME WHAT YOU WILL. YOU ARE MY SOVEREIGN.
YOU DESERVE PUNISH-MENT!
HMM... THE KNOT, THE RIDING CROP, OR THE WHIP?
YES, STRIKE ME!
YOU'RE SO BEAUTIFUL WHEN YOU PUNISH ME.
SILENCE, SLAVE!

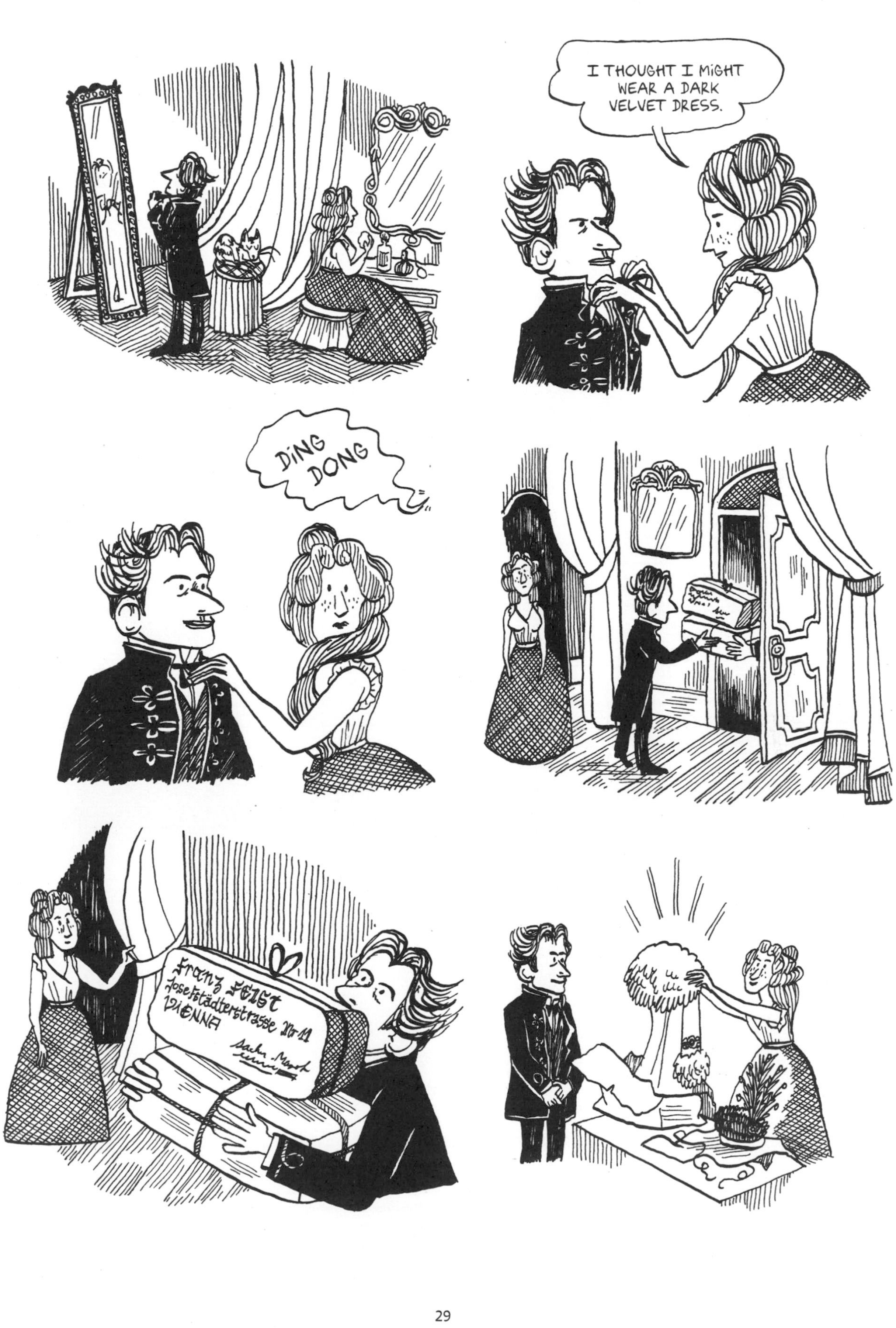
I THOUGHT I MIGHT WEAR A DARK VELVET DRESS.
DING DONG
Franz FEIST
Josefstädterstrasse Nr 11
VIENNA

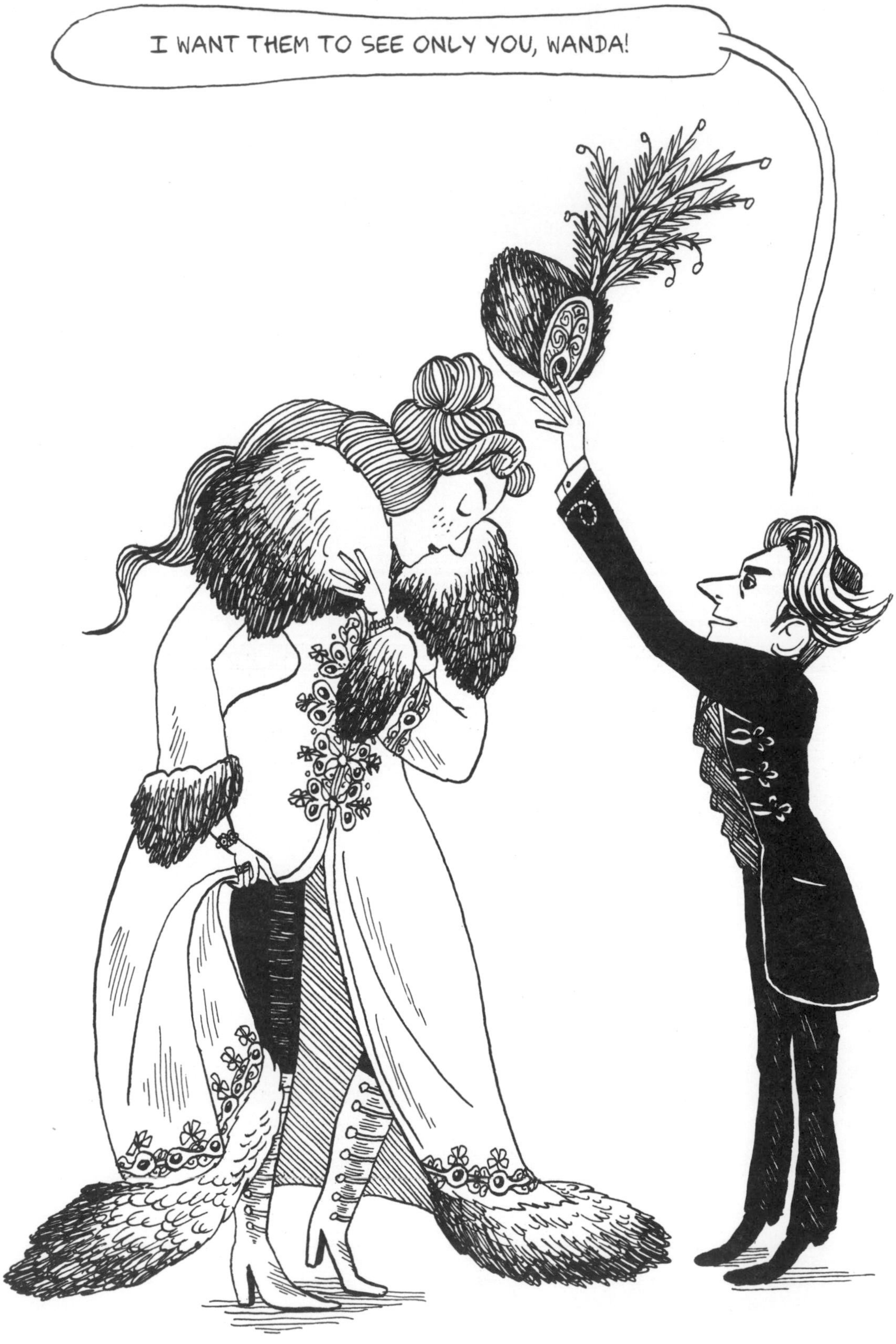
I WANT THEM TO SEE ONLY YOU, WANDA!

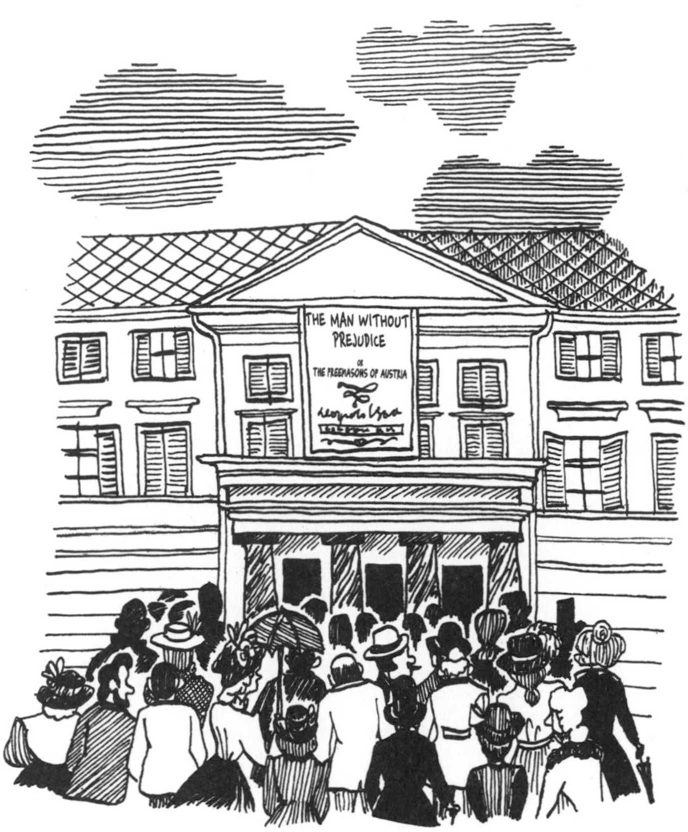
THE MAN WITHOUT PREJUDICE
OR
THE FREEMASONS OF AUSTRIA

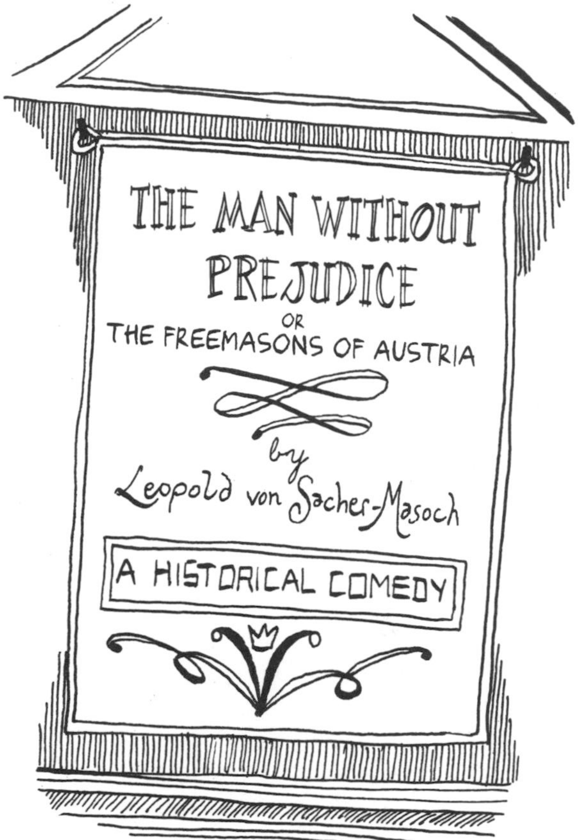
THE MAN WITHOUT PREJUDICE
OR
THE FREEMASONS OF AUSTRIA
by
Leopold von Sacher-Masoch
A HISTORICAL COMEDY

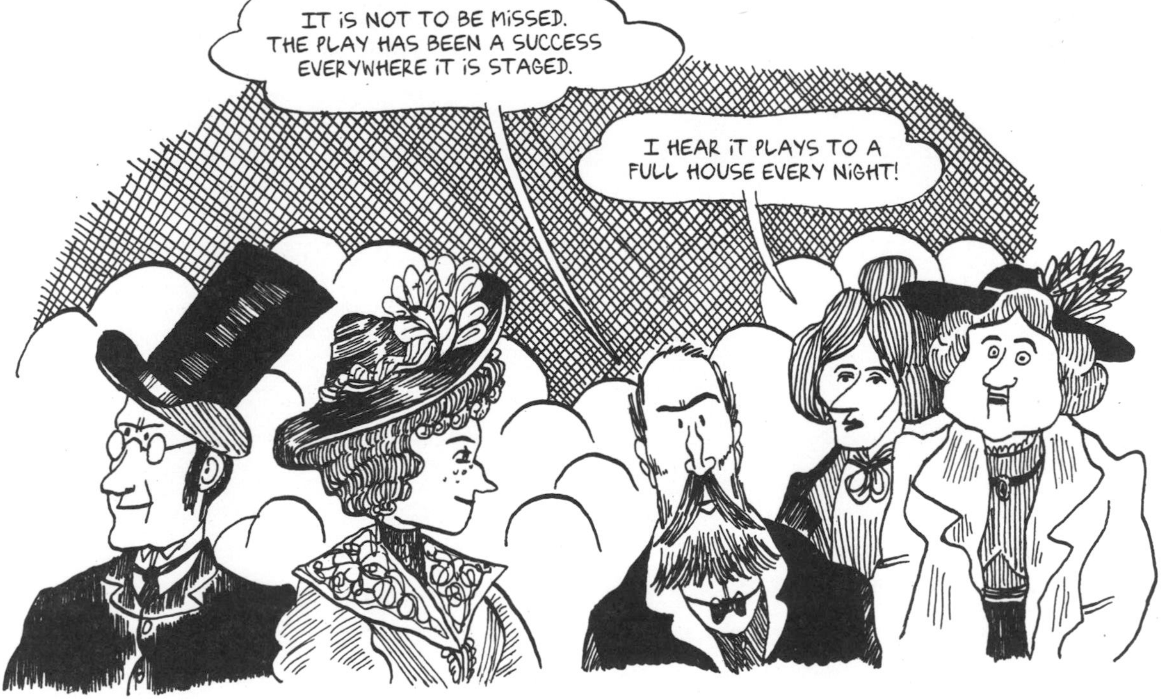
IT IS NOT TO BE MISSED. THE PLAY HAS BEEN A SUCCESS EVERYWHERE IT IS STAGED.
I HEAR IT PLAYS TO A FULL HOUSE EVERY NIGHT!

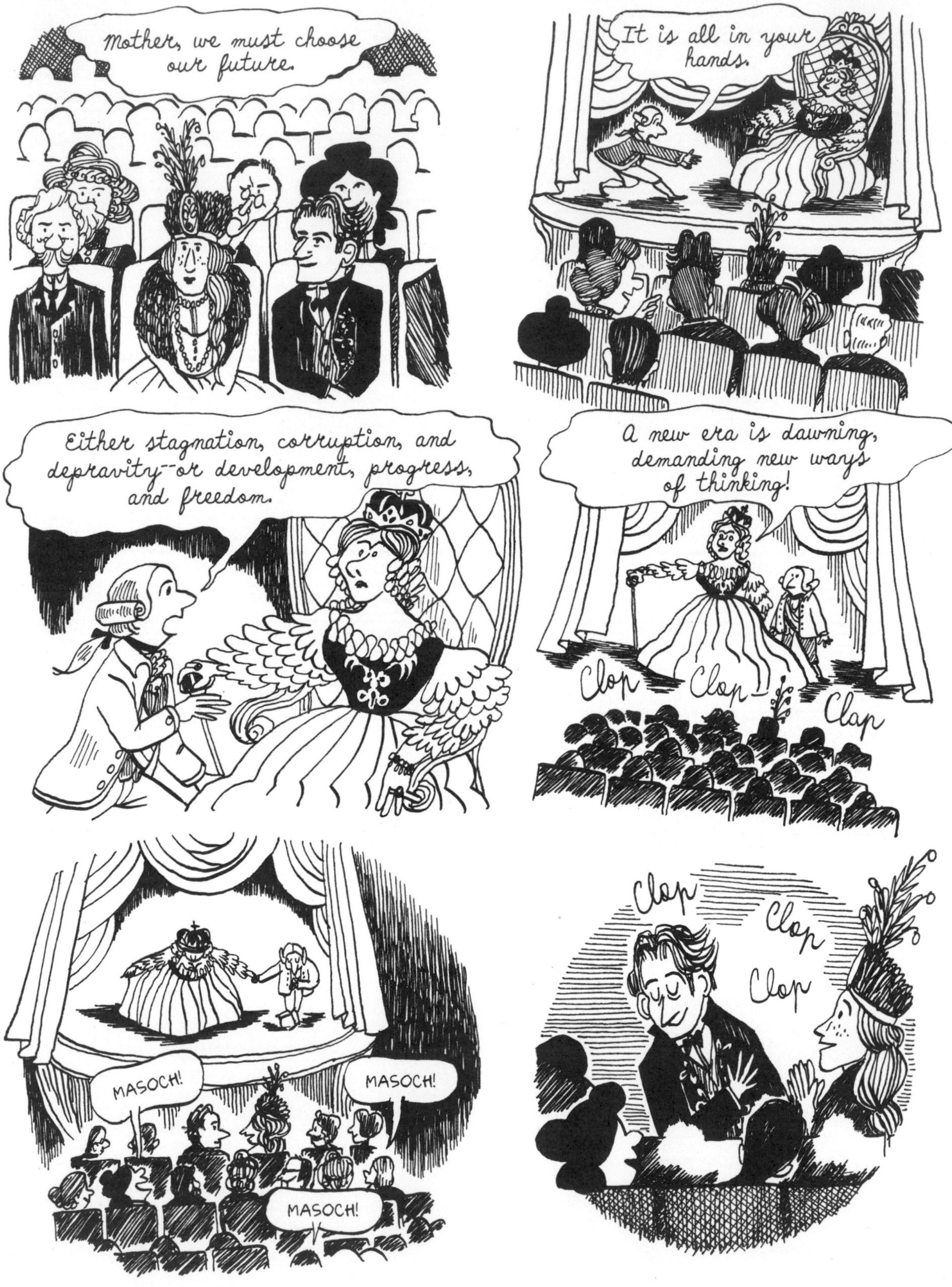
Mother, we must choose our future.
It is all in your hands.
Either stagnation, corruption, and depravity--or development, progress, and freedom.
A new era is dawning, demanding new ways of thinking!
Clop
Clop
Clap
MASOCH!
MASOCH!
MASOCH!
Clap
Clap
Clap

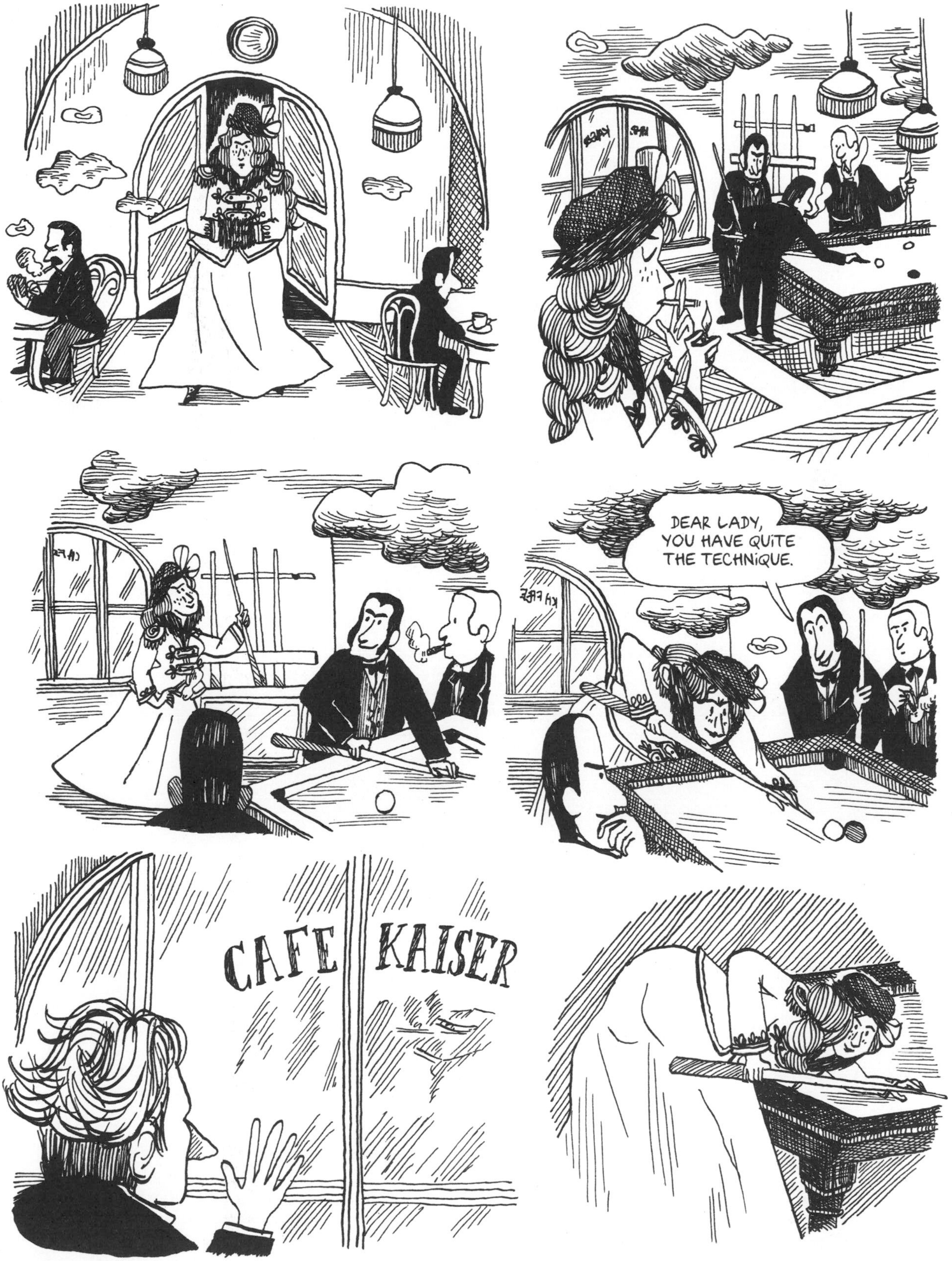
DEAR LADY, YOU HAVE QUITE THE TECHNIQUE.
CAFE KAISER

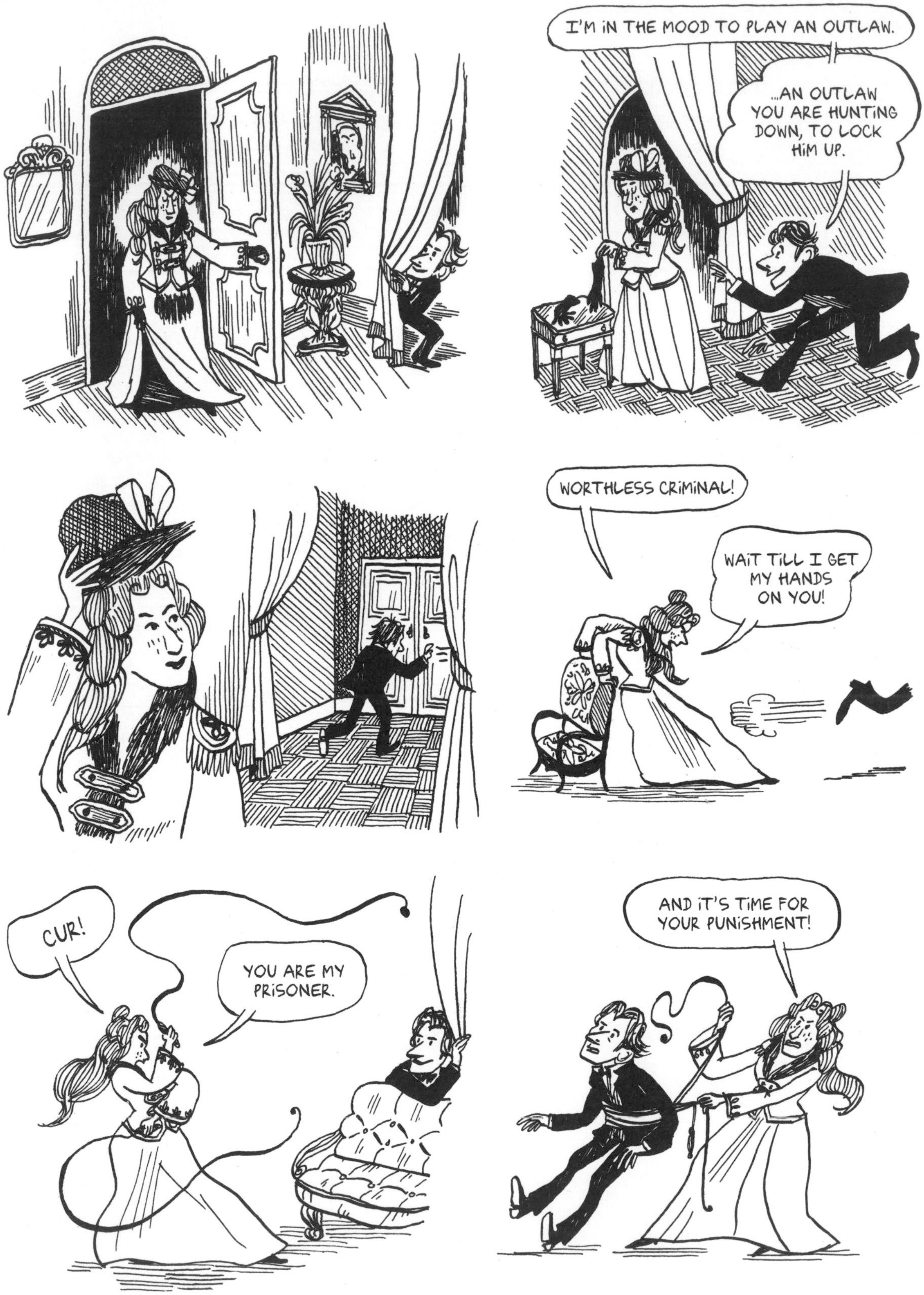
I'M IN THE MOOD TO PLAY AN OUTLAW.
...AN OUTLAW YOU ARE HUNTING DOWN, TO LOCK HIM UP.
WORTHLESS CRIMINAL!
WAIT TILL I GET MY HANDS ON YOU!
CUR!
YOU ARE MY PRISONER.
AND IT'S TIME FOR YOUR PUNISHMENT!

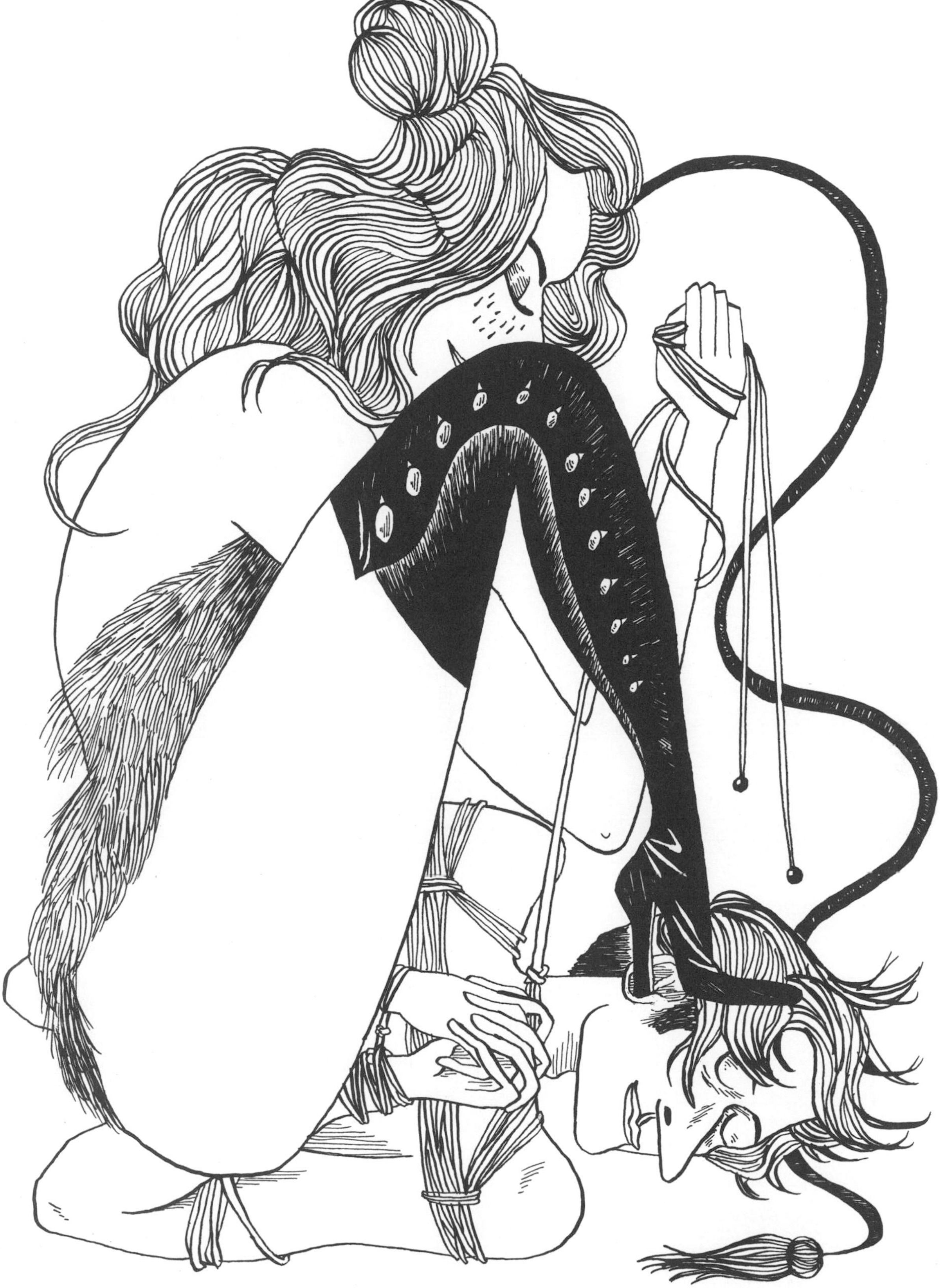

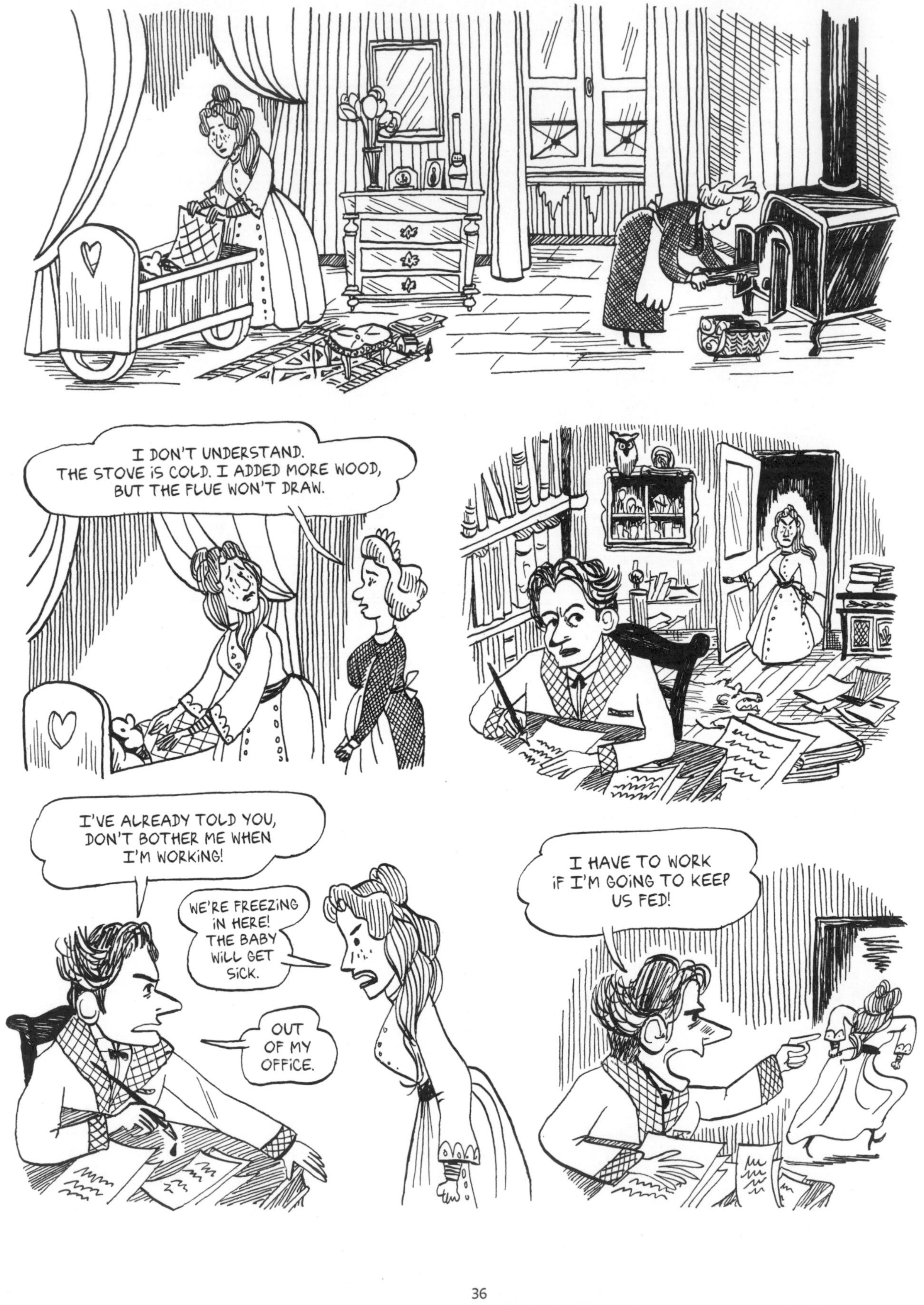

I DON'T UNDERSTAND. THE STOVE iS COLD. I ADDED MORE WOOD, BUT THE FLUE WON'T DRAW.
I'VE ALREADY TOLD YOU, DON'T BOTHER ME WHEN I'M WORKiNG!
WE'RE FREEZiNG iN HERE! THE BABY WiLL GET SiCK.
OUT OF MY OFFiCE.
I HAVE TO WORK iF I'M GOiNG TO KEEP US FED!

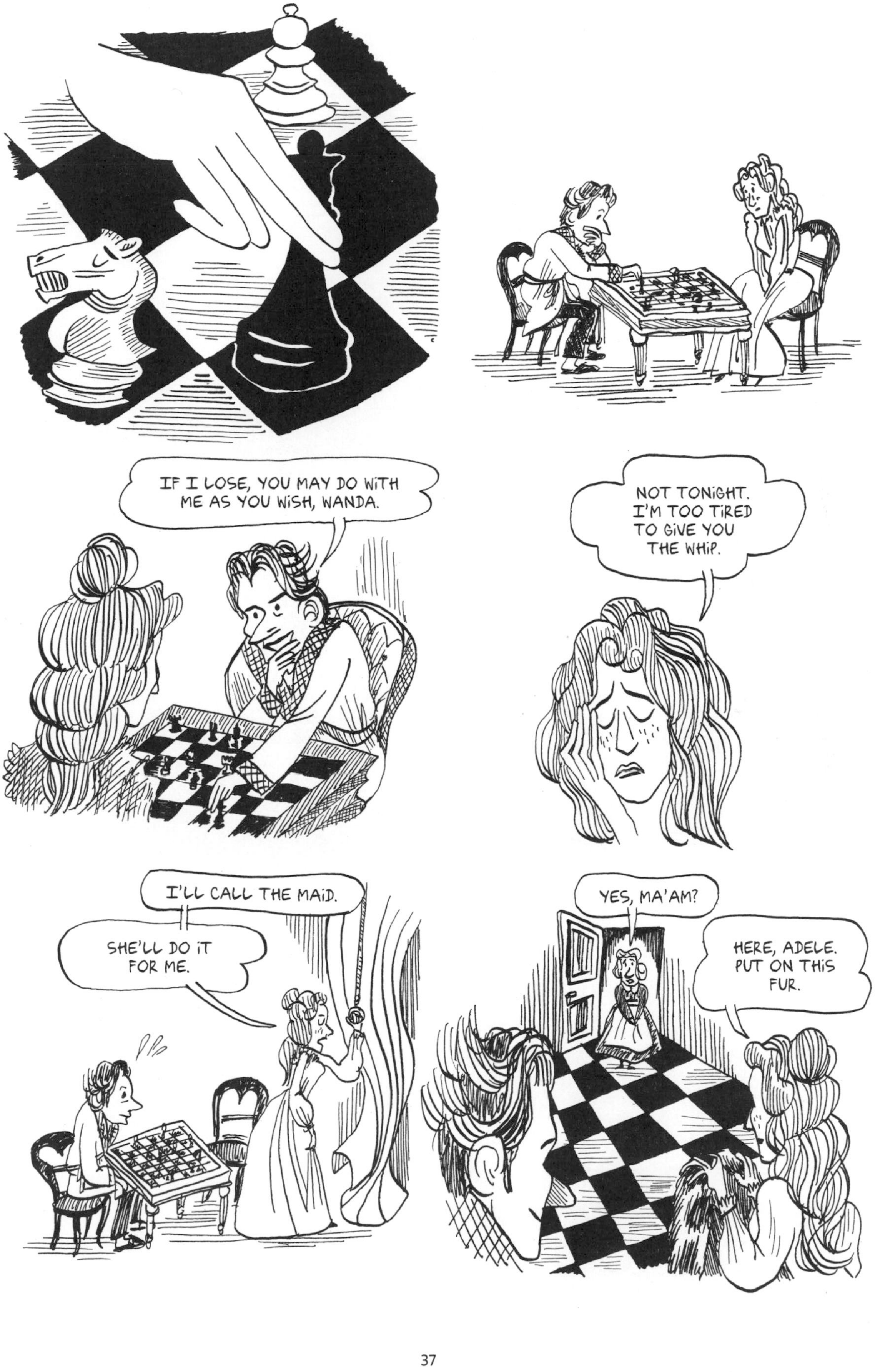
IF I LOSE, YOU MAY DO WITH ME AS YOU WISH, WANDA.
NOT TONIGHT. I'M TOO TIRED TO GIVE YOU THE WHIP.
I'LL CALL THE MAID.
SHE'LL DO IT FOR ME.
YES, MA'AM?
HERE, ADELE. PUT ON THIS FUR.

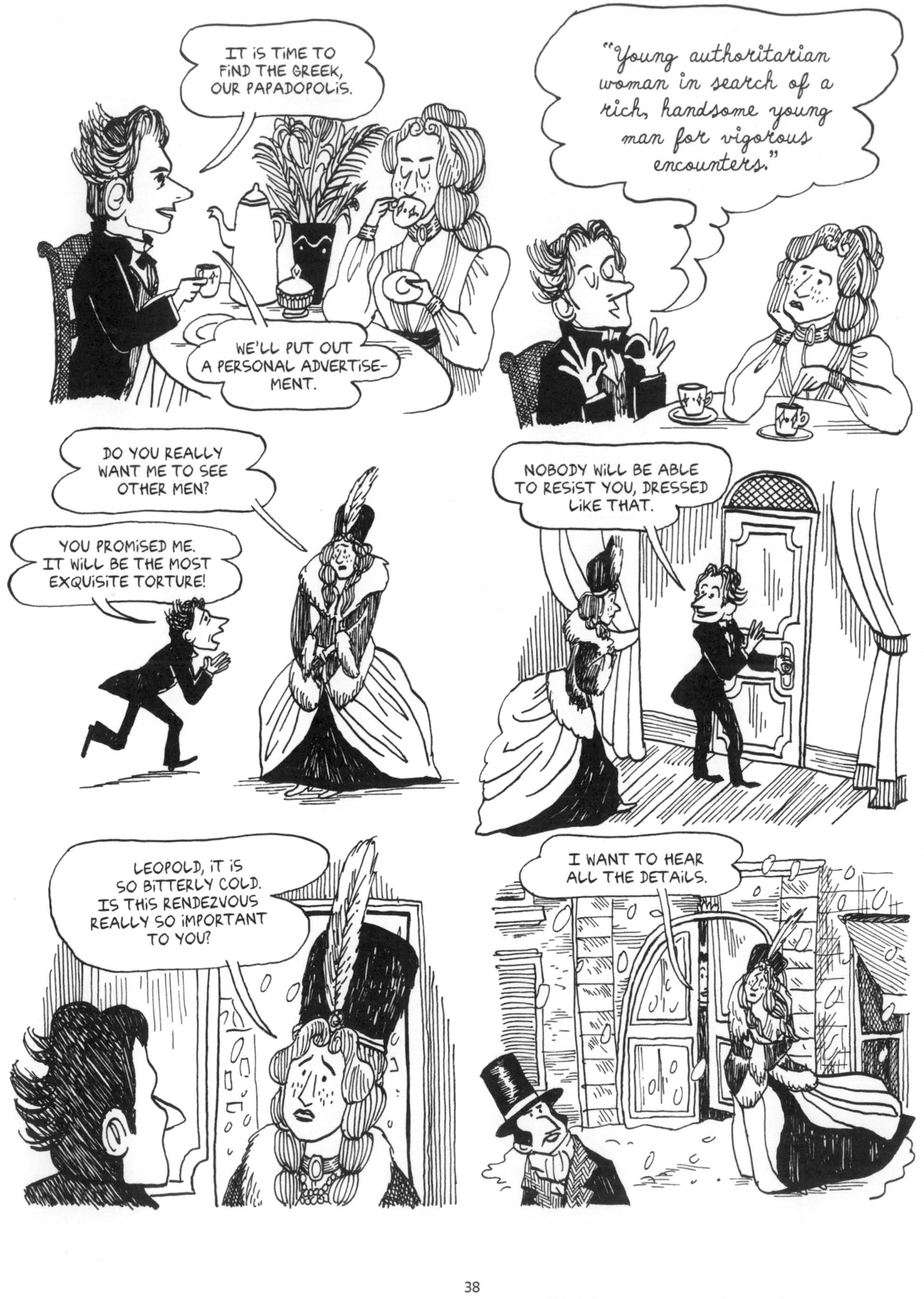
IT IS TIME TO FIND THE GREEK, OUR PAPADOPOLIS.
WE'LL PUT OUT A PERSONAL ADVERTISE-MENT.
"Young authoritarian woman in search of a rich, handsome young man for vigorous encounters."
DO YOU REALLY WANT ME TO SEE OTHER MEN?
YOU PROMISED ME. IT WILL BE THE MOST EXQUISITE TORTURE!
NOBODY WILL BE ABLE TO RESIST YOU, DRESSED LIKE THAT.
LEOPOLD, IT IS SO BITTERLY COLD. IS THIS RENDEZVOUS REALLY SO IMPORTANT TO YOU?
I WANT TO HEAR ALL THE DETAILS.

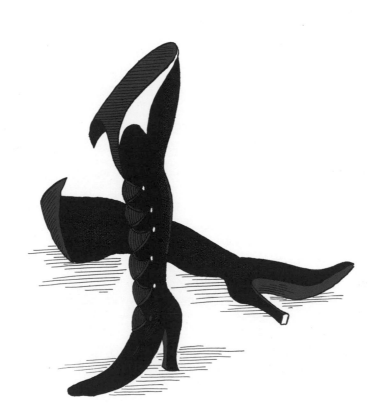

Eight years have passed. The couple has moved to Leipzig, Germany. Leopold continues to work a great deal. In addition to his books, he is the editor of the literary review *Auf der Höhe*. The strain of daily life, and the birth of their sons, Alexander and Demetrius, has taken its toll on Wanda and Leopold's relationship.

A LETTER FROM PARIS!

ONE OF MY STORIES WILL APPEAR IN *LA NOUVELLE REVUE*.

AH... THIS AFTERNOON, MADAME MARIE IS COMING TO GIVE ME A FRENCH LESSON.

SHE'S FROM PARIS, TOO.

I STARTED LEARNING THE LANGUAGE OF MOLIÈRE AT AGE TWO, WITH MY GOVERNESS. HER NAME WAS MADEMOISELLE MARTINET...

...DELIGHTFULLY STRICT.

I KNOW. YOU'VE TOLD ME A HUNDRED TIMES.

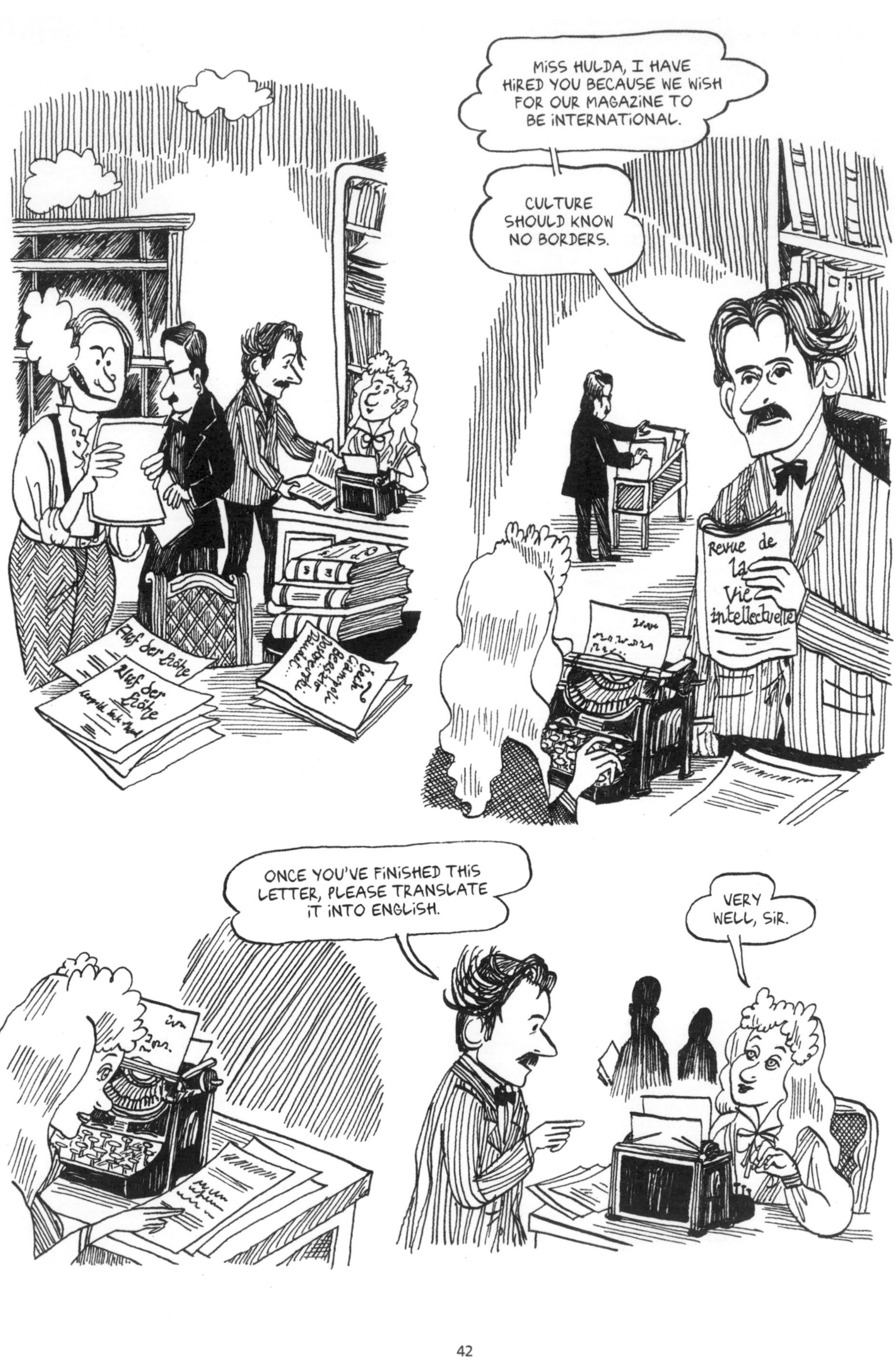
Auf der Höhe
Auf der Höhe
MISS HULDA, I HAVE HIRED YOU BECAUSE WE WISH FOR OUR MAGAZINE TO BE INTERNATIONAL.
CULTURE SHOULD KNOW NO BORDERS.
Revue de la Vie intellectuelle
ONCE YOU'VE FINISHED THIS LETTER, PLEASE TRANSLATE IT INTO ENGLISH.
VERY WELL, SIR.

OUR NEXT ISSUE WILL BE DEVOTED TO FRANCE, WITH POETRY BY VICTOR HUGO AND AN ARTICLE WRITTEN BY CAMILLE FLAMMARION.
DID YOU NOT ALSO MENTION A TEXT ON MUSIC BY SAINT-SAËNS?
INDEED. AND ONE OR TWO OF MY STORIES.
I SHALL LEAVE YOU TO YOUR WORK, MISS HULDA.
THANK YOU, SIR.

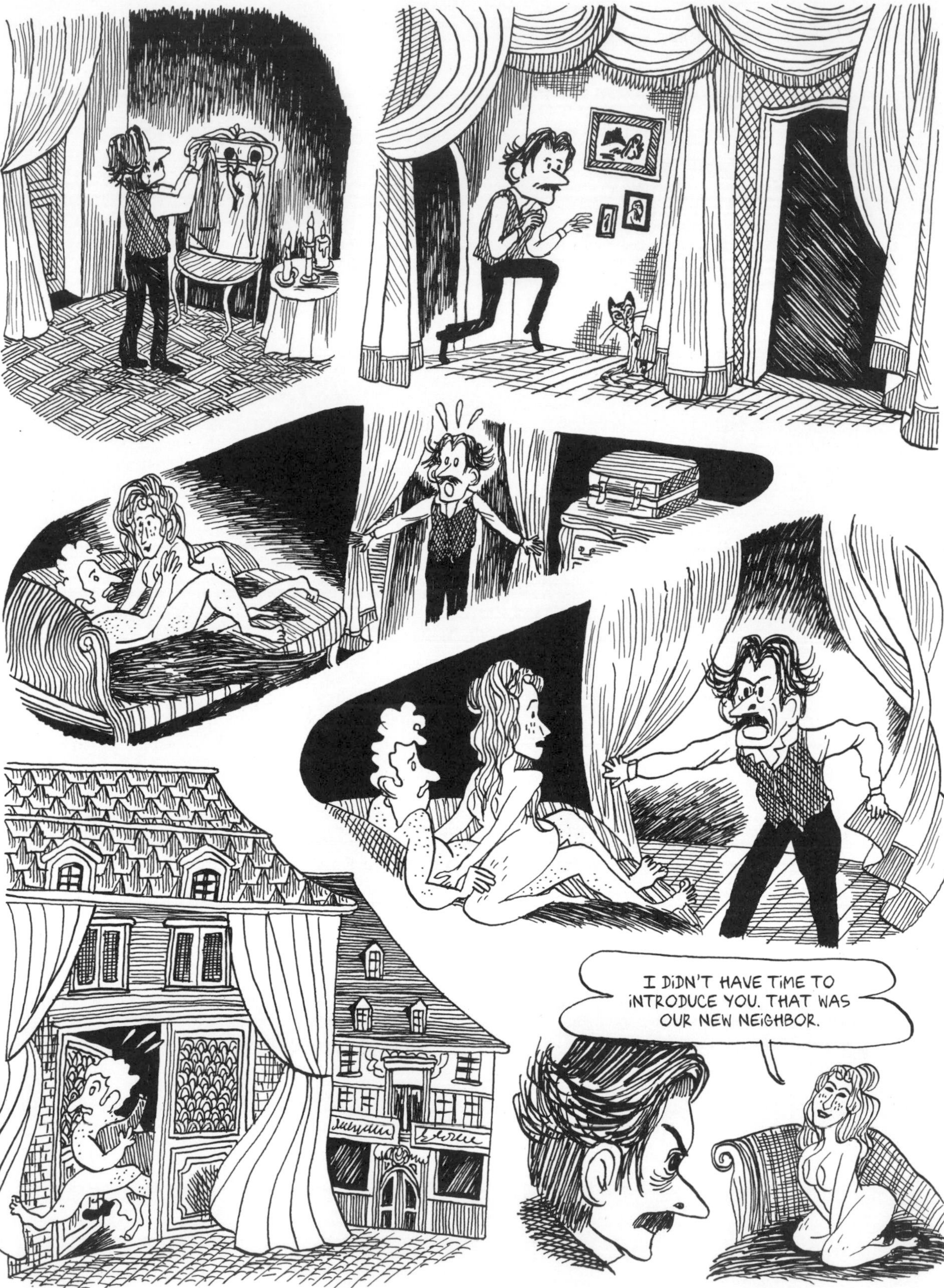
I DIDN'T HAVE TIME TO INTRODUCE YOU. THAT WAS OUR NEW NEIGHBOR.

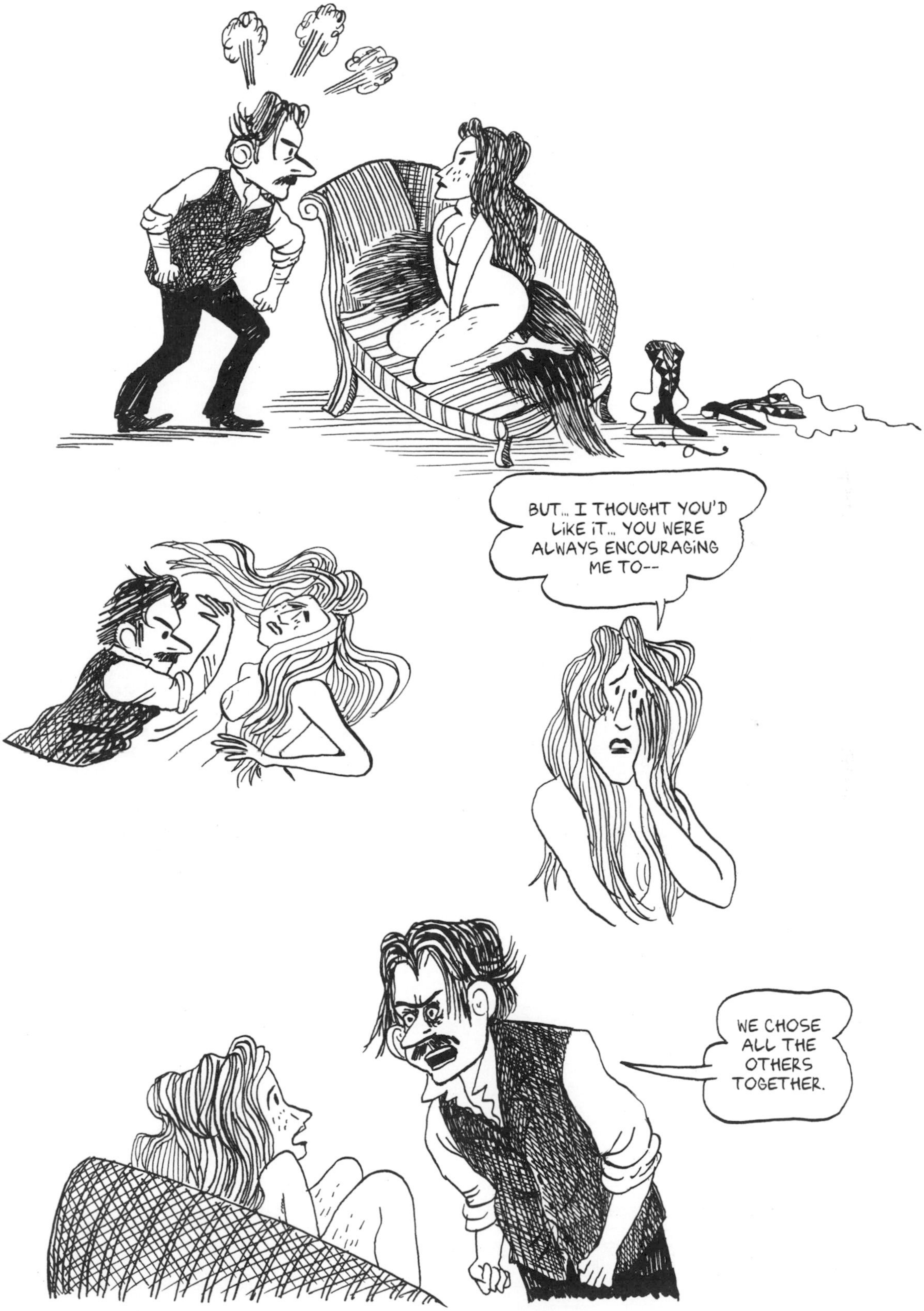
BUT... I THOUGHT YOU'D LIKE IT... YOU WERE ALWAYS ENCOURAGING ME TO--
WE CHOSE ALL THE OTHERS TOGETHER.

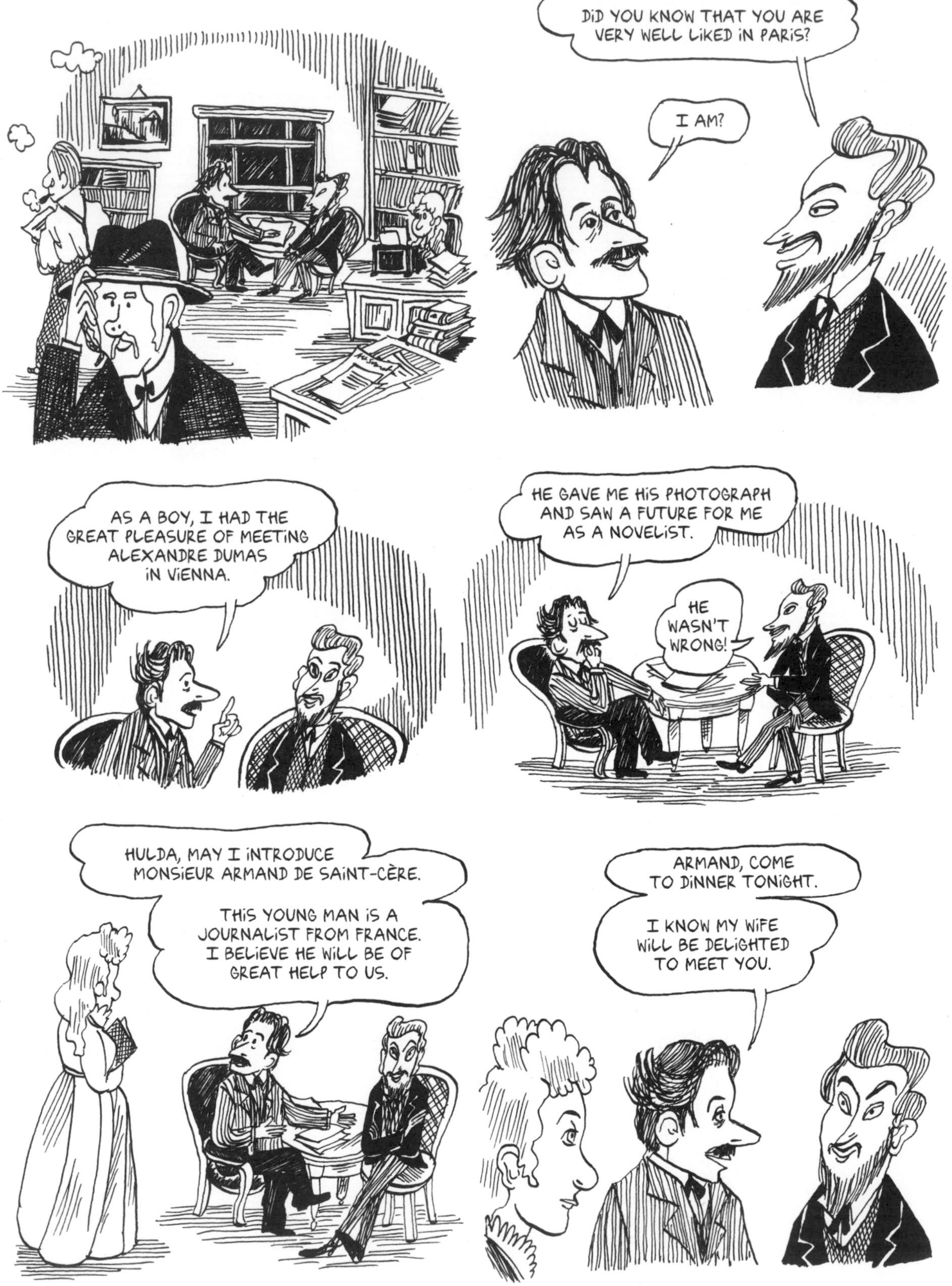
DID YOU KNOW THAT YOU ARE VERY WELL LIKED IN PARIS?
I AM?
AS A BOY, I HAD THE GREAT PLEASURE OF MEETING ALEXANDRE DUMAS IN VIENNA.
HE GAVE ME HIS PHOTOGRAPH AND SAW A FUTURE FOR ME AS A NOVELIST.
HE WASN'T WRONG!
HULDA, MAY I INTRODUCE MONSIEUR ARMAND DE SAINT-CÈRE.
THIS YOUNG MAN IS A JOURNALIST FROM FRANCE. I BELIEVE HE WILL BE OF GREAT HELP TO US.
ARMAND, COME TO DINNER TONIGHT.
I KNOW MY WIFE WILL BE DELIGHTED TO MEET YOU.

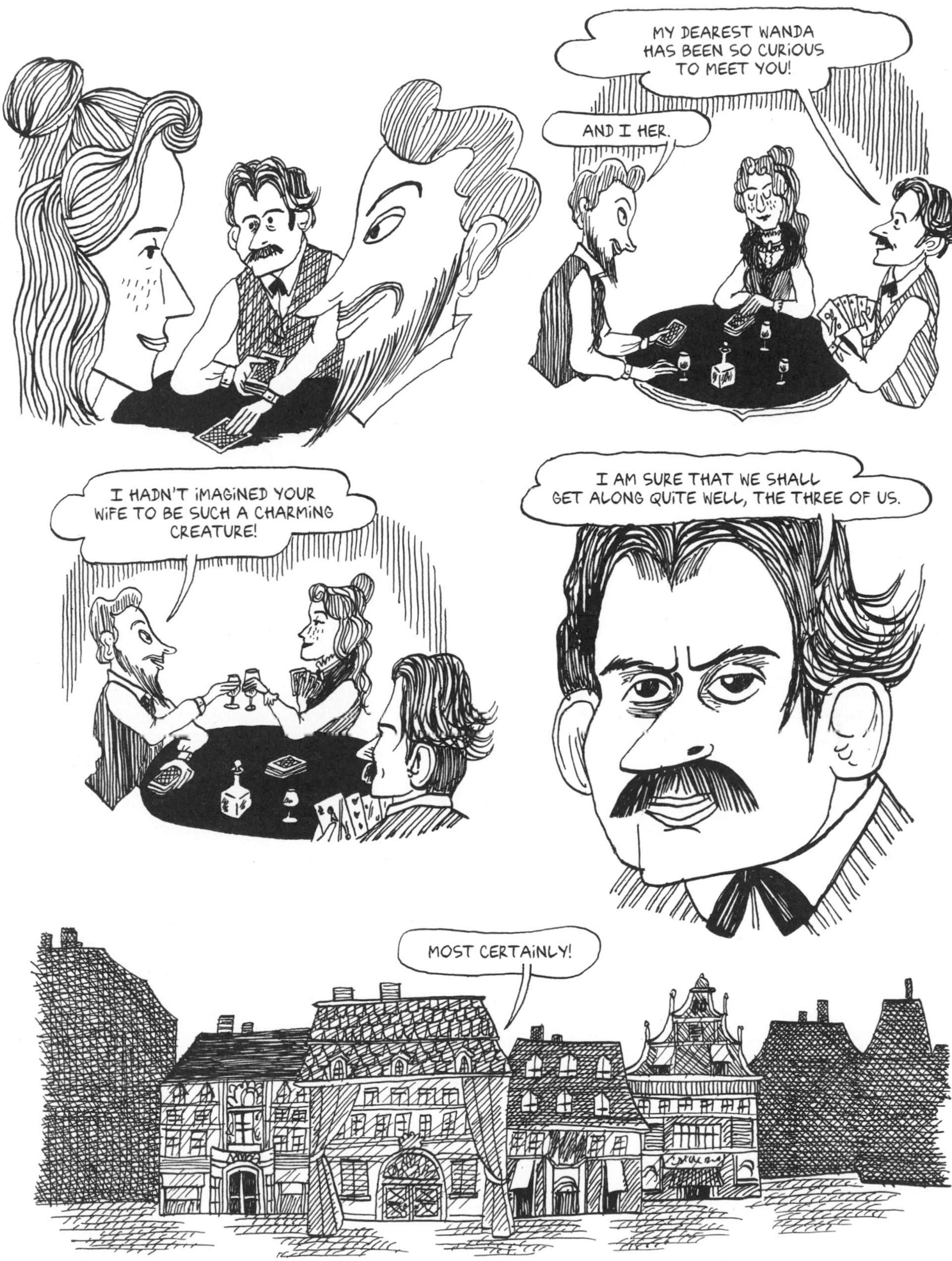
MY DEAREST WANDA HAS BEEN SO CURIOUS TO MEET YOU!
AND I HER.
I HADN'T IMAGINED YOUR WIFE TO BE SUCH A CHARMING CREATURE!
I AM SURE THAT WE SHALL GET ALONG QUITE WELL, THE THREE OF US.
MOST CERTAINLY!

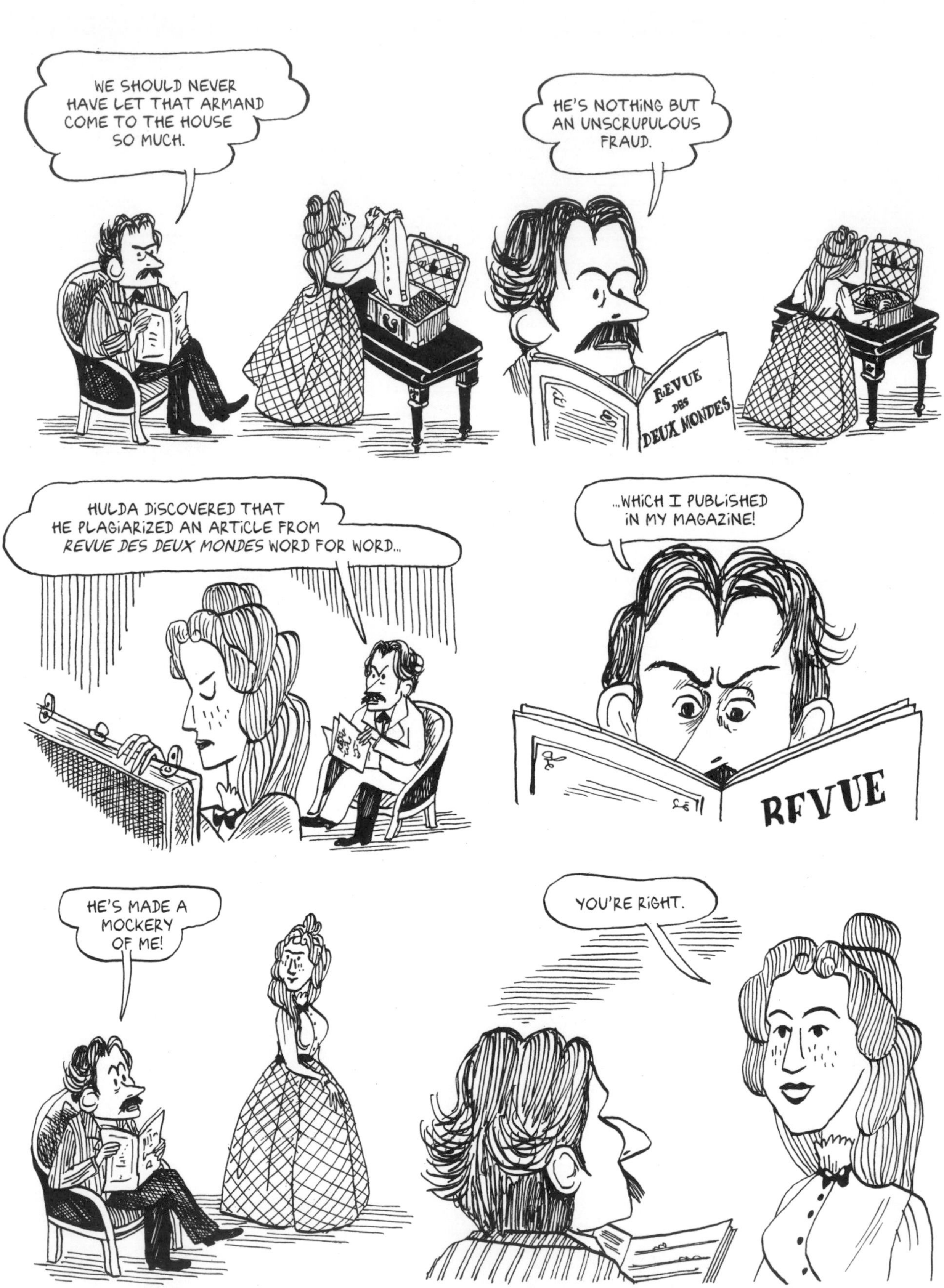
WE SHOULD NEVER HAVE LET THAT ARMAND COME TO THE HOUSE SO MUCH.
HE'S NOTHING BUT AN UNSCRUPULOUS FRAUD.
REVUE DES DEUX MONDES
HULDA DISCOVERED THAT HE PLAGIARIZED AN ARTICLE FROM *REVUE DES DEUX MONDES* WORD FOR WORD...
...WHICH I PUBLISHED IN MY MAGAZINE!
REVUE
HE'S MADE A MOCKERY OF ME!
YOU'RE RIGHT.

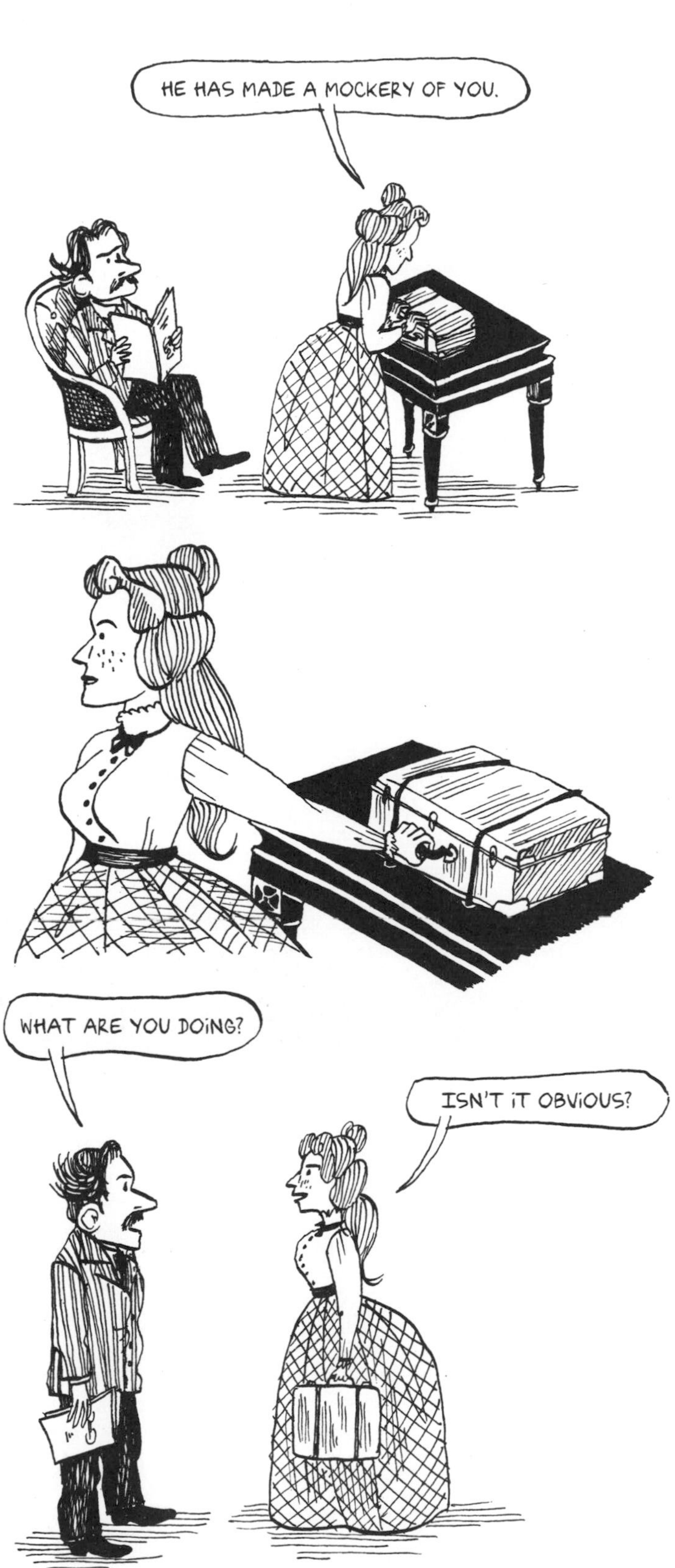
HE HAS MADE A MOCKERY OF YOU.
WHAT ARE YOU DOING?
ISN'T IT OBVIOUS?

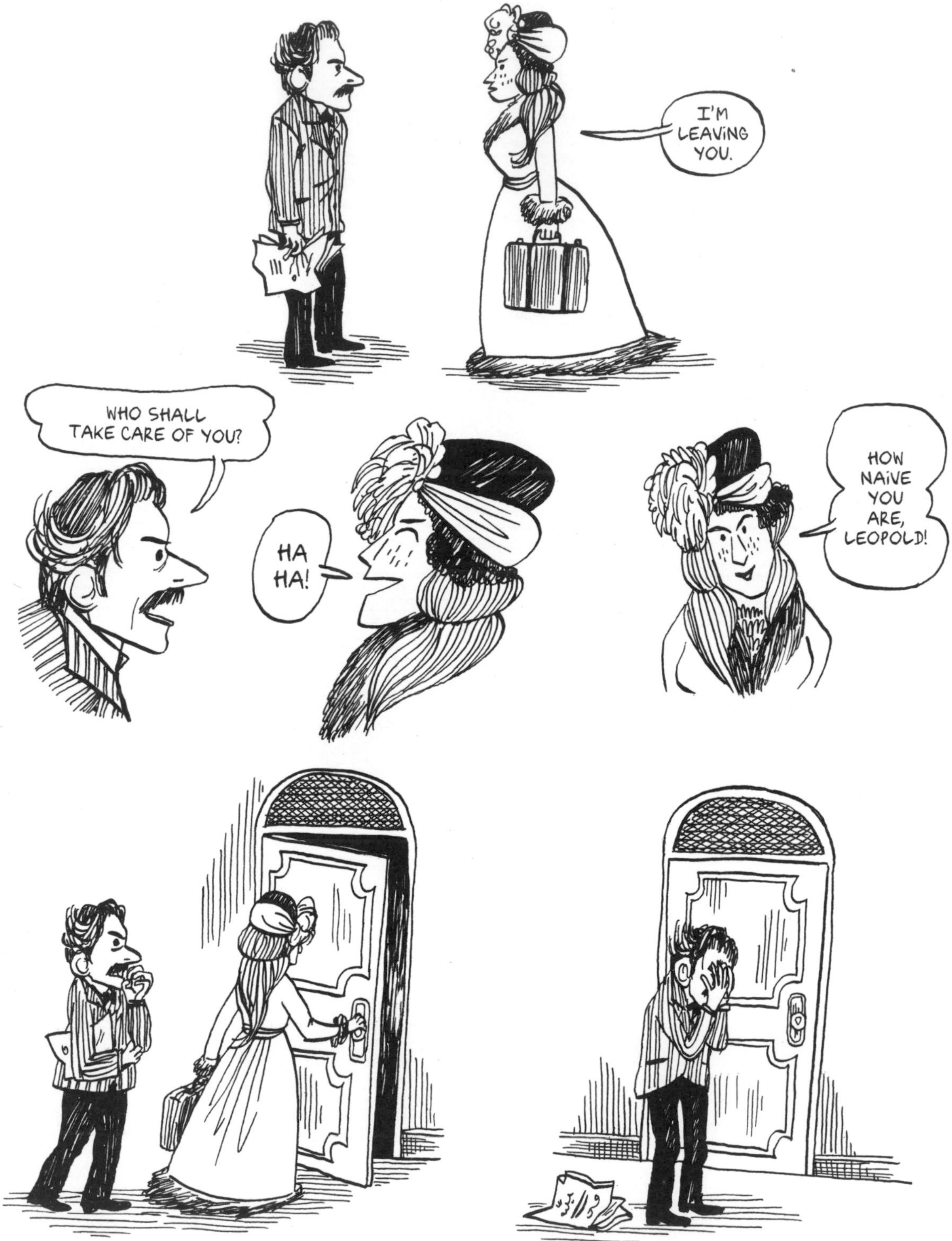
I'M LEAVING YOU.
WHO SHALL TAKE CARE OF YOU?
HA HA!
HOW NAIVE YOU ARE, LEOPOLD!

Three years have passed since Wanda left with Armand.
Leopold has gained custody of his son, Alexander,
and has fallen on hard times.

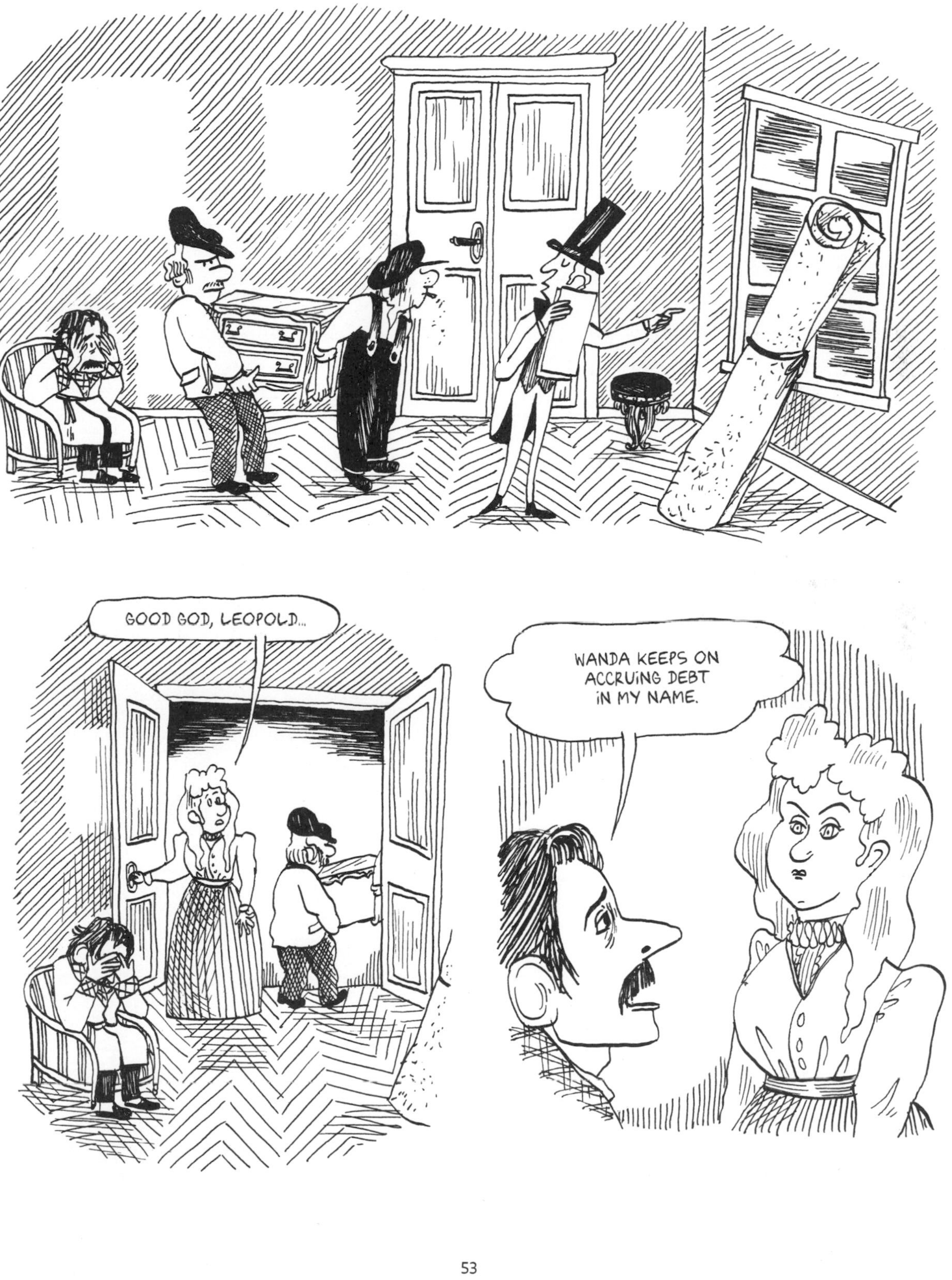
GOOD GOD, LEOPOLD...
WANDA KEEPS ON ACCRUING DEBT IN MY NAME.

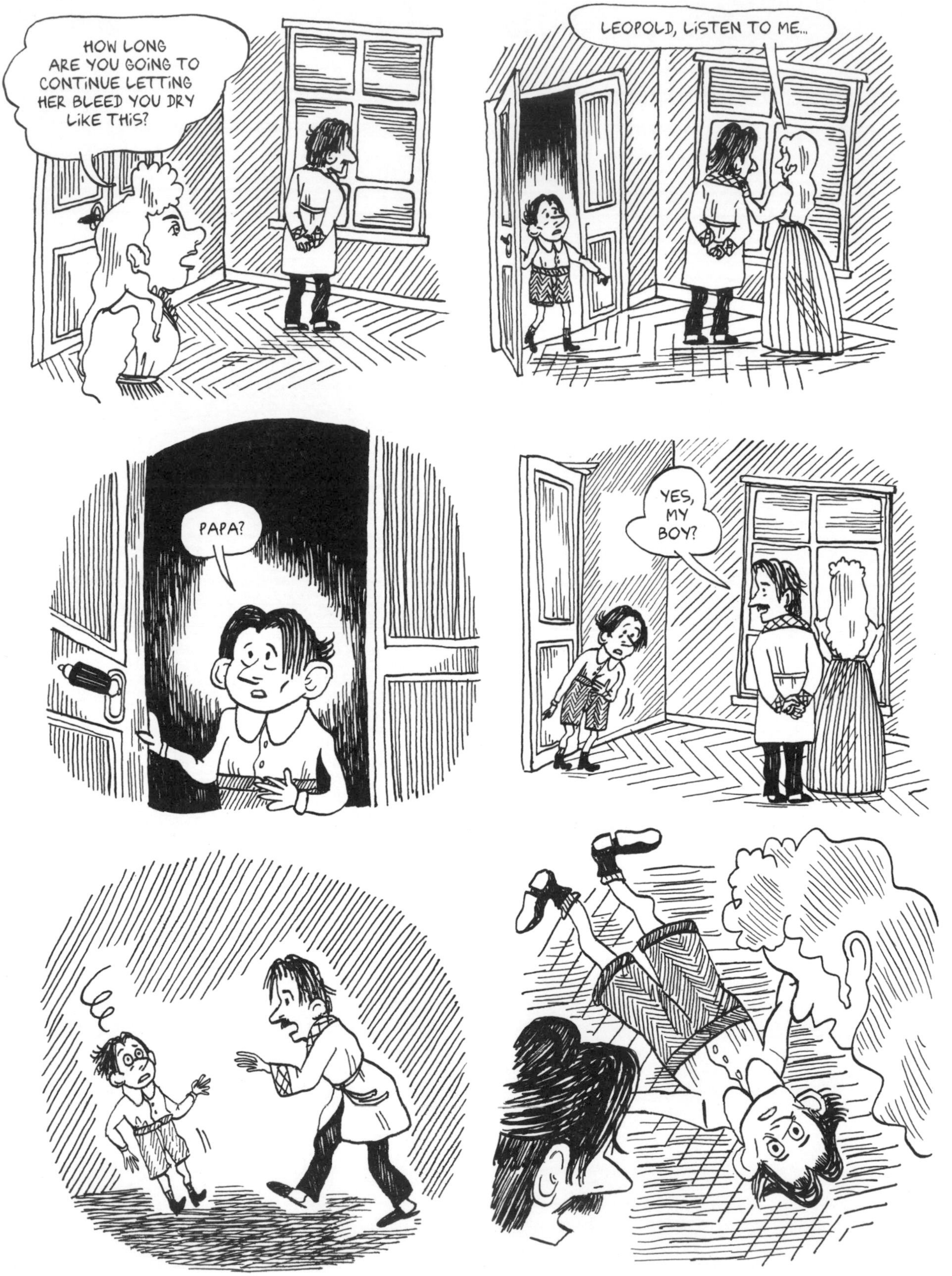
HOW LONG ARE YOU GOING TO CONTINUE LETTING HER BLEED YOU DRY LIKE THIS?
LEOPOLD, LISTEN TO ME...
PAPA?
YES, MY BOY?

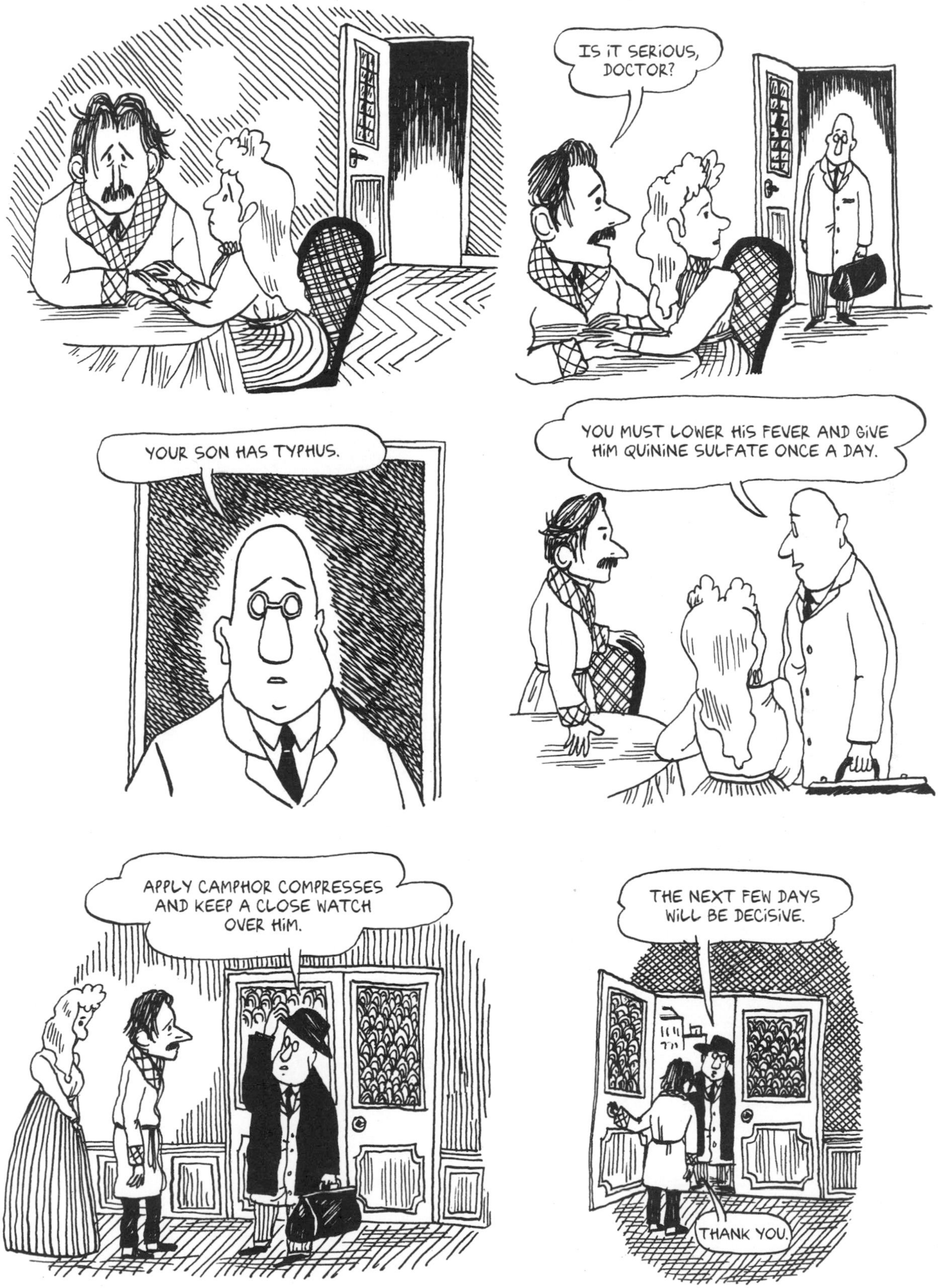
IS IT SERIOUS, DOCTOR?
YOUR SON HAS TYPHUS.
YOU MUST LOWER HIS FEVER AND GIVE HIM QUININE SULFATE ONCE A DAY.
APPLY CAMPHOR COMPRESSES AND KEEP A CLOSE WATCH OVER HIM.
THE NEXT FEW DAYS WILL BE DECISIVE.
THANK YOU.

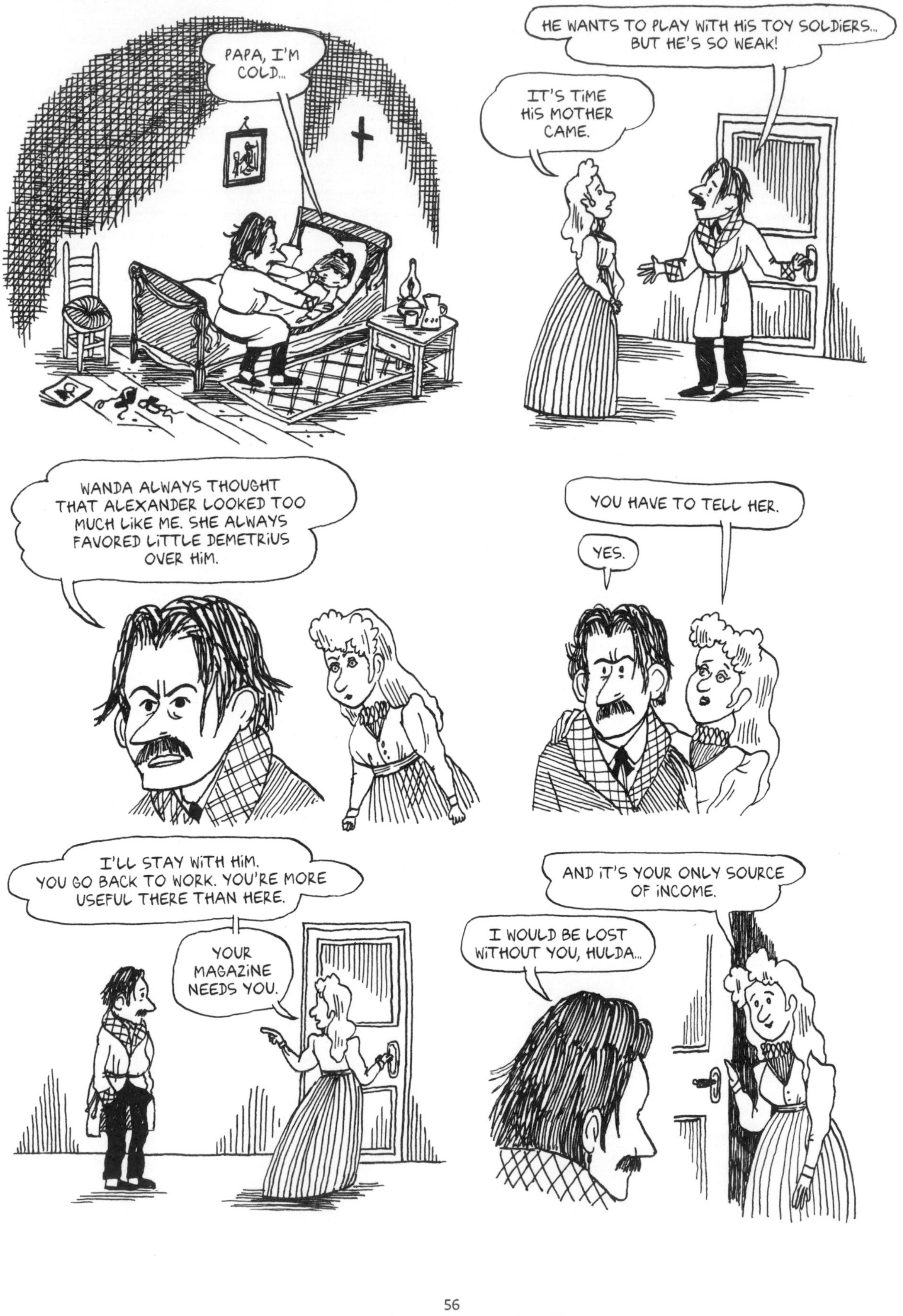
PAPA, I'M COLD...
HE WANTS TO PLAY WITH HIS TOY SOLDIERS... BUT HE'S SO WEAK!
IT'S TIME HIS MOTHER CAME.
WANDA ALWAYS THOUGHT THAT ALEXANDER LOOKED TOO MUCH LIKE ME. SHE ALWAYS FAVORED LITTLE DEMETRIUS OVER HIM.
YOU HAVE TO TELL HER.
YES.
I'LL STAY WITH HIM. YOU GO BACK TO WORK. YOU'RE MORE USEFUL THERE THAN HERE.
YOUR MAGAZINE NEEDS YOU.
AND IT'S YOUR ONLY SOURCE OF INCOME.
I WOULD BE LOST WITHOUT YOU, HULDA...

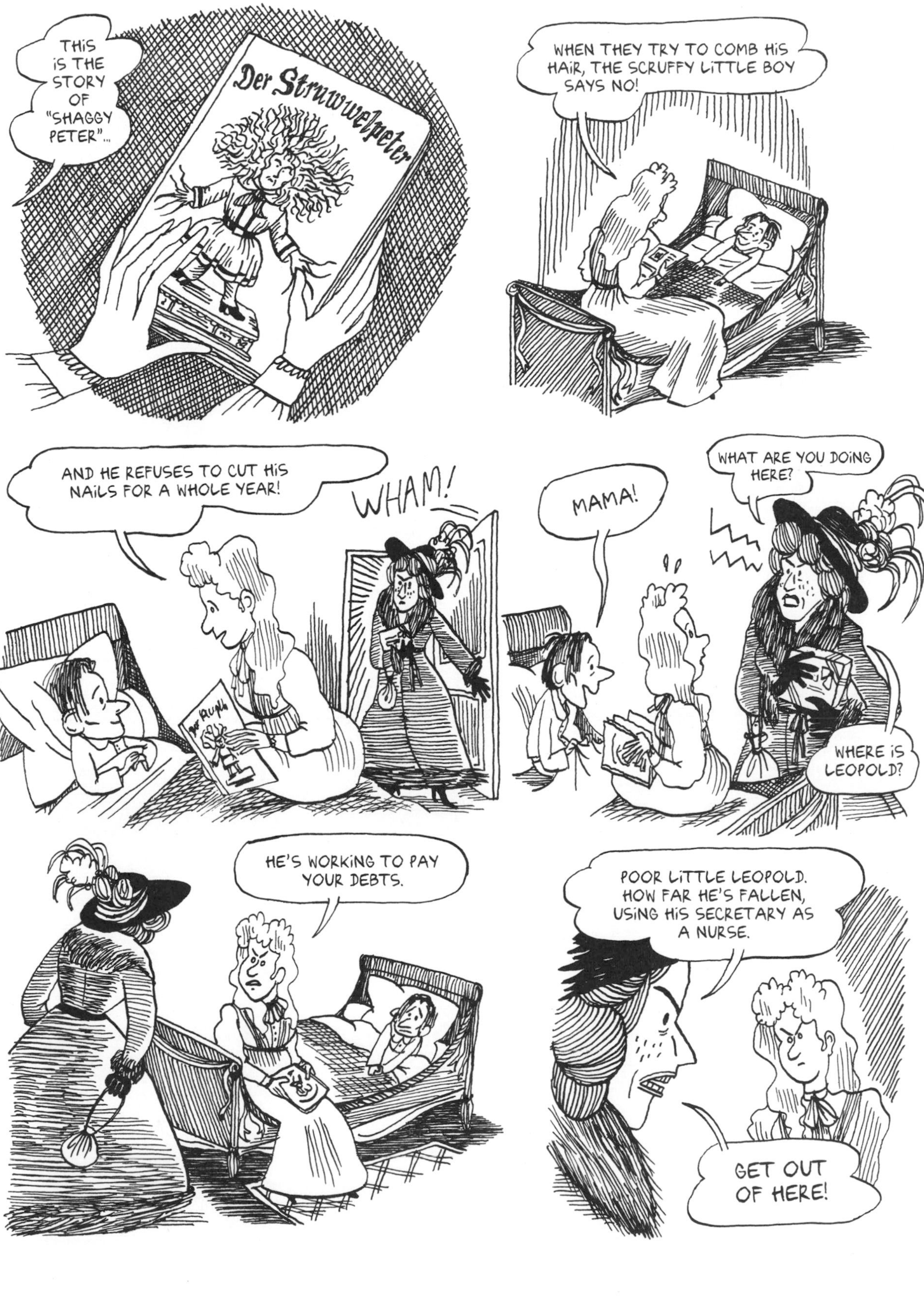
THIS IS THE STORY OF "SHAGGY PETER"...
Der Struwwelpeter
WHEN THEY TRY TO COMB HIS HAIR, THE SCRUFFY LITTLE BOY SAYS NO!
AND HE REFUSES TO CUT HIS NAILS FOR A WHOLE YEAR!
WHAM!
MAMA!
WHAT ARE YOU DOING HERE?
WHERE IS LEOPOLD?
HE'S WORKING TO PAY YOUR DEBTS.
POOR LITTLE LEOPOLD. HOW FAR HE'S FALLEN, USING HIS SECRETARY AS A NURSE.
GET OUT OF HERE!

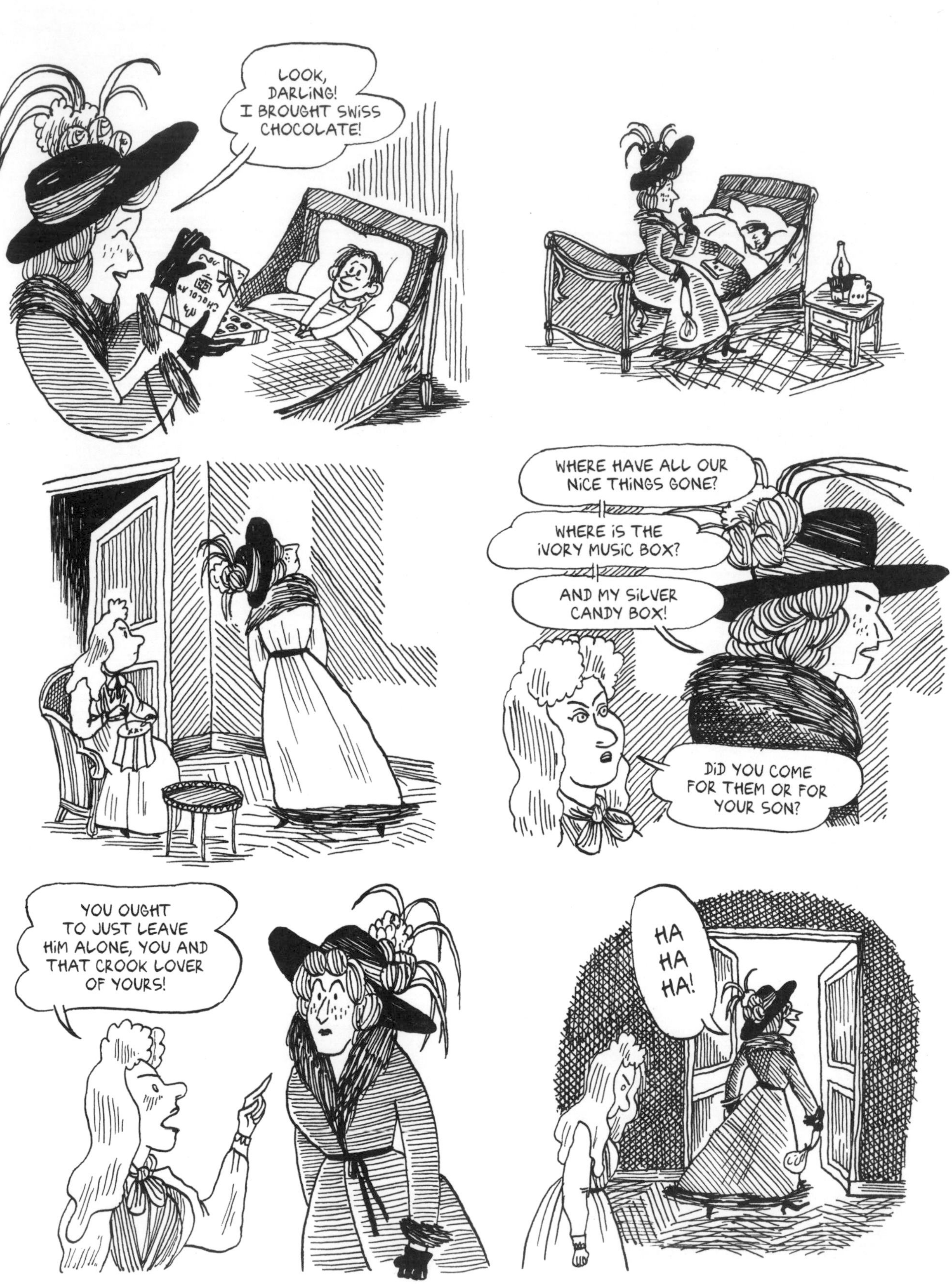
LOOK, DARLING! I BROUGHT SWISS CHOCOLATE!
WHERE HAVE ALL OUR NICE THINGS GONE?
WHERE IS THE IVORY MUSIC BOX?
AND MY SILVER CANDY BOX!
DID YOU COME FOR THEM OR FOR YOUR SON?
YOU OUGHT TO JUST LEAVE HIM ALONE, YOU AND THAT CROOK LOVER OF YOURS!
HA HA HA!

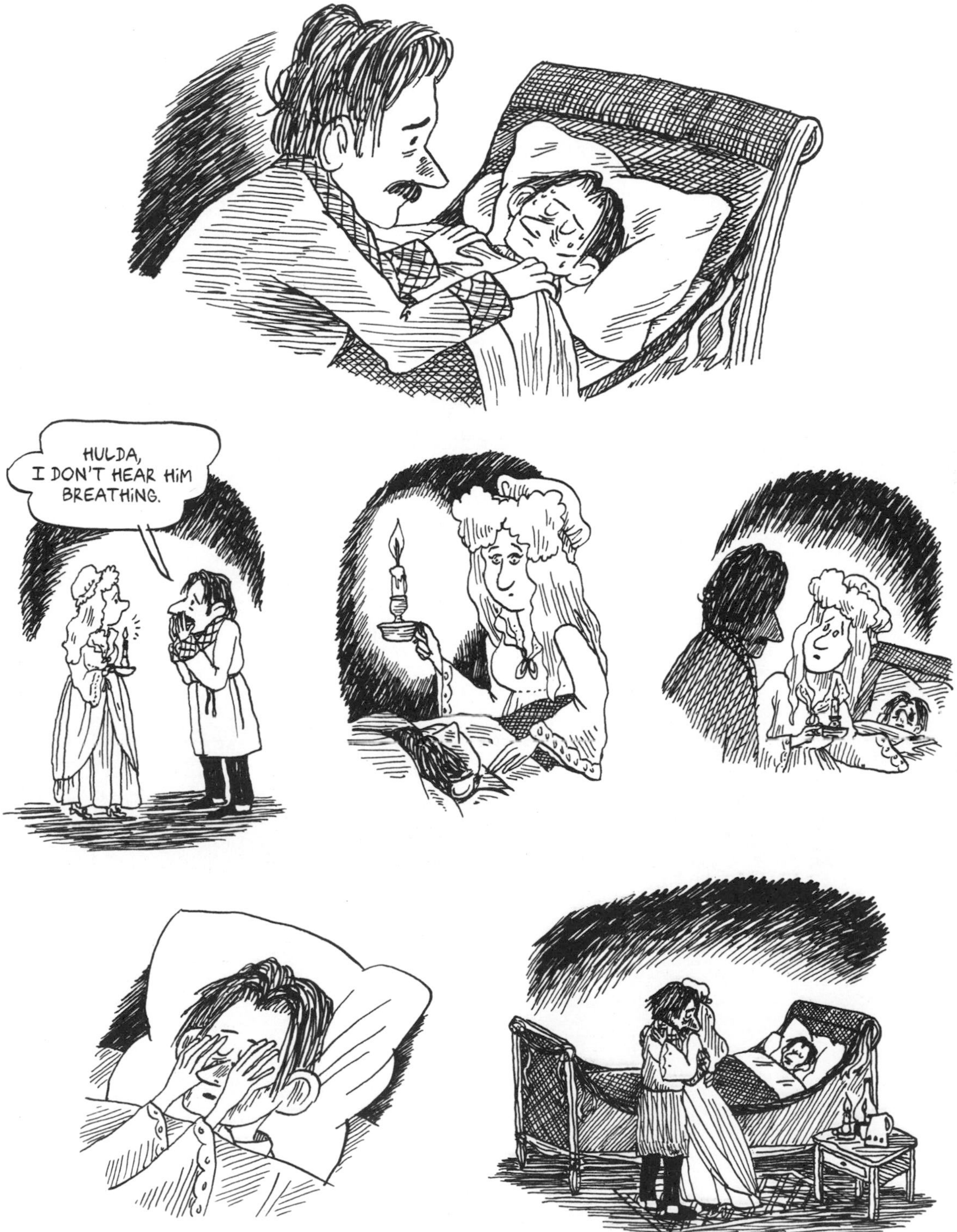
HULDA, I DON'T HEAR HIM BREATHING.

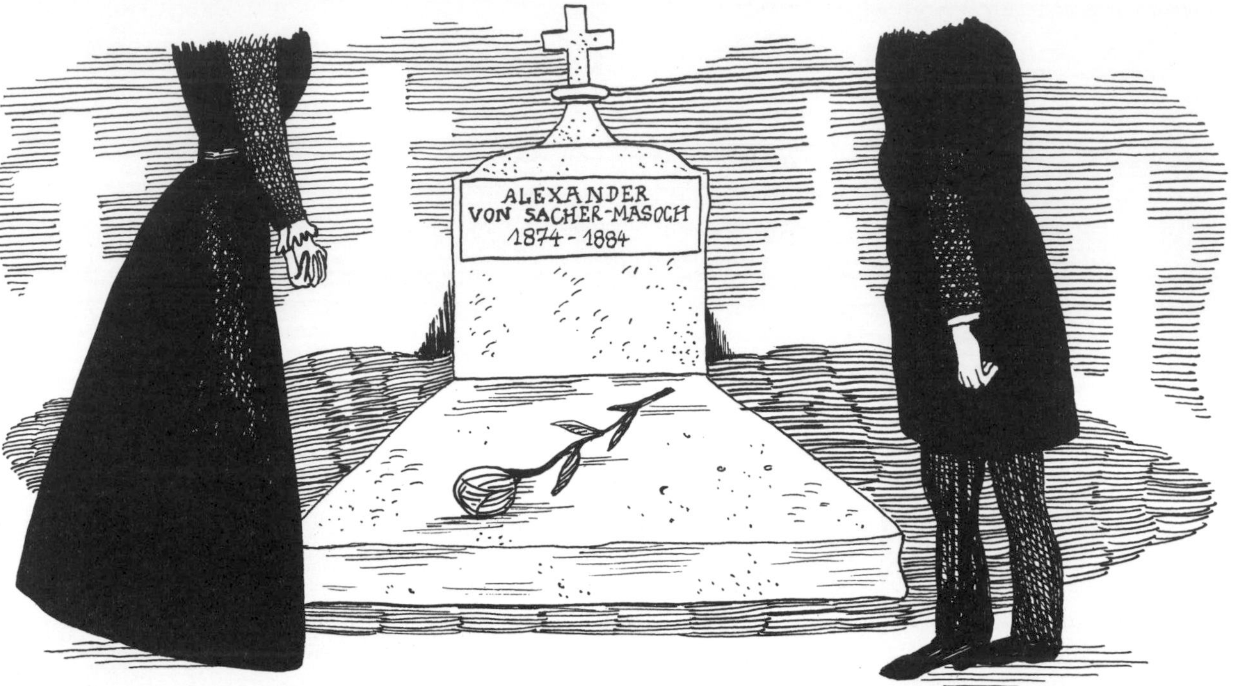
ALEXANDER
VON SACHER-MASOCH
1874 - 1884

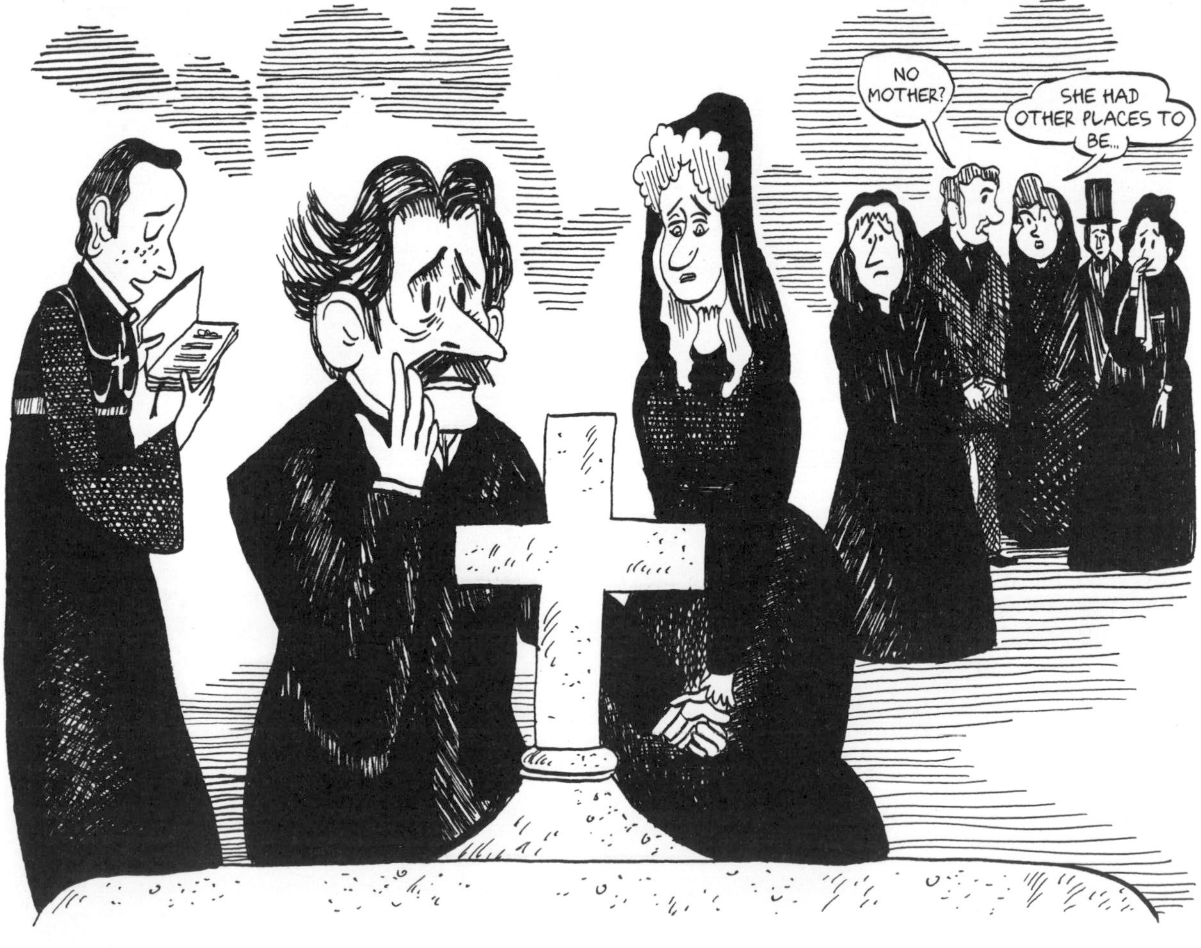
NO MOTHER?
SHE HAD OTHER PLACES TO BE...

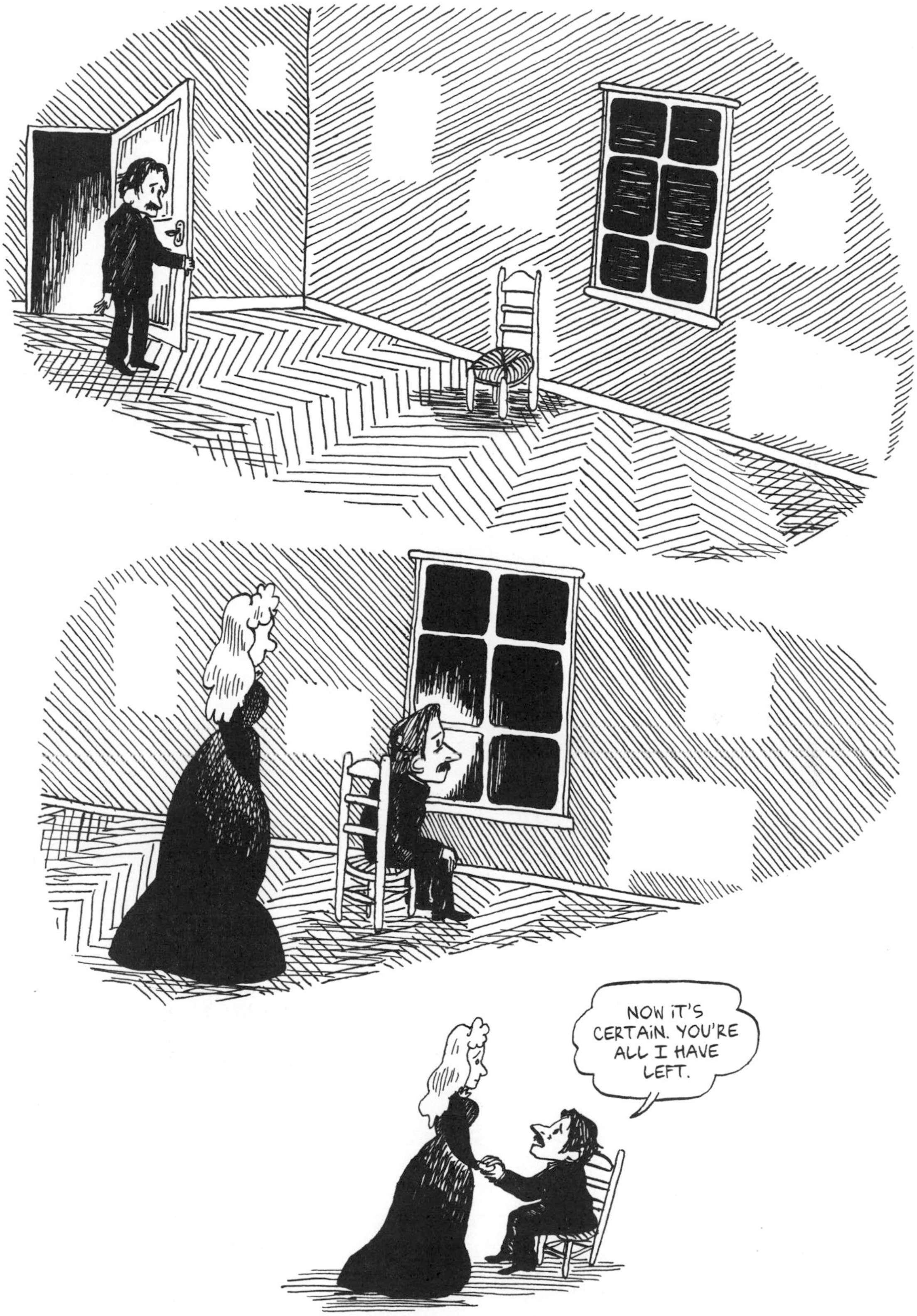
NOW iT'S CERTAiN. YOU'RE ALL I HAVE LEFT.

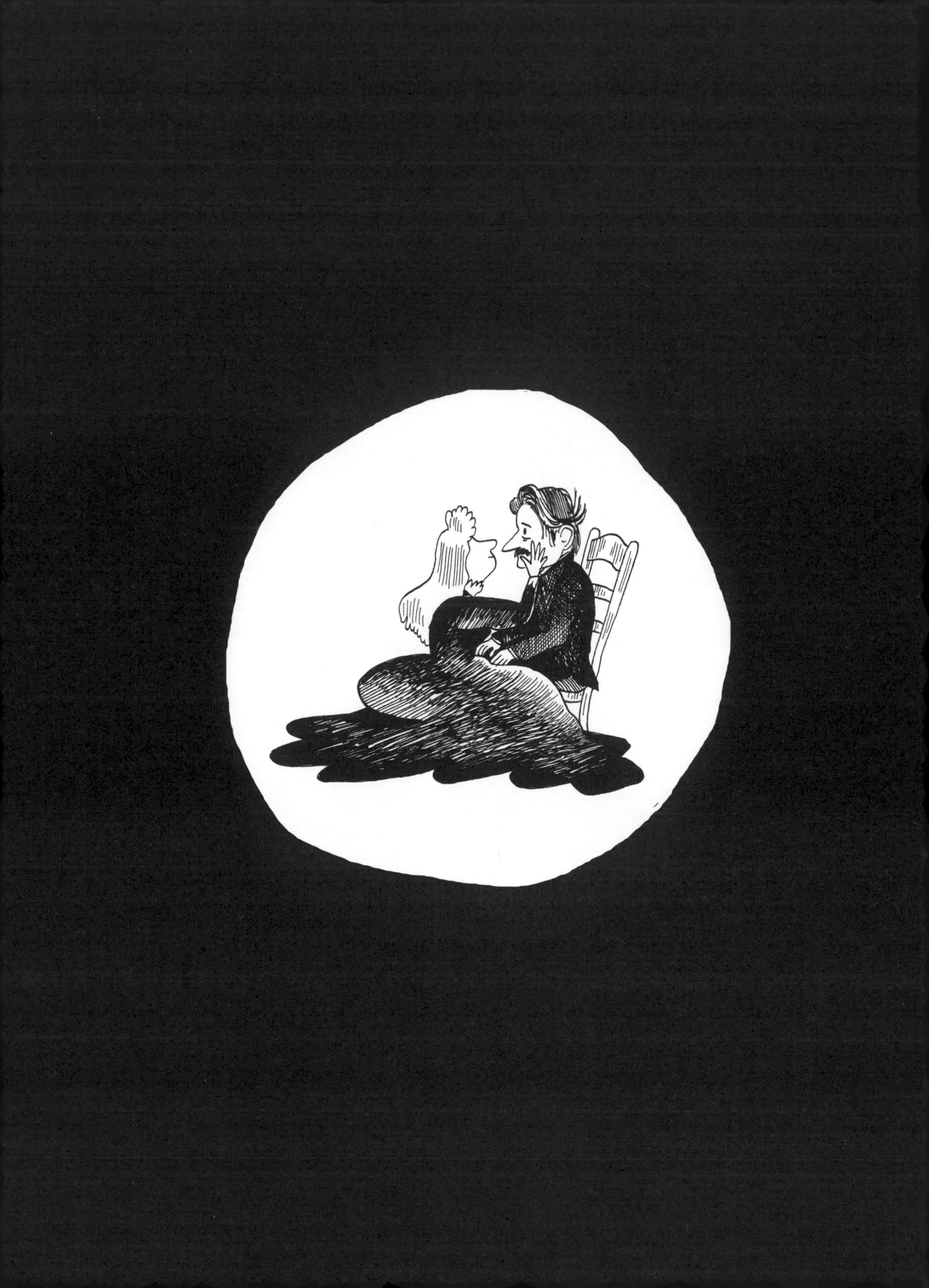

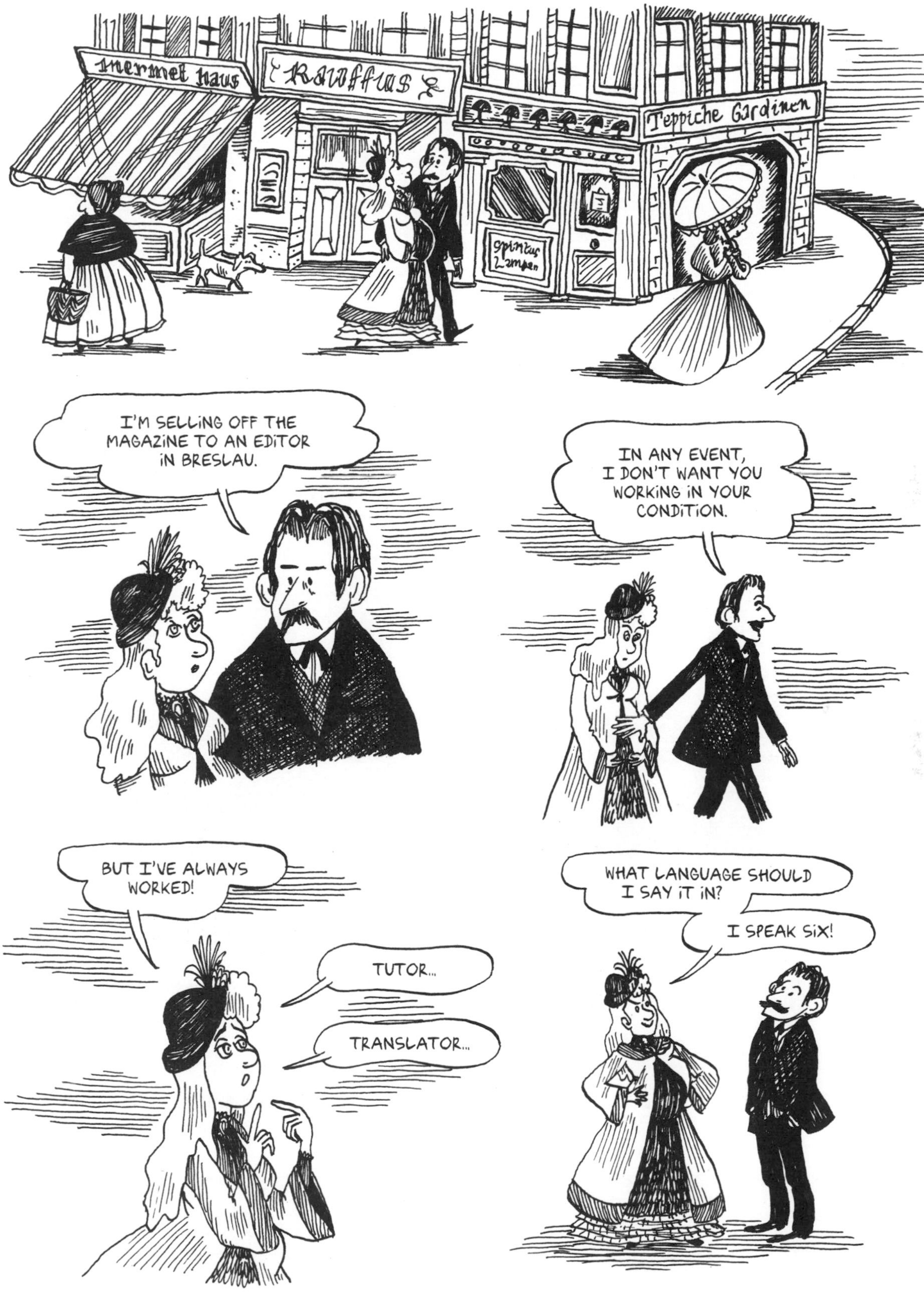
Teppiche Gardinen
I'M SELLING OFF THE MAGAZINE TO AN EDITOR IN BRESLAU.
IN ANY EVENT, I DON'T WANT YOU WORKING IN YOUR CONDITION.
BUT I'VE ALWAYS WORKED!
TUTOR...
TRANSLATOR...
WHAT LANGUAGE SHOULD I SAY IT IN?
I SPEAK SIX!

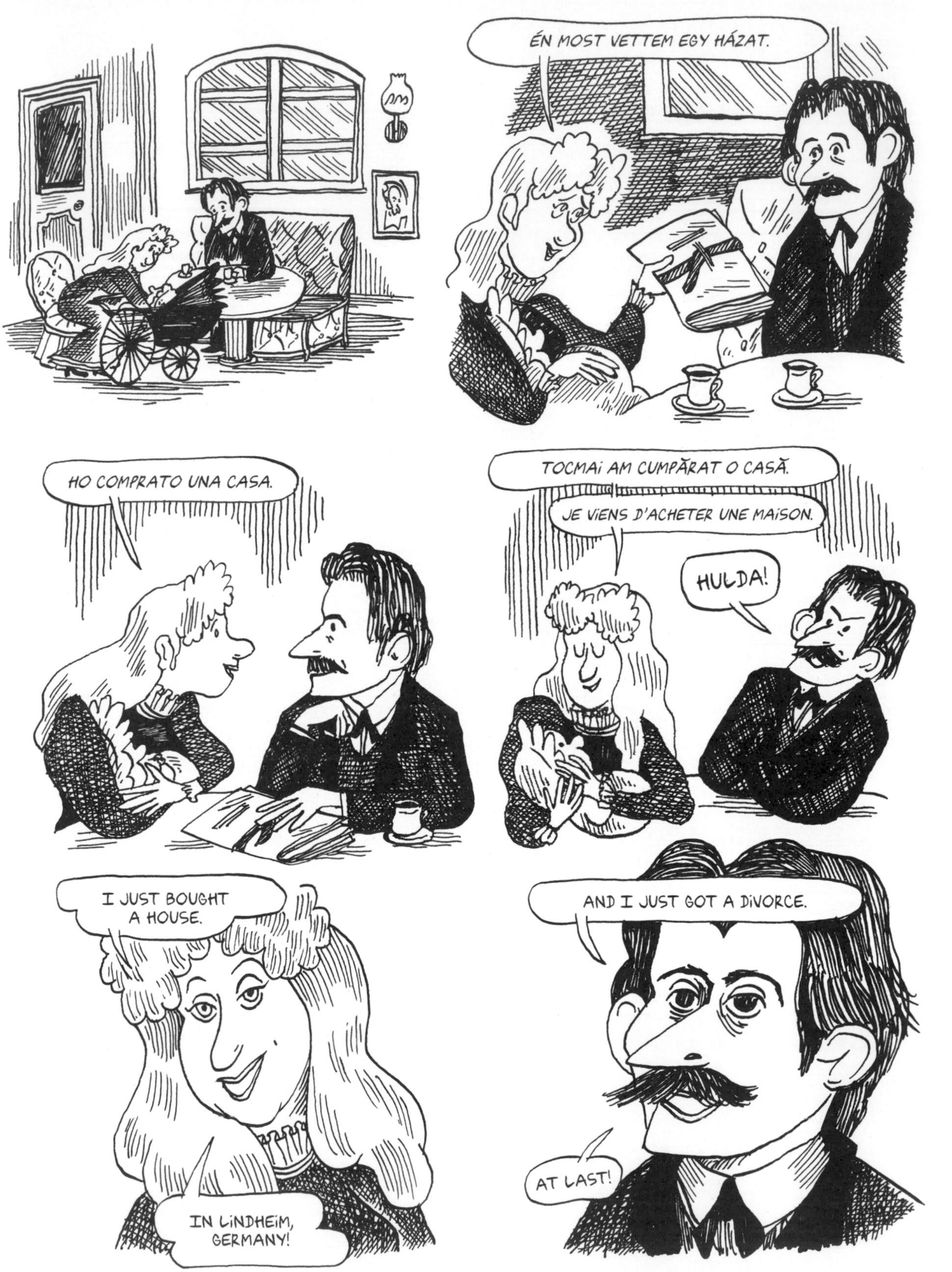
ÉN MOST VETTEM EGY HÁZAT.
HO COMPRATO UNA CASA.
TOCMAI AM CUMPĂRAT O CASĂ.
JE VIENS D'ACHETER UNE MAISON.
HULDA!
I JUST BOUGHT A HOUSE.
IN LINDHEIM, GERMANY!
AND I JUST GOT A DIVORCE.
AT LAST!

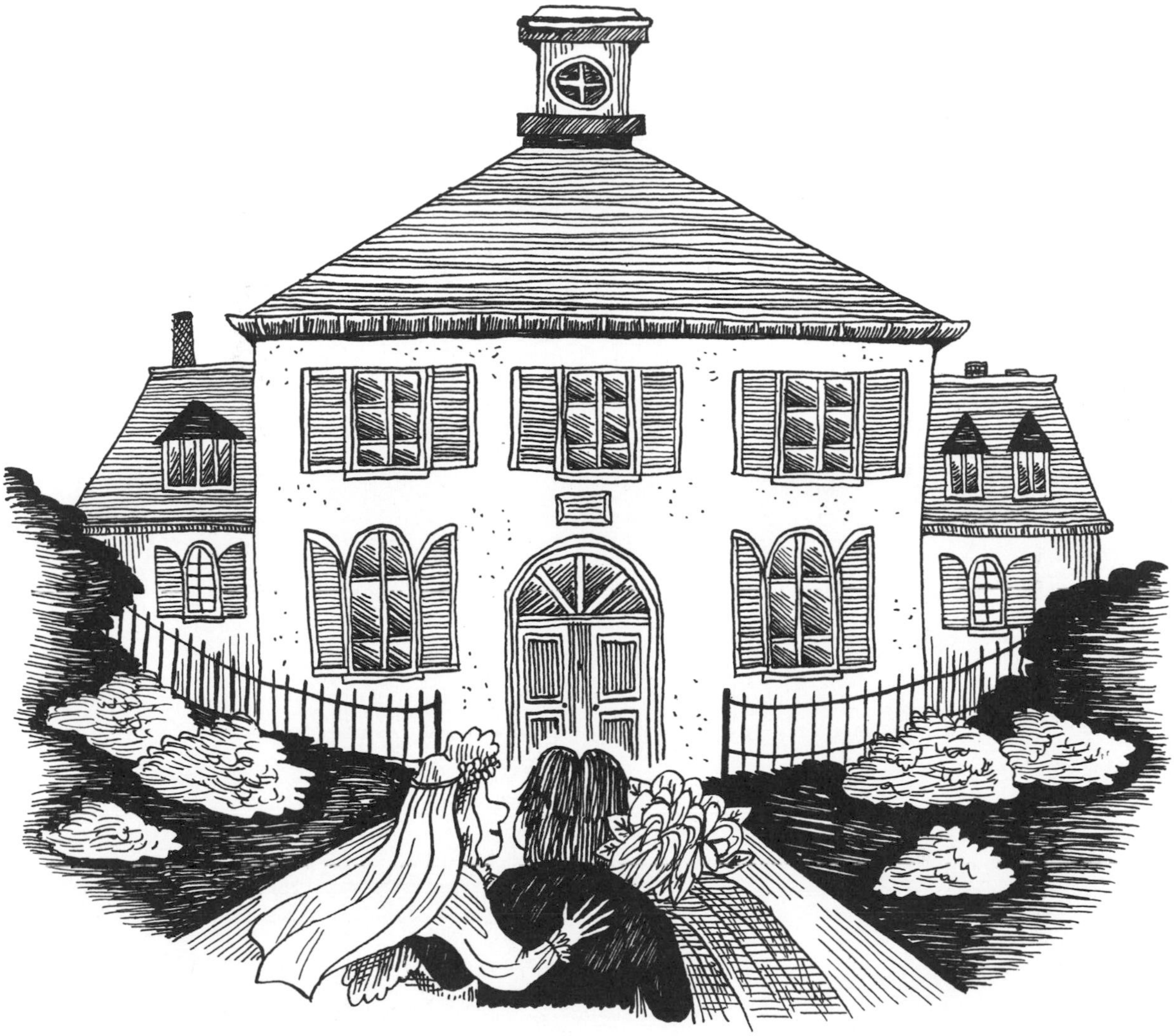

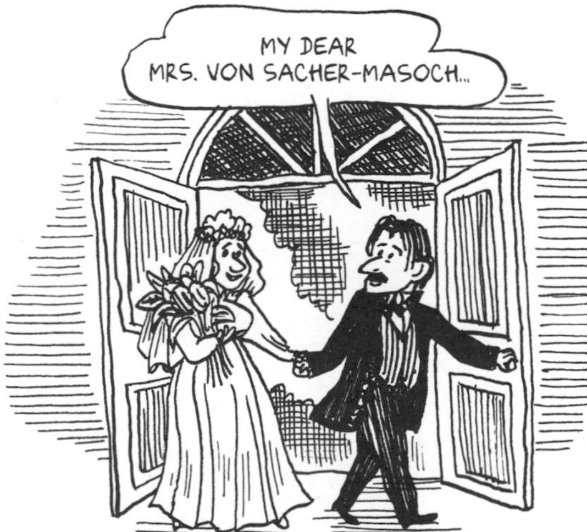
MY DEAR
MRS. VON SACHER-MASOCH...

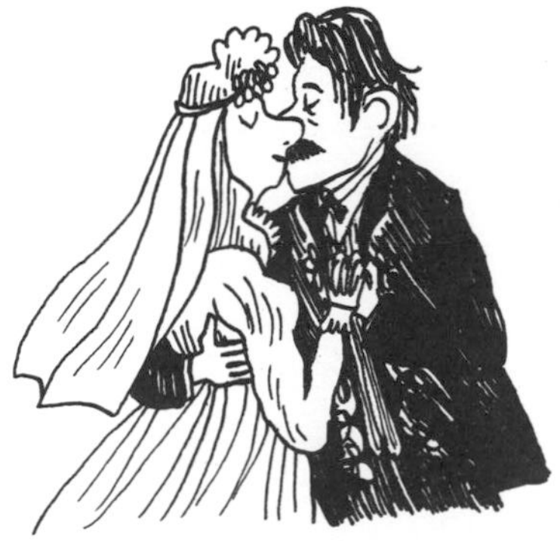

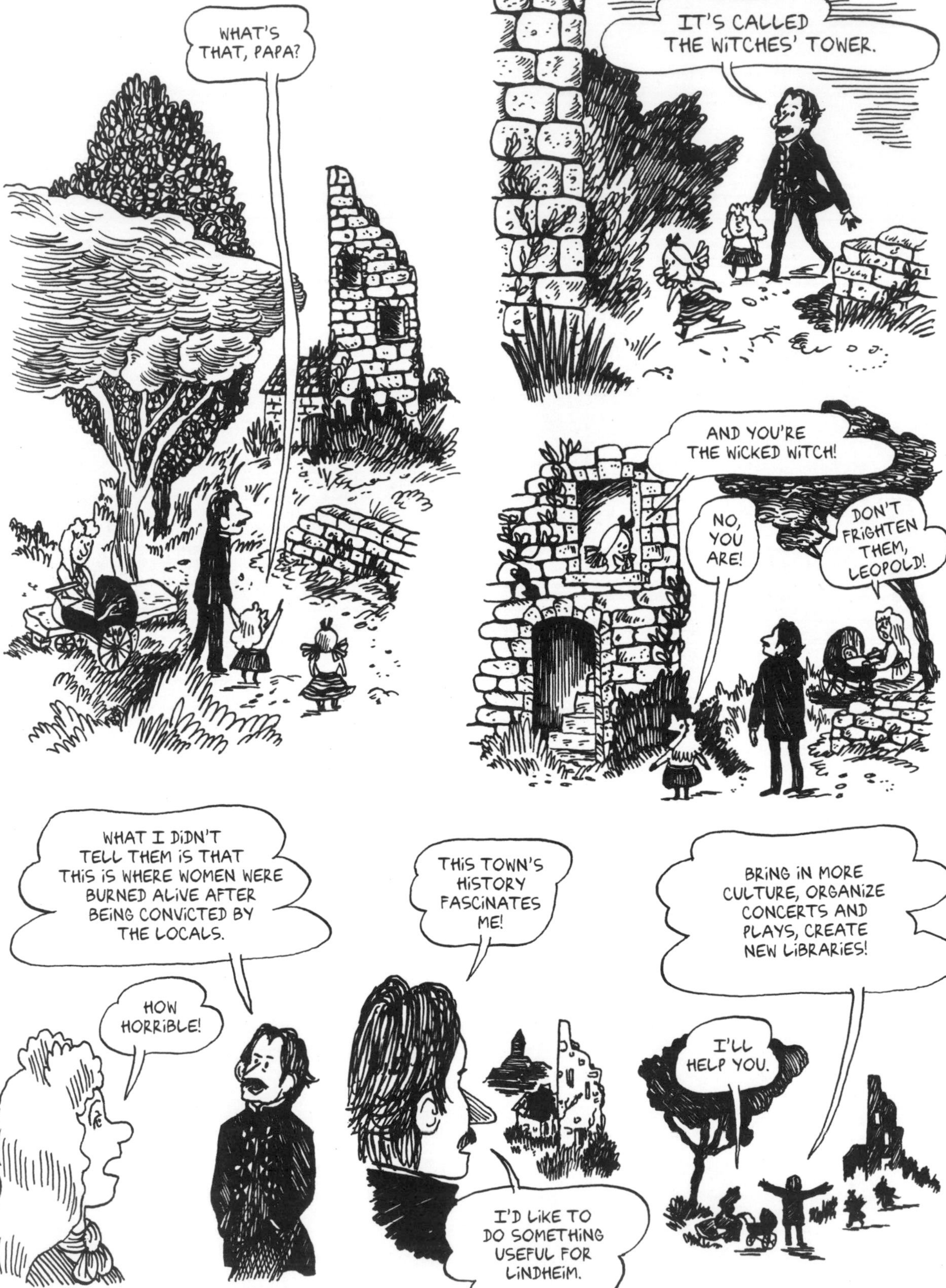
WHAT'S THAT, PAPA?
IT'S CALLED THE WITCHES' TOWER.
AND YOU'RE THE WICKED WITCH!
NO, YOU ARE!
DON'T FRIGHTEN THEM, LEOPOLD!
WHAT I DIDN'T TELL THEM IS THAT THIS IS WHERE WOMEN WERE BURNED ALIVE AFTER BEING CONVICTED BY THE LOCALS.
HOW HORRIBLE!
THIS TOWN'S HISTORY FASCINATES ME!
I'D LIKE TO DO SOMETHING USEFUL FOR LINDHEIM.
BRING IN MORE CULTURE, ORGANIZE CONCERTS AND PLAYS, CREATE NEW LIBRARIES!
I'LL HELP YOU.

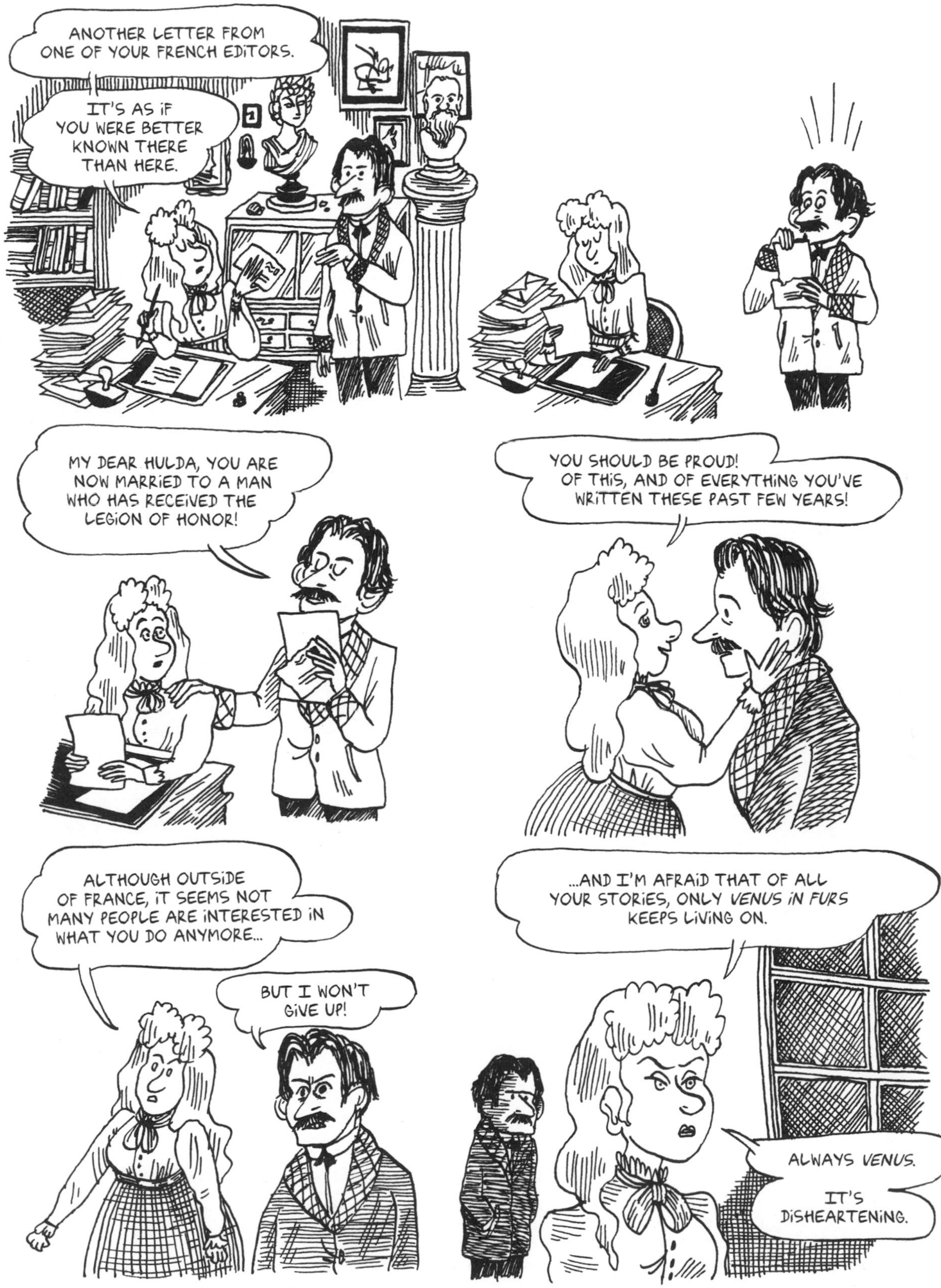
ANOTHER LETTER FROM ONE OF YOUR FRENCH EDITORS.
IT'S AS IF YOU WERE BETTER KNOWN THERE THAN HERE.
MY DEAR HULDA, YOU ARE NOW MARRIED TO A MAN WHO HAS RECEIVED THE LEGION OF HONOR!
YOU SHOULD BE PROUD! OF THIS, AND OF EVERYTHING YOU'VE WRITTEN THESE PAST FEW YEARS!
ALTHOUGH OUTSIDE OF FRANCE, IT SEEMS NOT MANY PEOPLE ARE INTERESTED IN WHAT YOU DO ANYMORE...
BUT I WON'T GIVE UP!
...AND I'M AFRAID THAT OF ALL YOUR STORIES, ONLY *VENUS IN FURS* KEEPS LIVING ON.
ALWAYS *VENUS.*
IT'S DISHEARTENING.

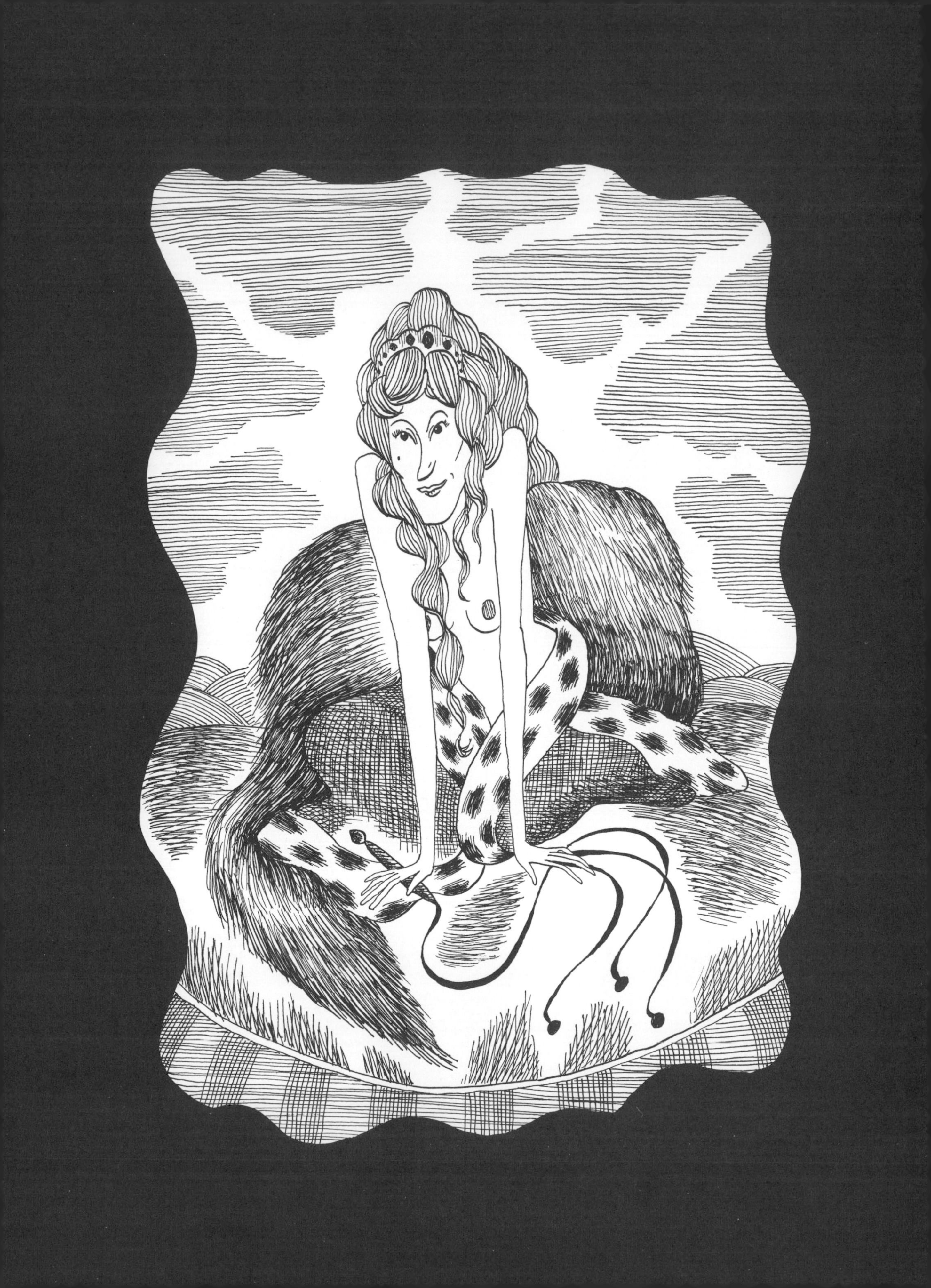

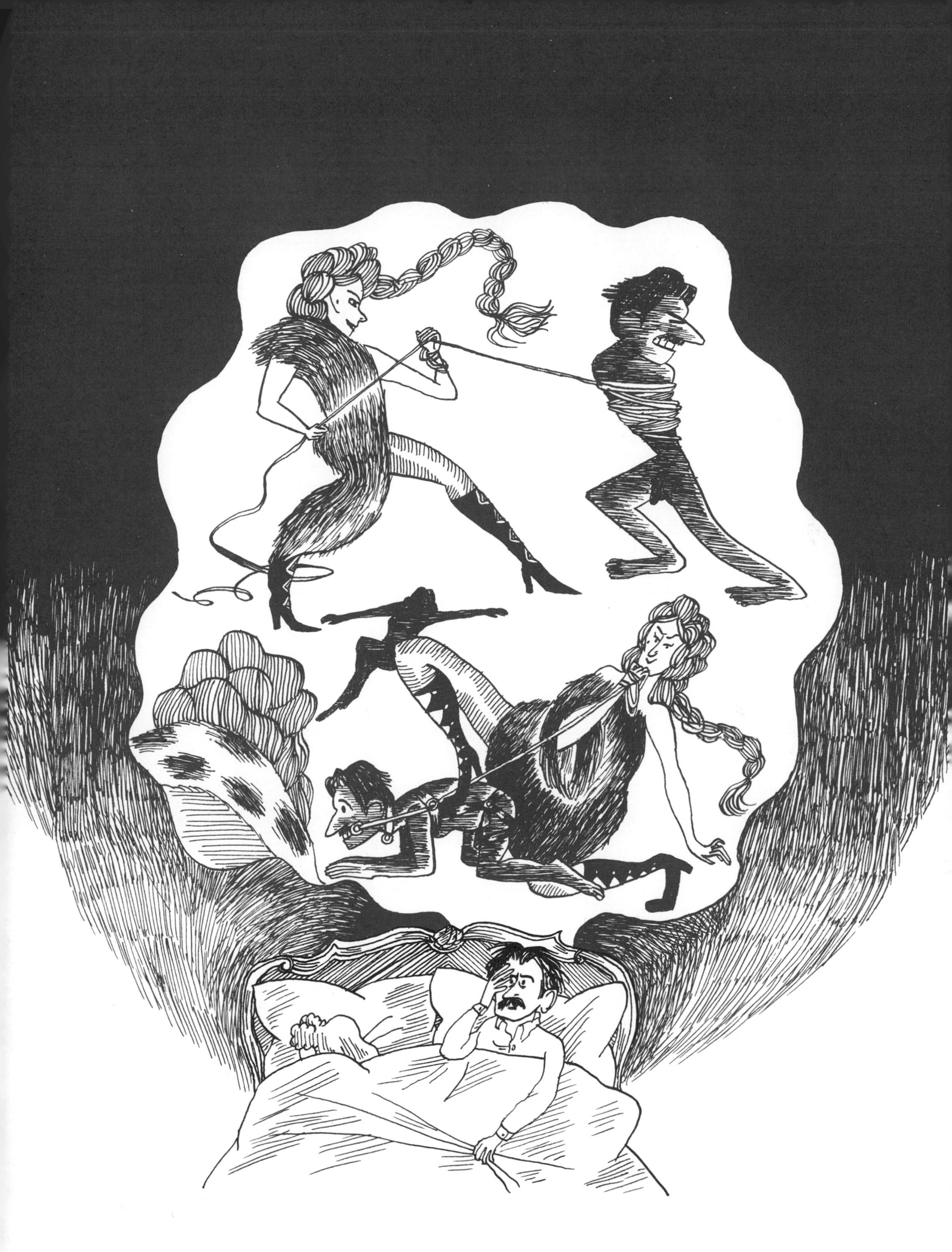

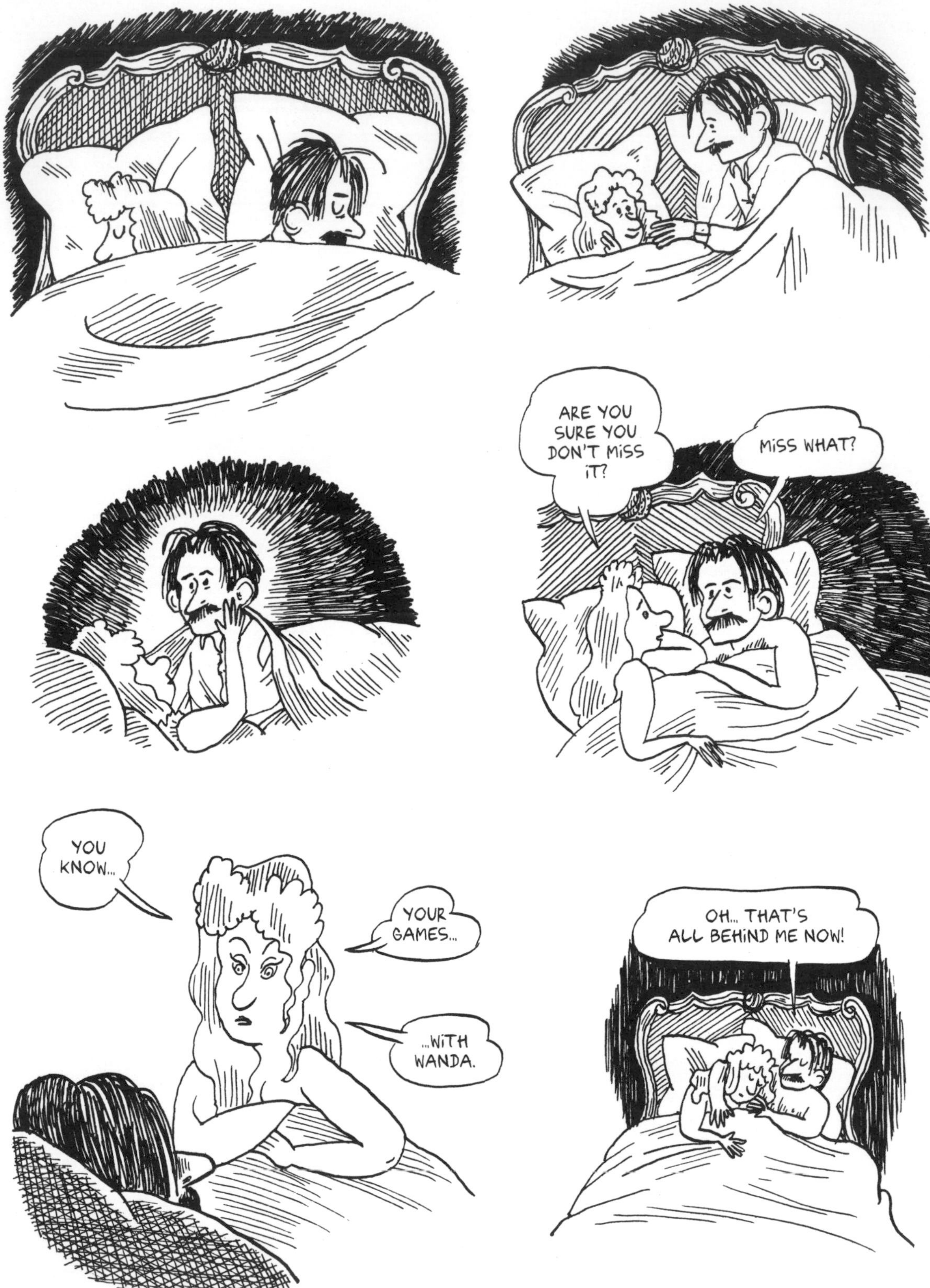
ARE YOU SURE YOU DON'T MISS IT?
MISS WHAT?
YOU KNOW...
YOUR GAMES...
...WITH WANDA.
OH... THAT'S ALL BEHIND ME NOW!

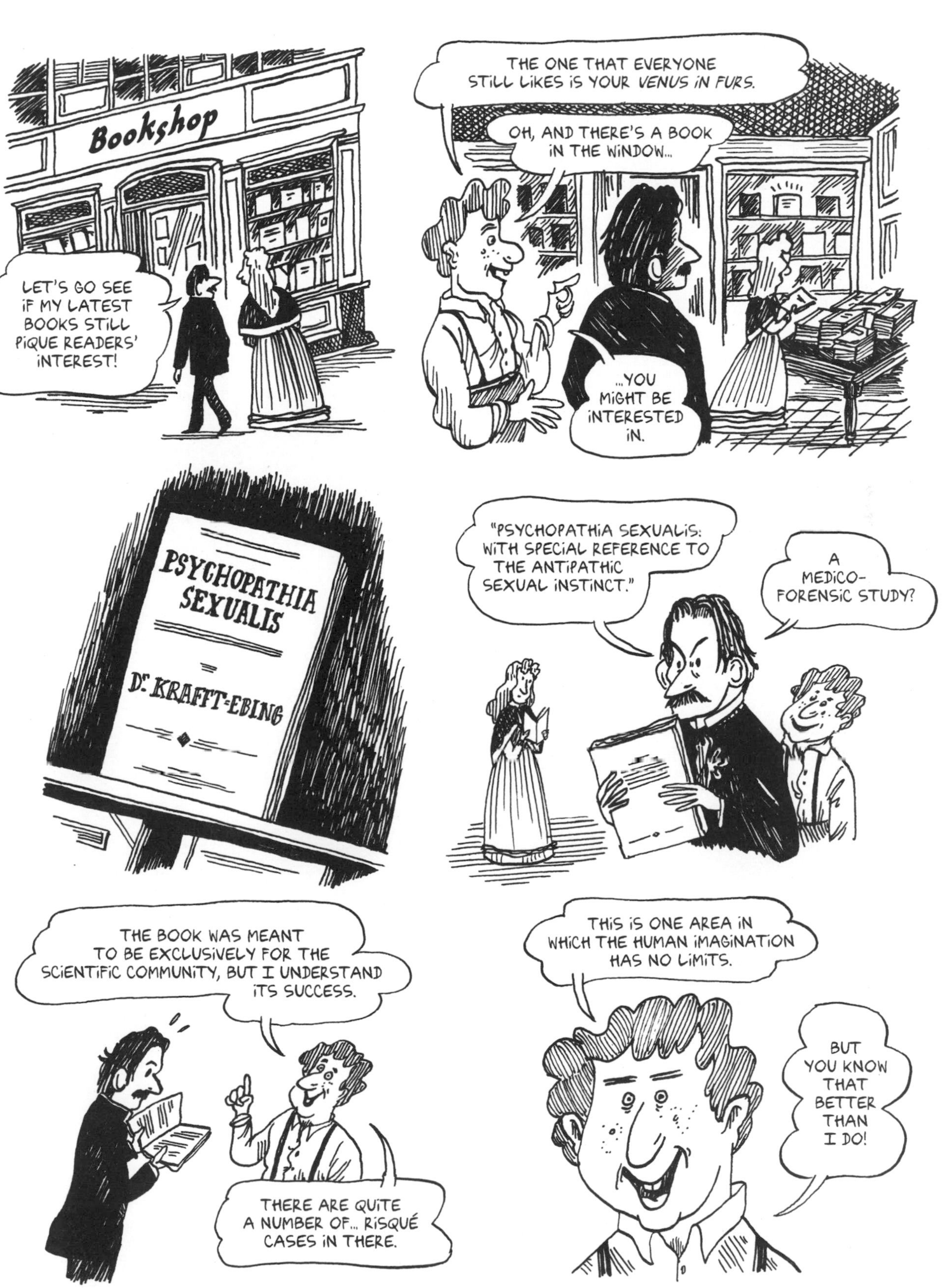
Bookshop
LET'S GO SEE IF MY LATEST BOOKS STILL PIQUE READERS' INTEREST!
THE ONE THAT EVERYONE STILL LIKES IS YOUR *VENUS IN FURS*.
OH, AND THERE'S A BOOK IN THE WINDOW...
...YOU MIGHT BE INTERESTED IN.
PSYCHOPATHIA SEXUALIS
Dr. KRAFFT-EBING
"PSYCHOPATHIA SEXUALIS: WITH SPECIAL REFERENCE TO THE ANTIPATHIC SEXUAL INSTINCT."
A MEDICO-FORENSIC STUDY?
THE BOOK WAS MEANT TO BE EXCLUSIVELY FOR THE SCIENTIFIC COMMUNITY, BUT I UNDERSTAND ITS SUCCESS.
THERE ARE QUITE A NUMBER OF... RISQUÉ CASES IN THERE.
THIS IS ONE AREA IN WHICH THE HUMAN IMAGINATION HAS NO LIMITS.
BUT YOU KNOW THAT BETTER THAN I DO!

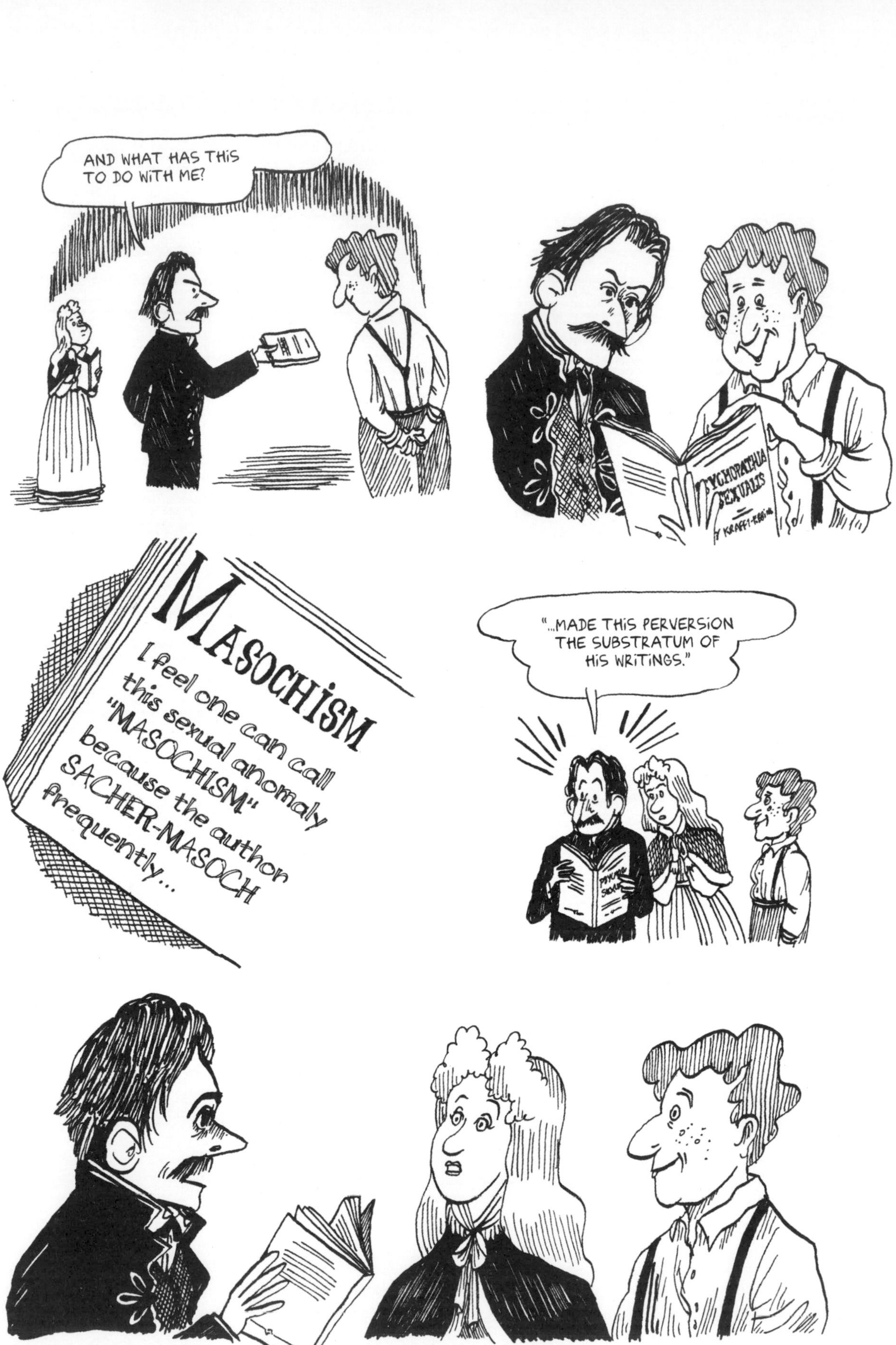
AND WHAT HAS THIS TO DO WITH ME?
PSYCHOPATHIA SEXUALIS
KRAFFT-EBING
MASOCHISM
I feel one can call this sexual anomaly "MASOCHISM" because the author SACHER-MASOCH frequently...
"...MADE THIS PERVERSION THE SUBSTRATUM OF HIS WRITINGS."

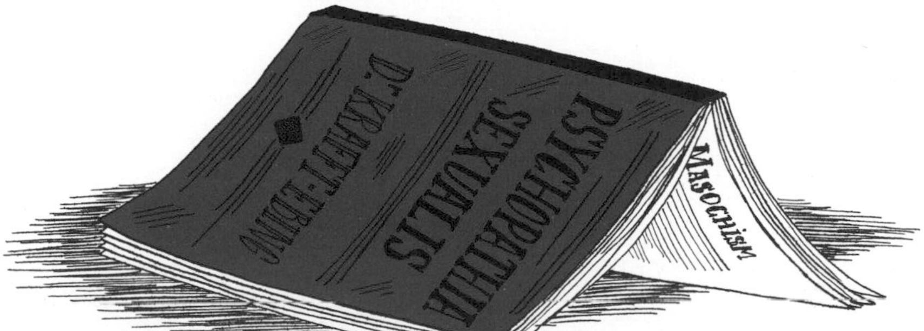
PSYCHOPATHIA
SEXUALIS
Dr. KRAFFT-EBING
Masochism

Leopold realizes with horror that he has unwittingly become the inspiration for masochism. His name will forevermore be associated with the Marquis de Sade, whose work was rejected, and who was thrown first into prison, then an insane asylum.

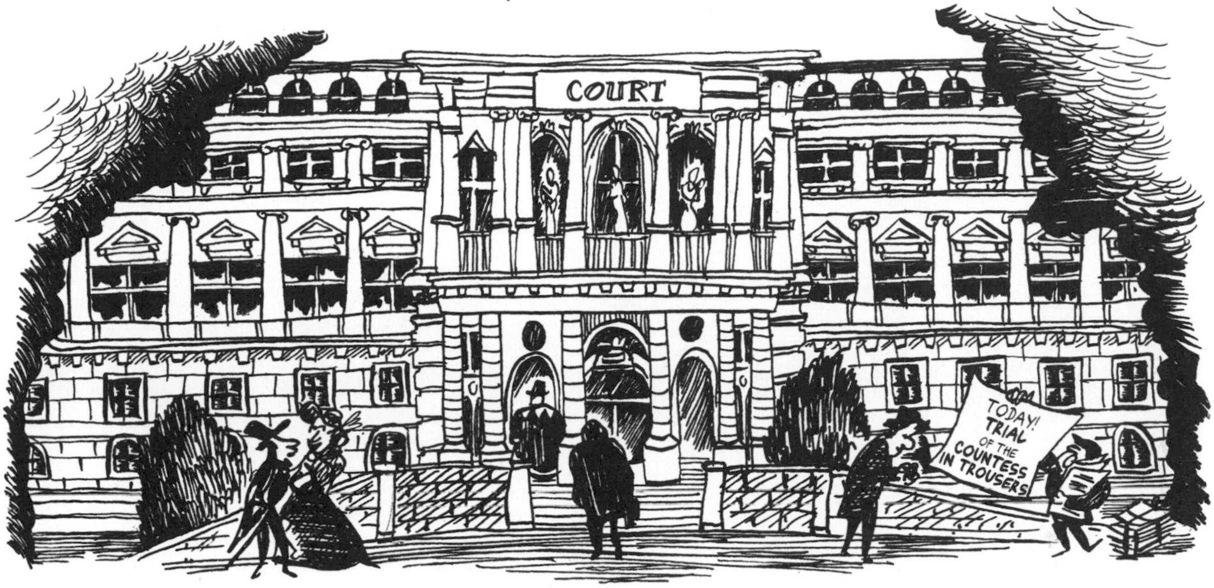
COURT
TODAY! TRIAL OF THE COUNTESS IN TROUSERS

Meanwhile, in Vienna, psychiatric medicine seems to be venturing down new roads.

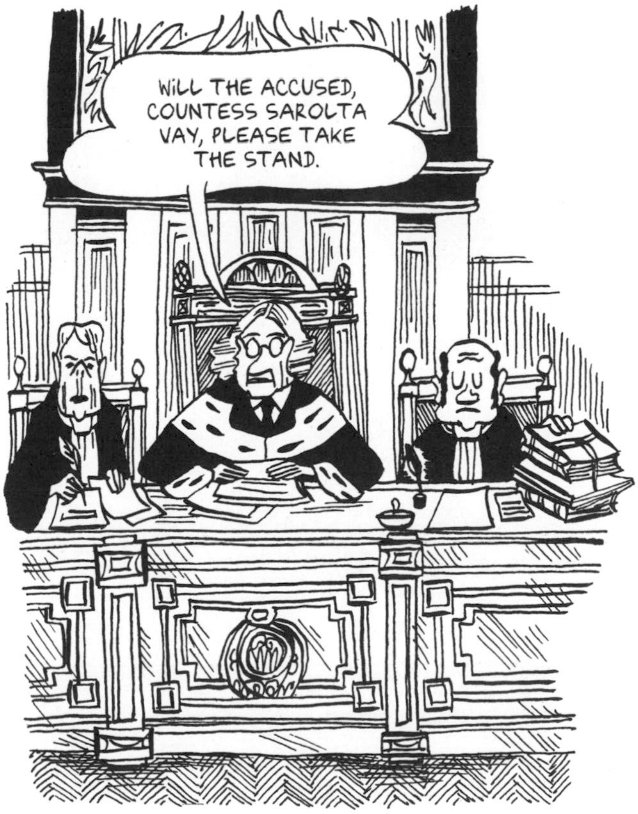
WILL THE ACCUSED, COUNTESS SAROLTA VAY, PLEASE TAKE THE STAND.

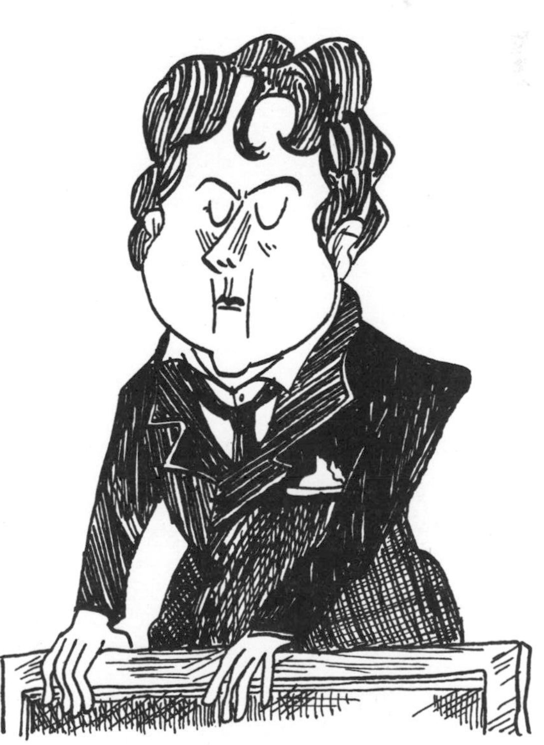

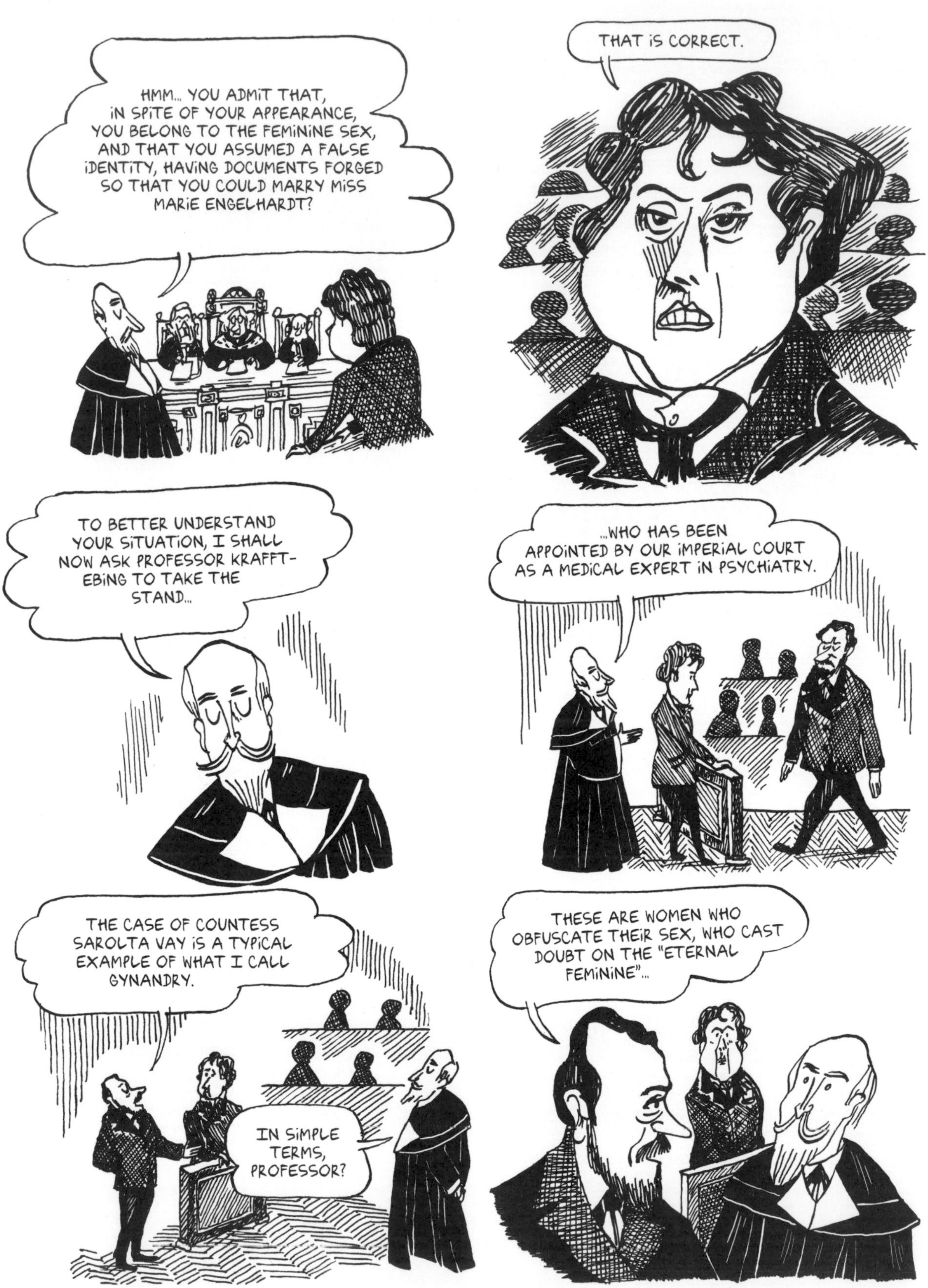
HMM... YOU ADMIT THAT, IN SPITE OF YOUR APPEARANCE, YOU BELONG TO THE FEMININE SEX, AND THAT YOU ASSUMED A FALSE IDENTITY, HAVING DOCUMENTS FORGED SO THAT YOU COULD MARRY MISS MARIE ENGELHARDT?
THAT IS CORRECT.
TO BETTER UNDERSTAND YOUR SITUATION, I SHALL NOW ASK PROFESSOR KRAFFT-EBING TO TAKE THE STAND...
...WHO HAS BEEN APPOINTED BY OUR IMPERIAL COURT AS A MEDICAL EXPERT IN PSYCHIATRY.
THE CASE OF COUNTESS SAROLTA VAY IS A TYPICAL EXAMPLE OF WHAT I CALL GYNANDRY.
IN SIMPLE TERMS, PROFESSOR?
THESE ARE WOMEN WHO OBFUSCATE THEIR SEX, WHO CAST DOUBT ON THE "ETERNAL FEMININE"...

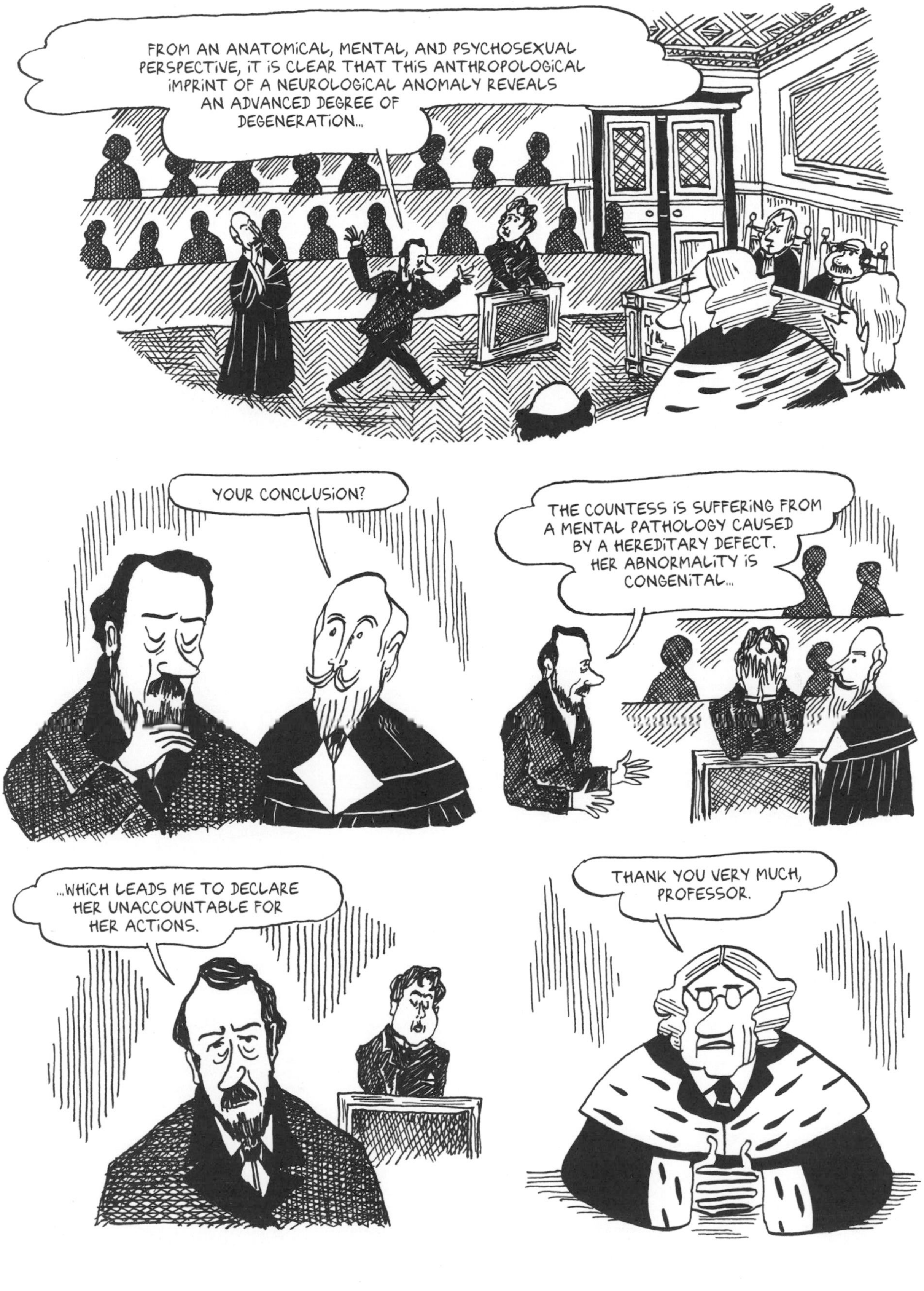
FROM AN ANATOMICAL, MENTAL, AND PSYCHOSEXUAL PERSPECTIVE, IT IS CLEAR THAT THIS ANTHROPOLOGICAL IMPRINT OF A NEUROLOGICAL ANOMALY REVEALS AN ADVANCED DEGREE OF DEGENERATION...
YOUR CONCLUSION?
THE COUNTESS IS SUFFERING FROM A MENTAL PATHOLOGY CAUSED BY A HEREDITARY DEFECT. HER ABNORMALITY IS CONGENITAL...
...WHICH LEADS ME TO DECLARE HER UNACCOUNTABLE FOR HER ACTIONS.
THANK YOU VERY MUCH, PROFESSOR.

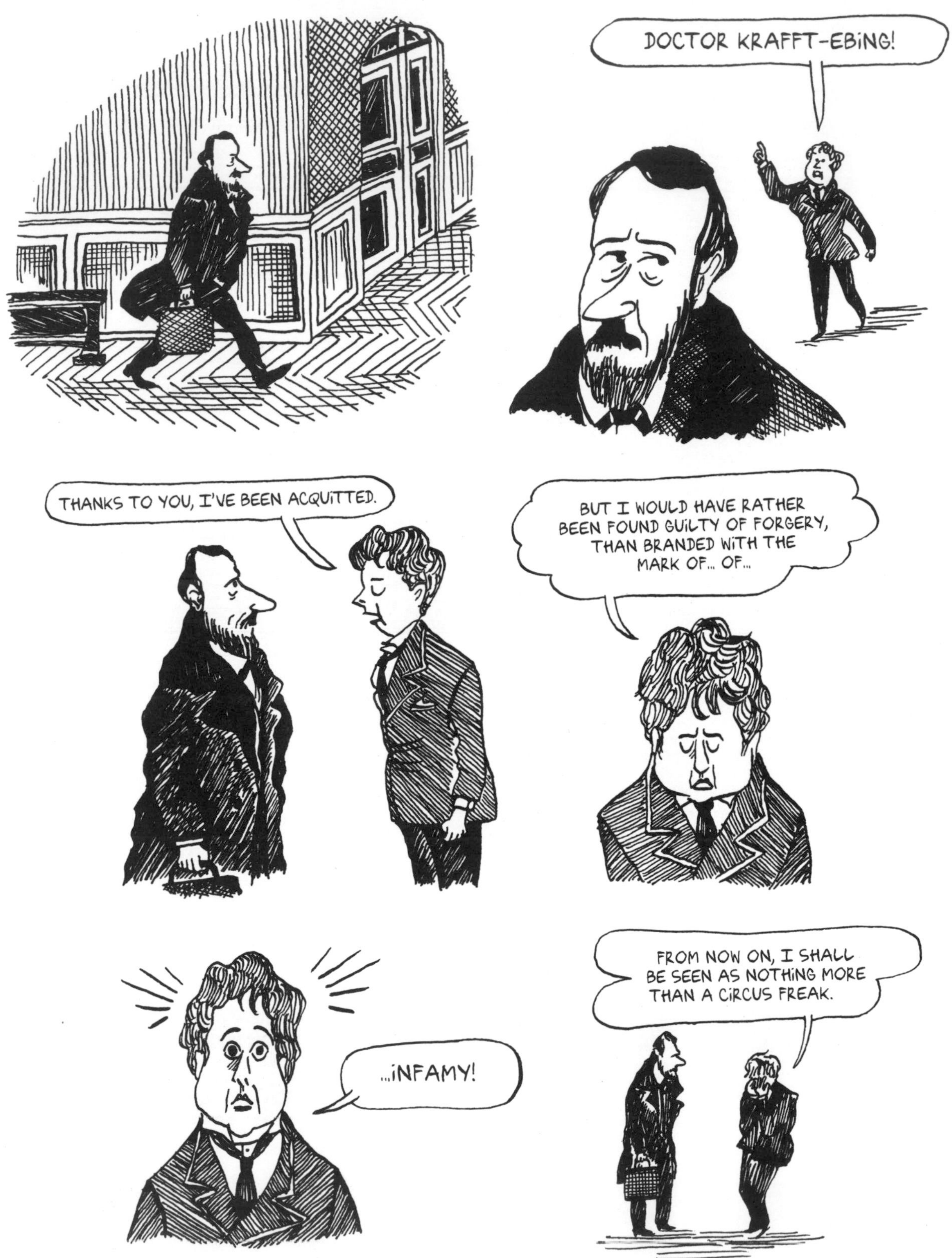
DOCTOR KRAFFT-EBING!
THANKS TO YOU, I'VE BEEN ACQUITTED.
BUT I WOULD HAVE RATHER BEEN FOUND GUILTY OF FORGERY, THAN BRANDED WITH THE MARK OF... OF...
...INFAMY!
FROM NOW ON, I SHALL BE SEEN AS NOTHING MORE THAN A CIRCUS FREAK.

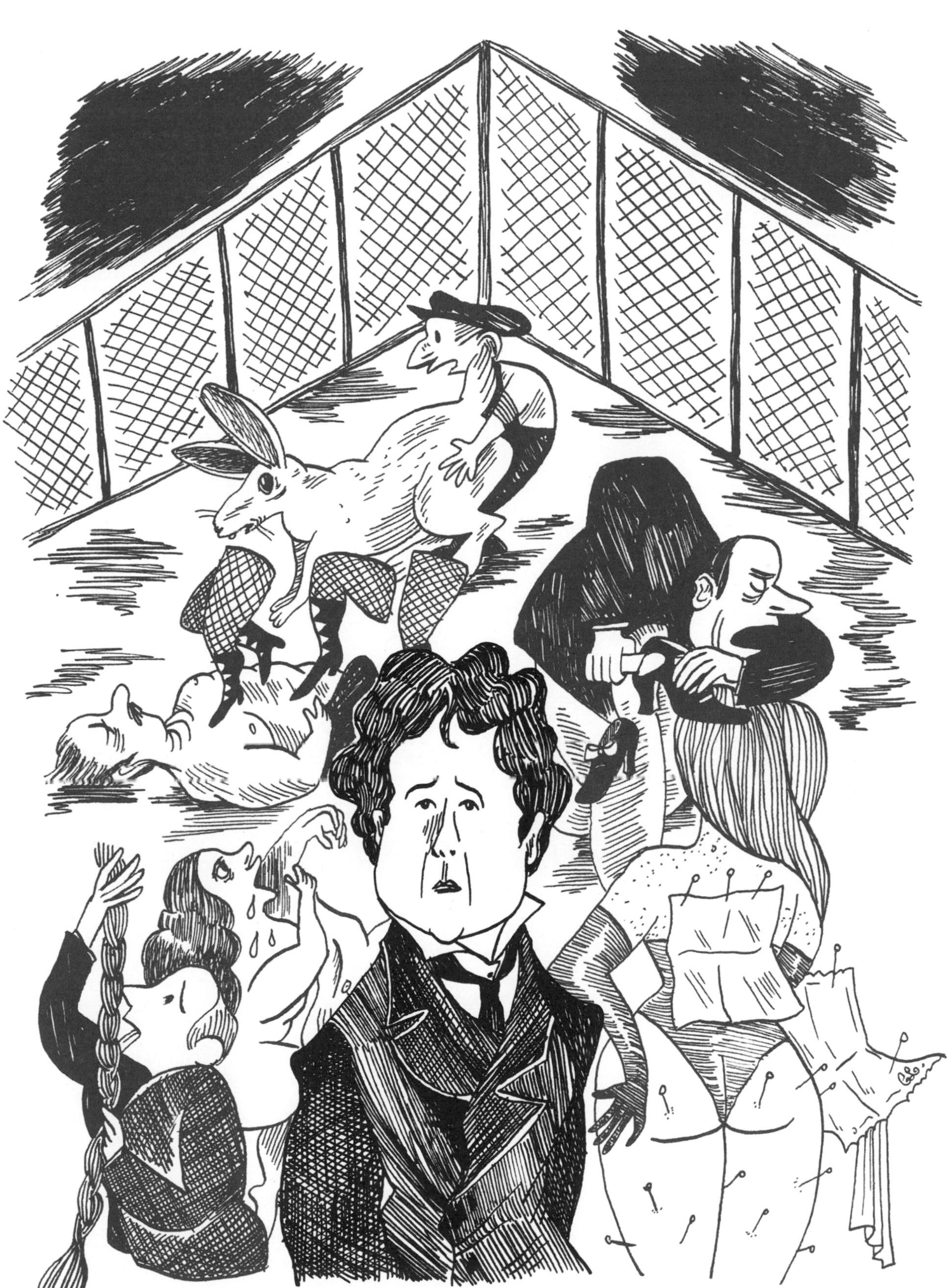

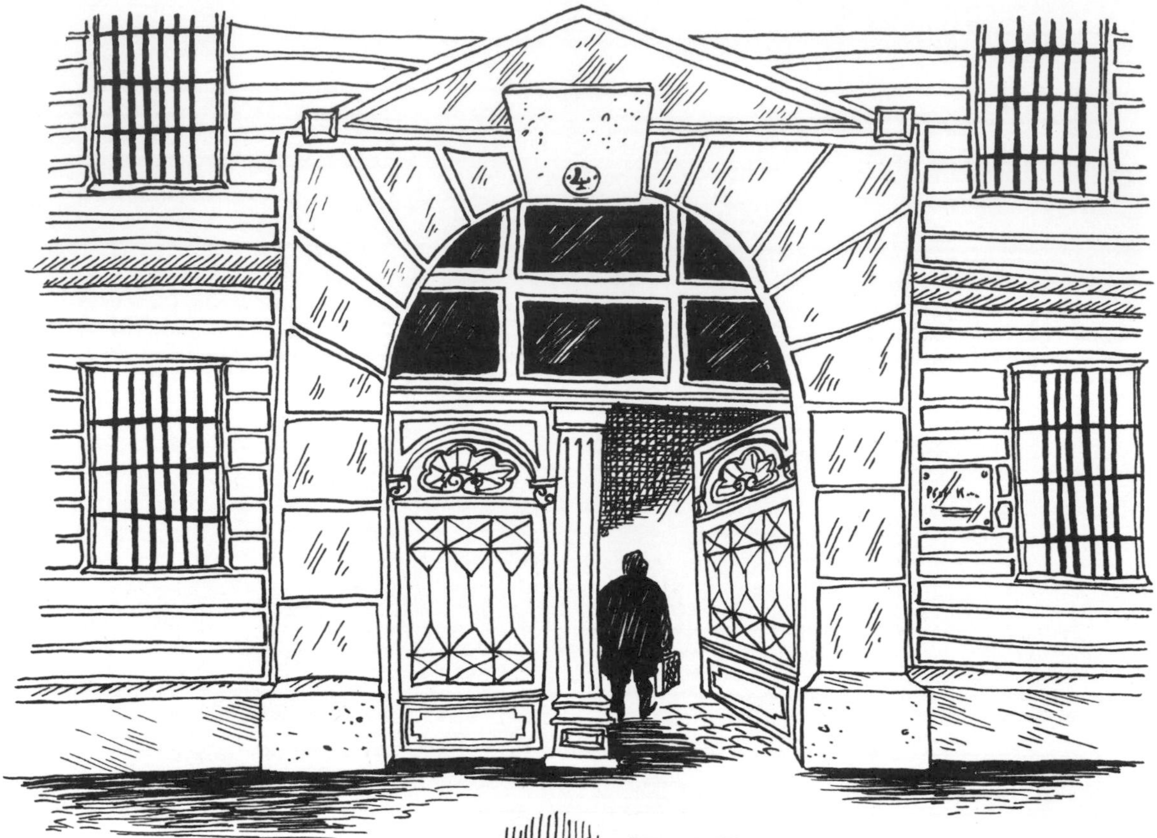

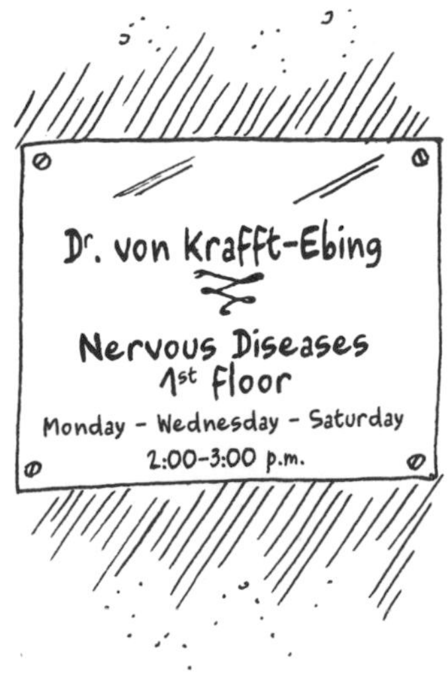
Dr. von Krafft-Ebing
Nervous Diseases
1st Floor
Monday - Wednesday - Saturday
2:00-3:00 p.m.

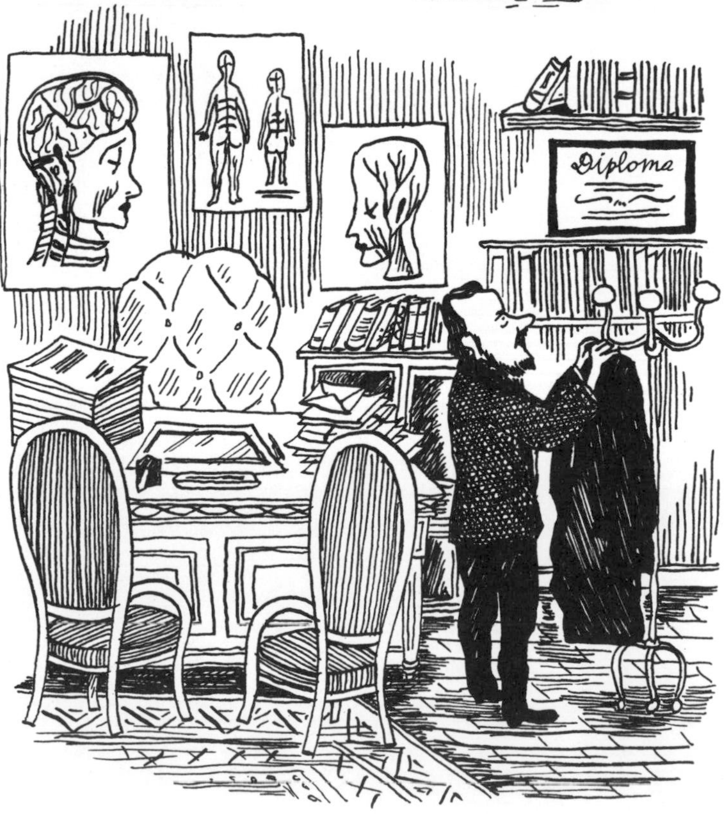
Diploma

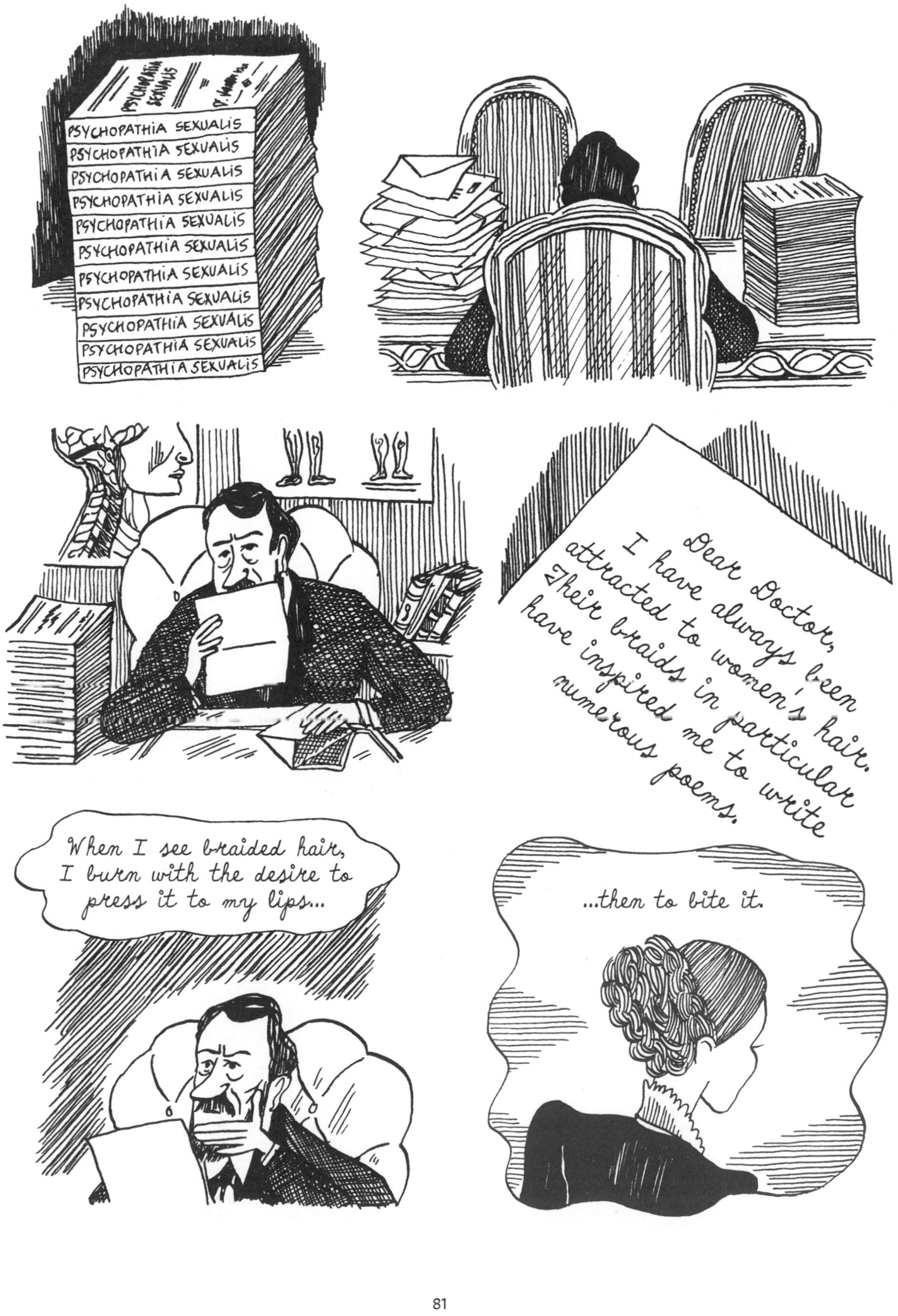
PSYCHOPATHIA SEXUALIS
PSYCHOPATHIA SEXUALIS
PSYCHOPATHIA SEXUALIS
PSYCHOPATHIA SEXUALIS
PSYCHOPATHIA SEXUALIS
PSYCHOPATHIA SEXUALIS
PSYCHOPATHIA SEXUALIS
PSYCHOPATHIA SEXUALIS
PSYCHOPATHIA SEXUALIS
PSYCHOPATHIA SEXUALIS
PSYCHOPATHIA SEXUALIS
PSYCHOPATHIA SEXUALIS
Dear Doctor,
I have always been attracted to women's hair. Their braids in particular have inspired me to write numerous poems.
When I see braided hair, I burn with the desire to press it to my lips...
...then to bite it.

When I'm in the street, I can't resist the temptation to take my scissors and cut the braids that I most covet.

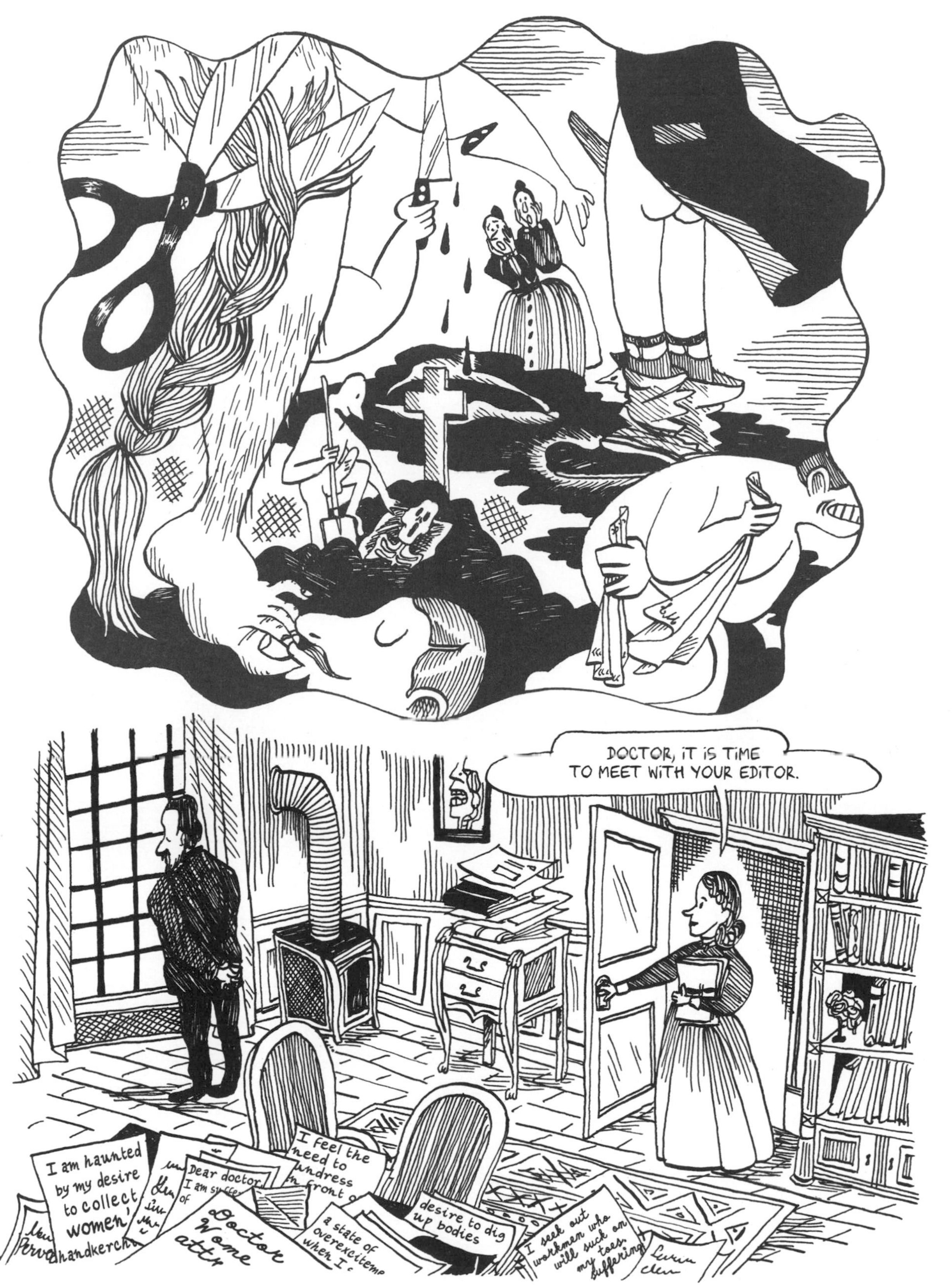
DOCTOR, IT IS TIME TO MEET WITH YOUR EDITOR.
I am haunted by my desire to collect women' handkerch
Dear doctor, I am succ
I feel the need to undress in front o
Doctor
desire to dig up bodies
a state of overexcitem when I
I seek out workmen who will suck on my toes. suffering

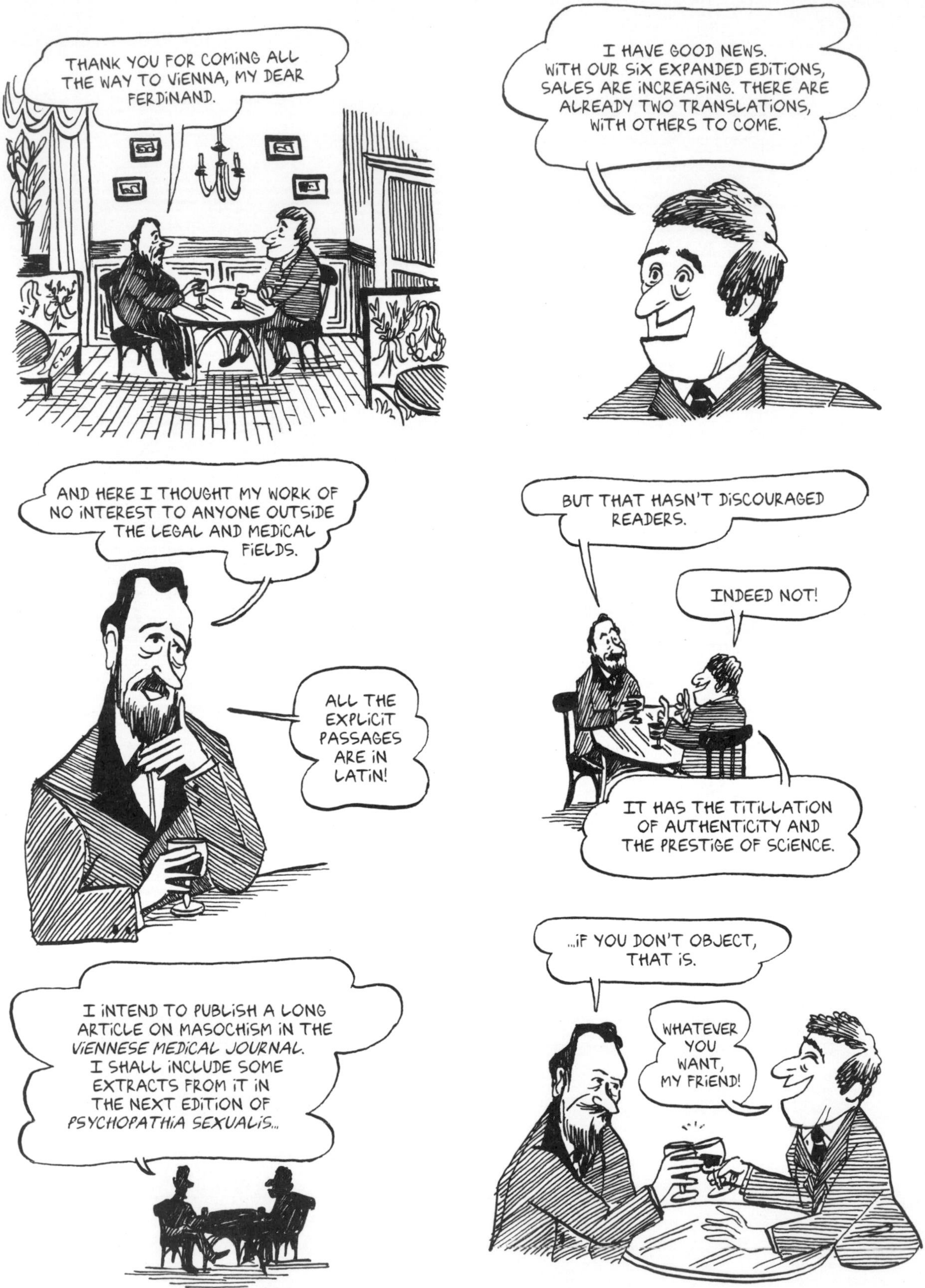
THANK YOU FOR COMING ALL THE WAY TO VIENNA, MY DEAR FERDINAND.
I HAVE GOOD NEWS. WITH OUR SIX EXPANDED EDITIONS, SALES ARE INCREASING. THERE ARE ALREADY TWO TRANSLATIONS, WITH OTHERS TO COME.
AND HERE I THOUGHT MY WORK OF NO INTEREST TO ANYONE OUTSIDE THE LEGAL AND MEDICAL FIELDS.
ALL THE EXPLICIT PASSAGES ARE IN LATIN!
BUT THAT HASN'T DISCOURAGED READERS.
INDEED NOT!
IT HAS THE TITILLATION OF AUTHENTICITY AND THE PRESTIGE OF SCIENCE.
I INTEND TO PUBLISH A LONG ARTICLE ON MASOCHISM IN THE *VIENNESE MEDICAL JOURNAL*. I SHALL INCLUDE SOME EXTRACTS FROM IT IN THE NEXT EDITION OF *PSYCHOPATHIA SEXUALIS*...
...IF YOU DON'T OBJECT, THAT IS.
WHATEVER YOU WANT, MY FRIEND!

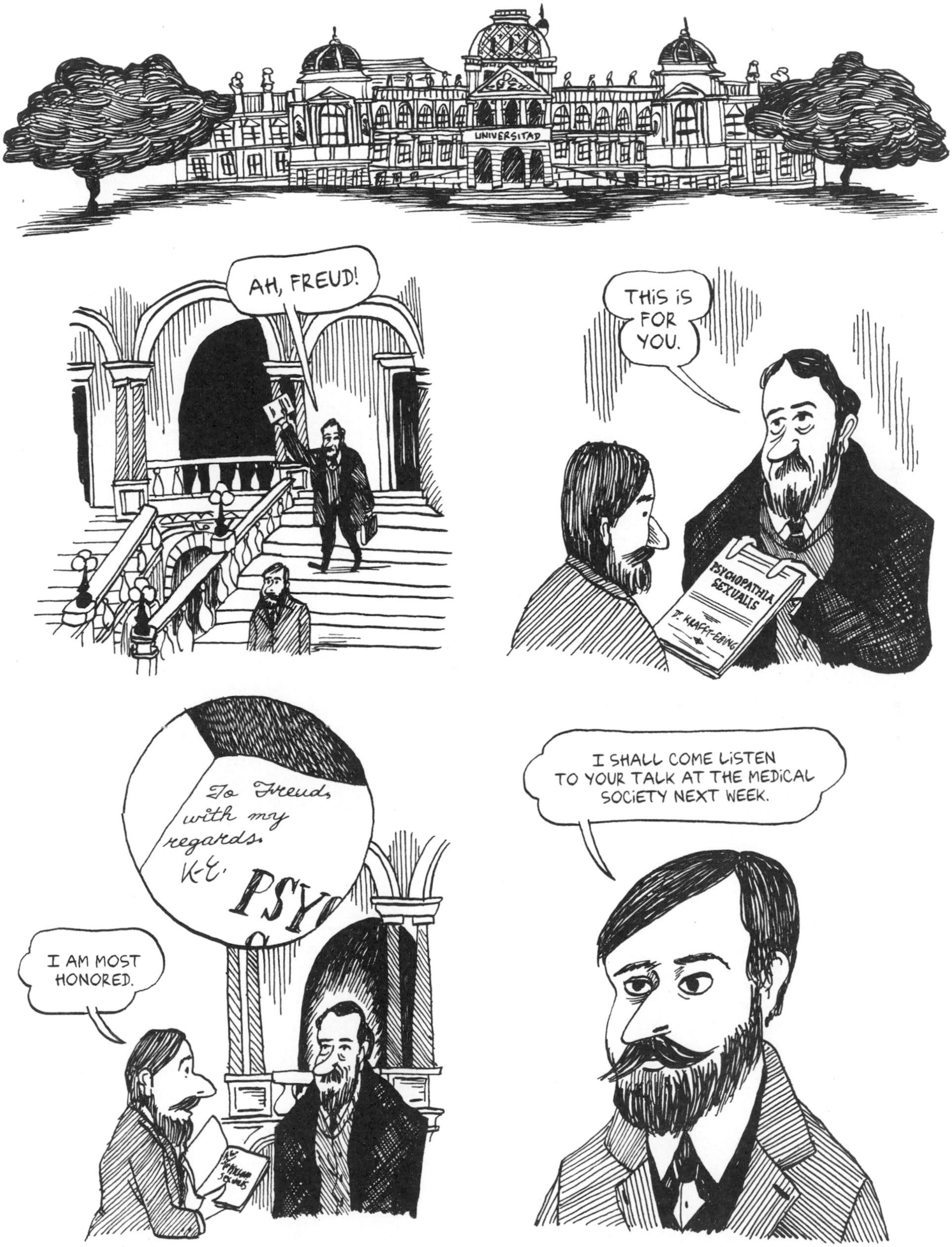
UNIVERSITAD
AH, FREUD!
THIS IS FOR YOU.
PSYCHOPATHIA SEXUALIS
Dr. KRAFFT-EBING
To Freud, with my regards. K-E.
PSY
I AM MOST HONORED.
I SHALL COME LISTEN TO YOUR TALK AT THE MEDICAL SOCIETY NEXT WEEK.

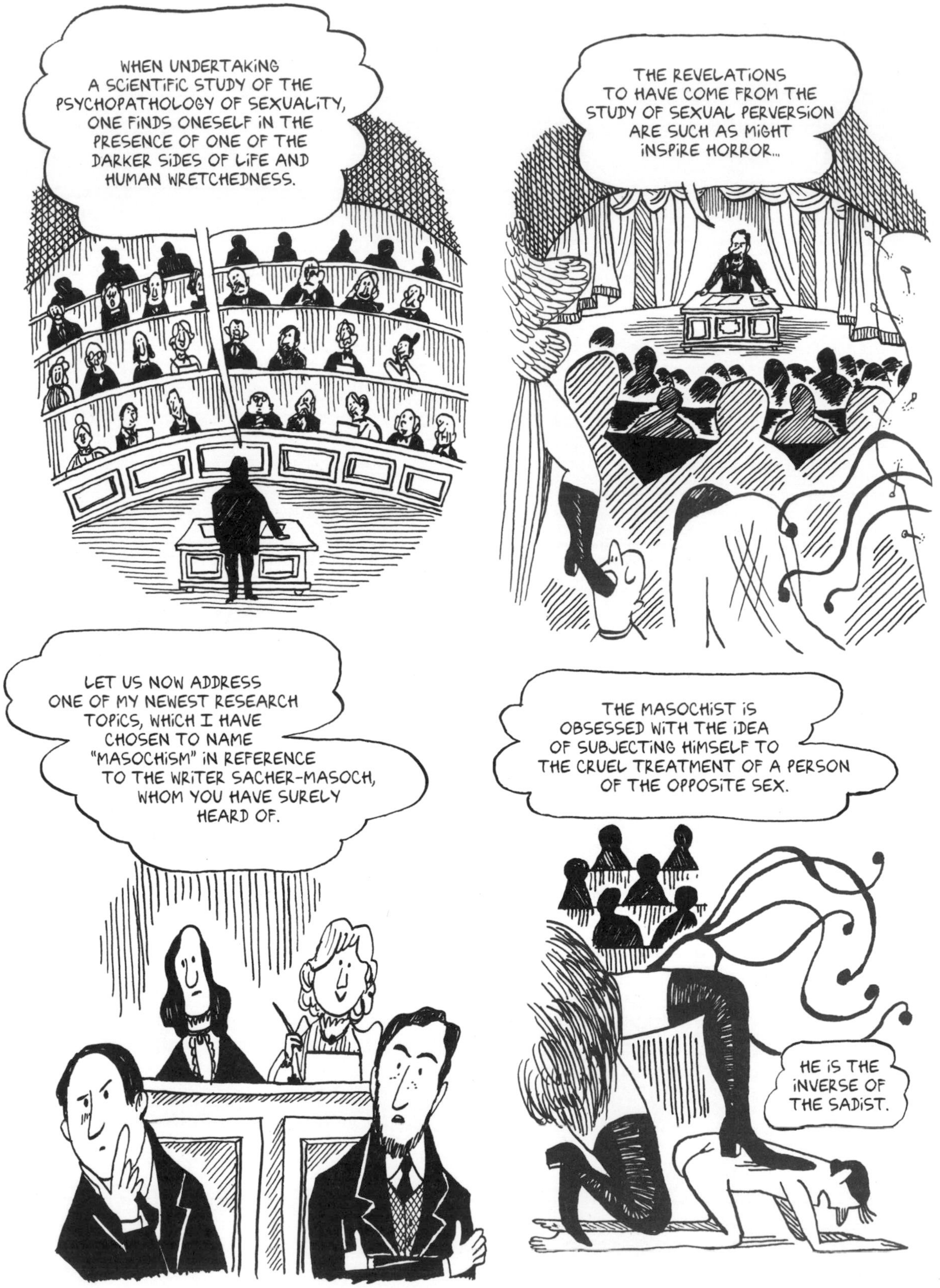

WHEN UNDERTAKING A SCIENTIFIC STUDY OF THE PSYCHOPATHOLOGY OF SEXUALITY, ONE FINDS ONESELF IN THE PRESENCE OF ONE OF THE DARKER SIDES OF LIFE AND HUMAN WRETCHEDNESS.
THE REVELATIONS TO HAVE COME FROM THE STUDY OF SEXUAL PERVERSION ARE SUCH AS MIGHT INSPIRE HORROR...
LET US NOW ADDRESS ONE OF MY NEWEST RESEARCH TOPICS, WHICH I HAVE CHOSEN TO NAME "MASOCHISM" IN REFERENCE TO THE WRITER SACHER-MASOCH, WHOM YOU HAVE SURELY HEARD OF.
THE MASOCHIST IS OBSESSED WITH THE IDEA OF SUBJECTING HIMSELF TO THE CRUEL TREATMENT OF A PERSON OF THE OPPOSITE SEX.
HE IS THE INVERSE OF THE SADIST.

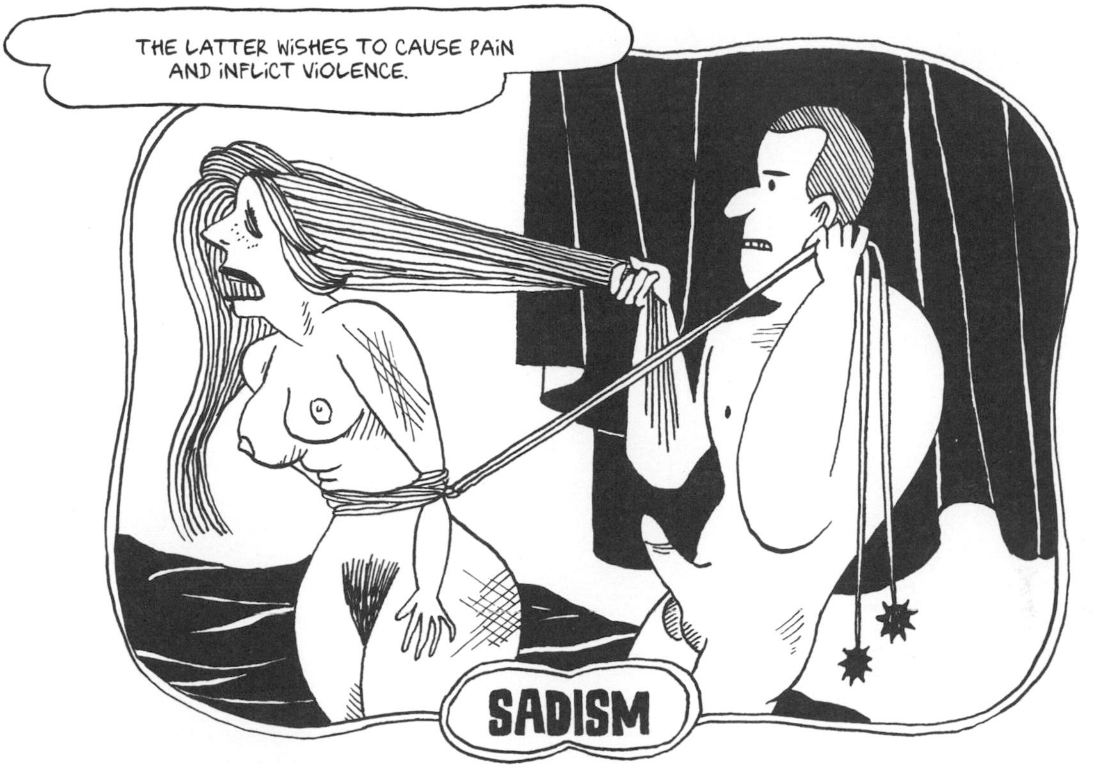
THE LATTER WISHES TO CAUSE PAIN AND INFLICT VIOLENCE.
SADISM

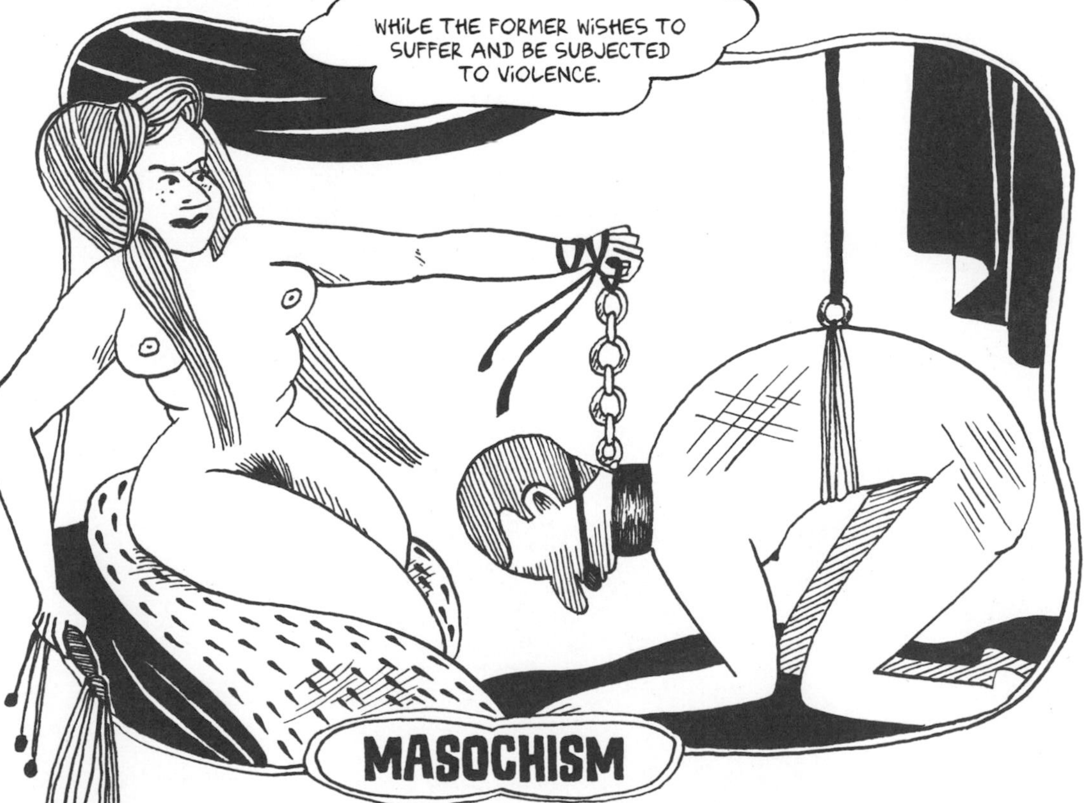
WHILE THE FORMER WISHES TO SUFFER AND BE SUBJECTED TO VIOLENCE.
MASOCHISM

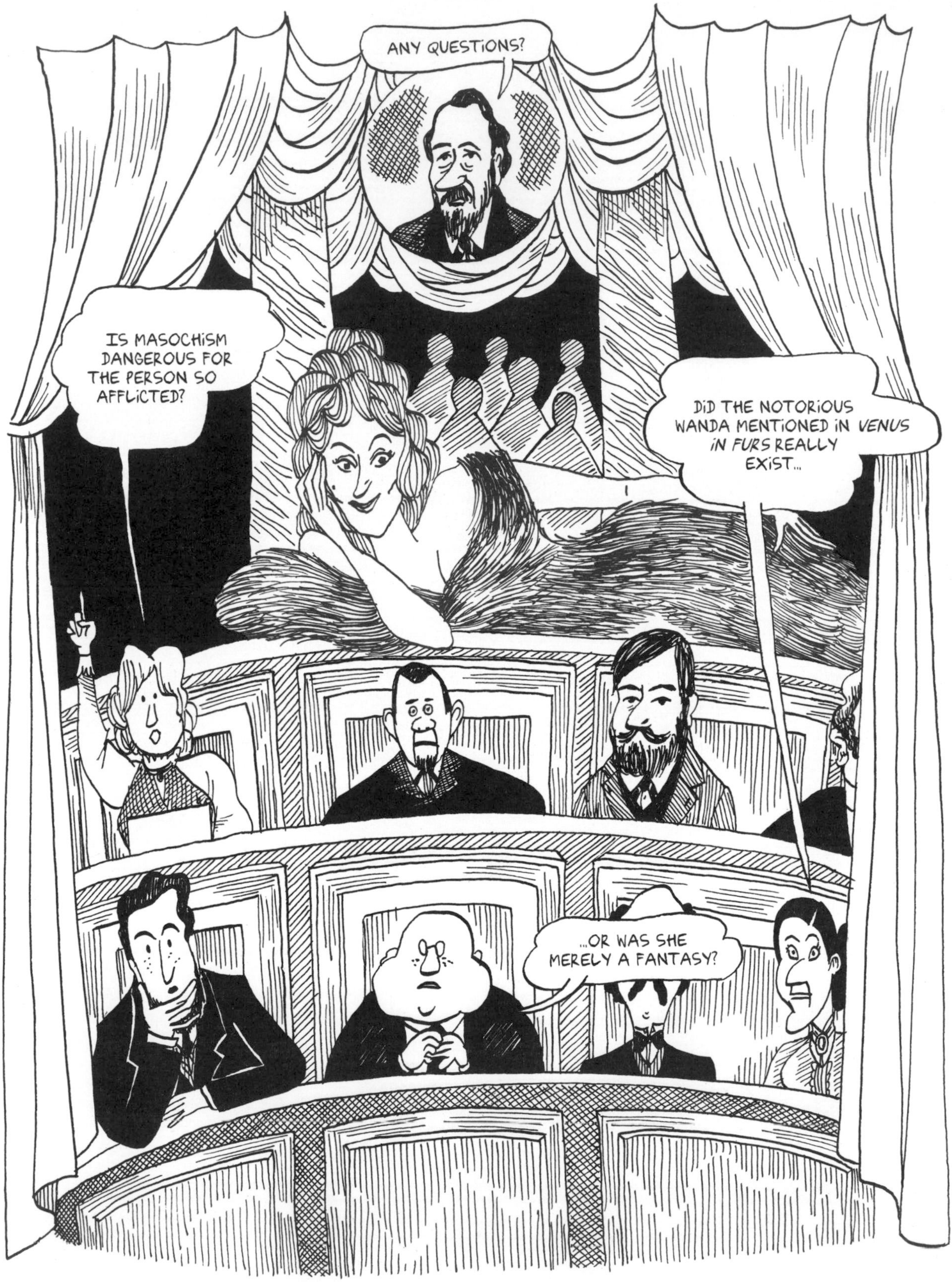
ANY QUESTIONS?
IS MASOCHISM DANGEROUS FOR THE PERSON SO AFFLICTED?
DID THE NOTORIOUS WANDA MENTIONED IN *VENUS IN FURS* REALLY EXIST...
...OR WAS SHE MERELY A FANTASY?

After several opulent years in Paris, Wanda is sinking into poverty. Her relationship with Armand is at an end, and her son, Demetrius, who has lived with her since the separation, would like to return to his father.

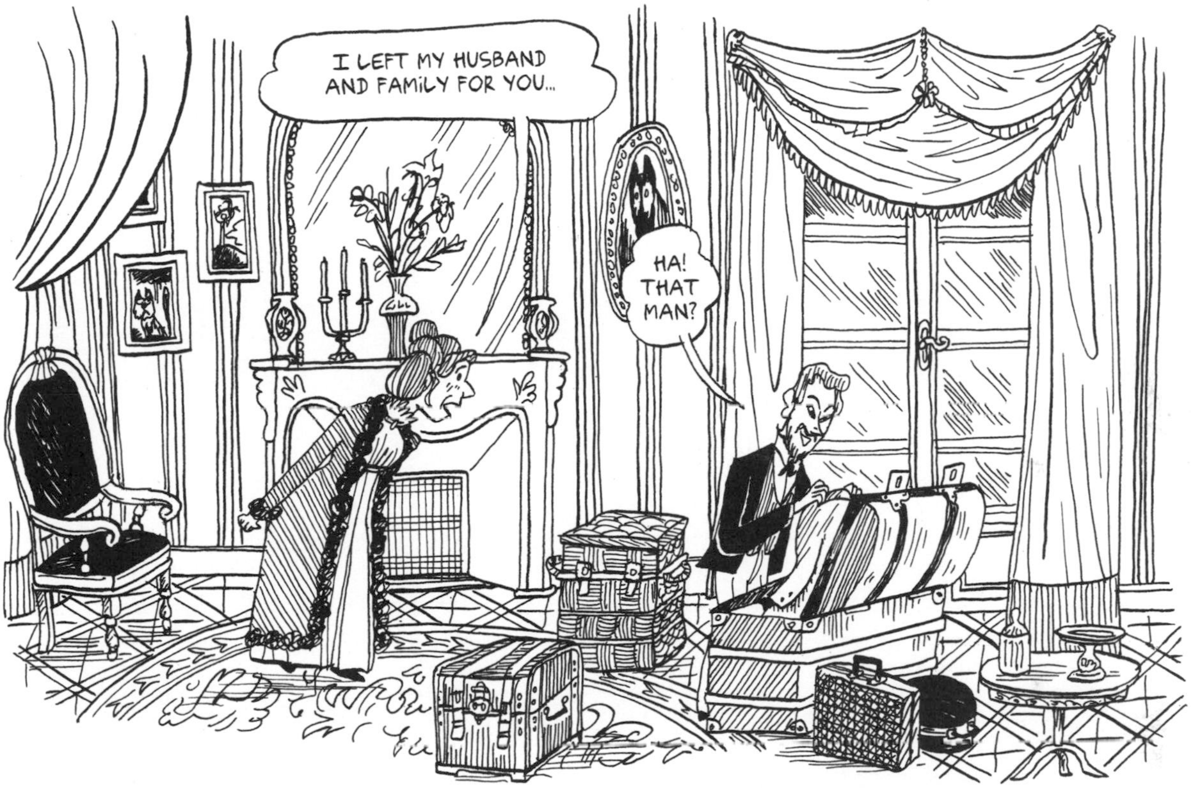

I LEFT MY HUSBAND AND FAMILY FOR YOU...
HA! THAT MAN?

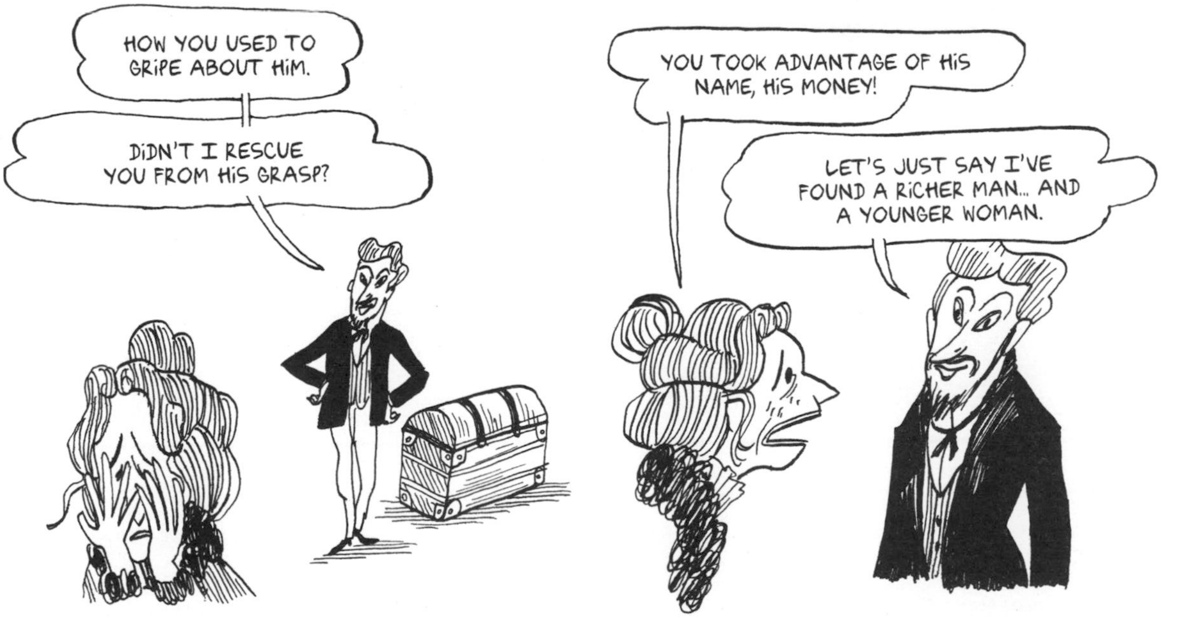

HOW YOU USED TO GRIPE ABOUT HIM.
DIDN'T I RESCUE YOU FROM HIS GRASP?
YOU TOOK ADVANTAGE OF HIS NAME, HIS MONEY!
LET'S JUST SAY I'VE FOUND A RICHER MAN... AND A YOUNGER WOMAN.

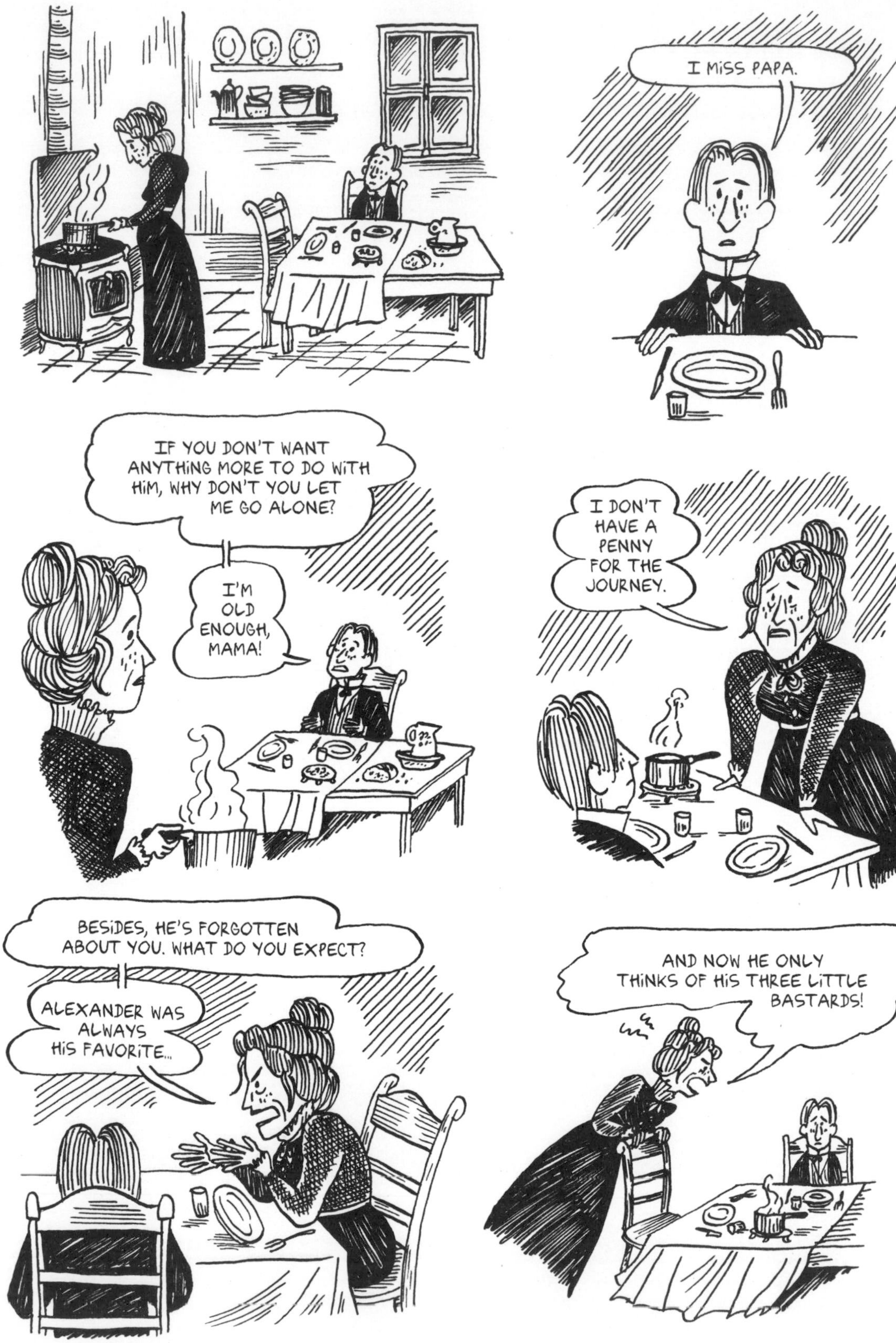
I MISS PAPA.
IF YOU DON'T WANT ANYTHING MORE TO DO WITH HIM, WHY DON'T YOU LET ME GO ALONE?
I'M OLD ENOUGH, MAMA!
I DON'T HAVE A PENNY FOR THE JOURNEY.
BESIDES, HE'S FORGOTTEN ABOUT YOU. WHAT DO YOU EXPECT?
ALEXANDER WAS ALWAYS HIS FAVORITE...
AND NOW HE ONLY THINKS OF HIS THREE LITTLE BASTARDS!

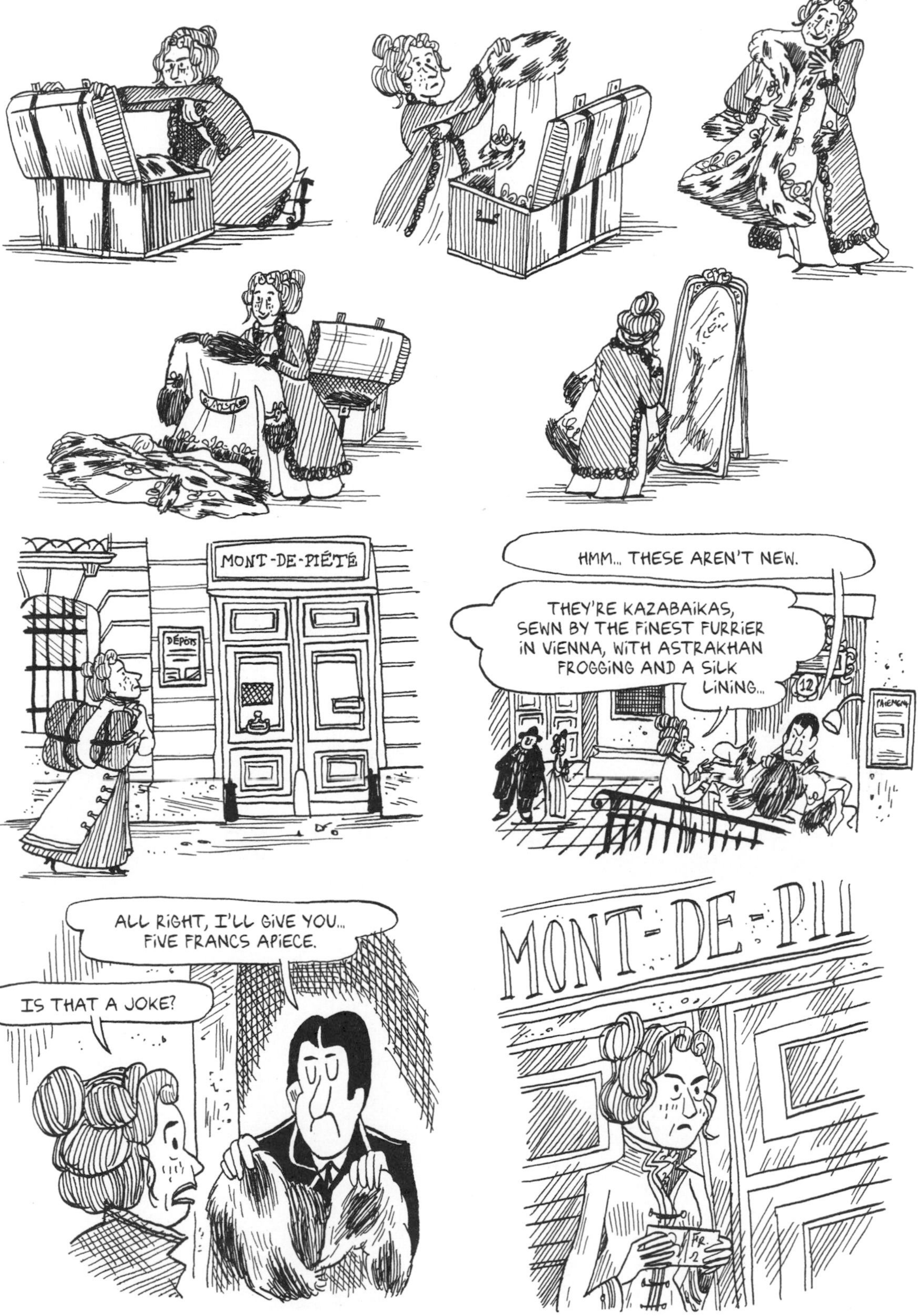
MONT-DE-PIÉTÉ
DÉPÔTS
HMM... THESE AREN'T NEW.
THEY'RE KAZABAIKAS, SEWN BY THE FINEST FURRIER IN VIENNA, WITH ASTRAKHAN FROGGING AND A SILK LINING...
12
ALL RIGHT, I'LL GIVE YOU... FIVE FRANCS APIECE.
IS THAT A JOKE?
MONT-DE-PI

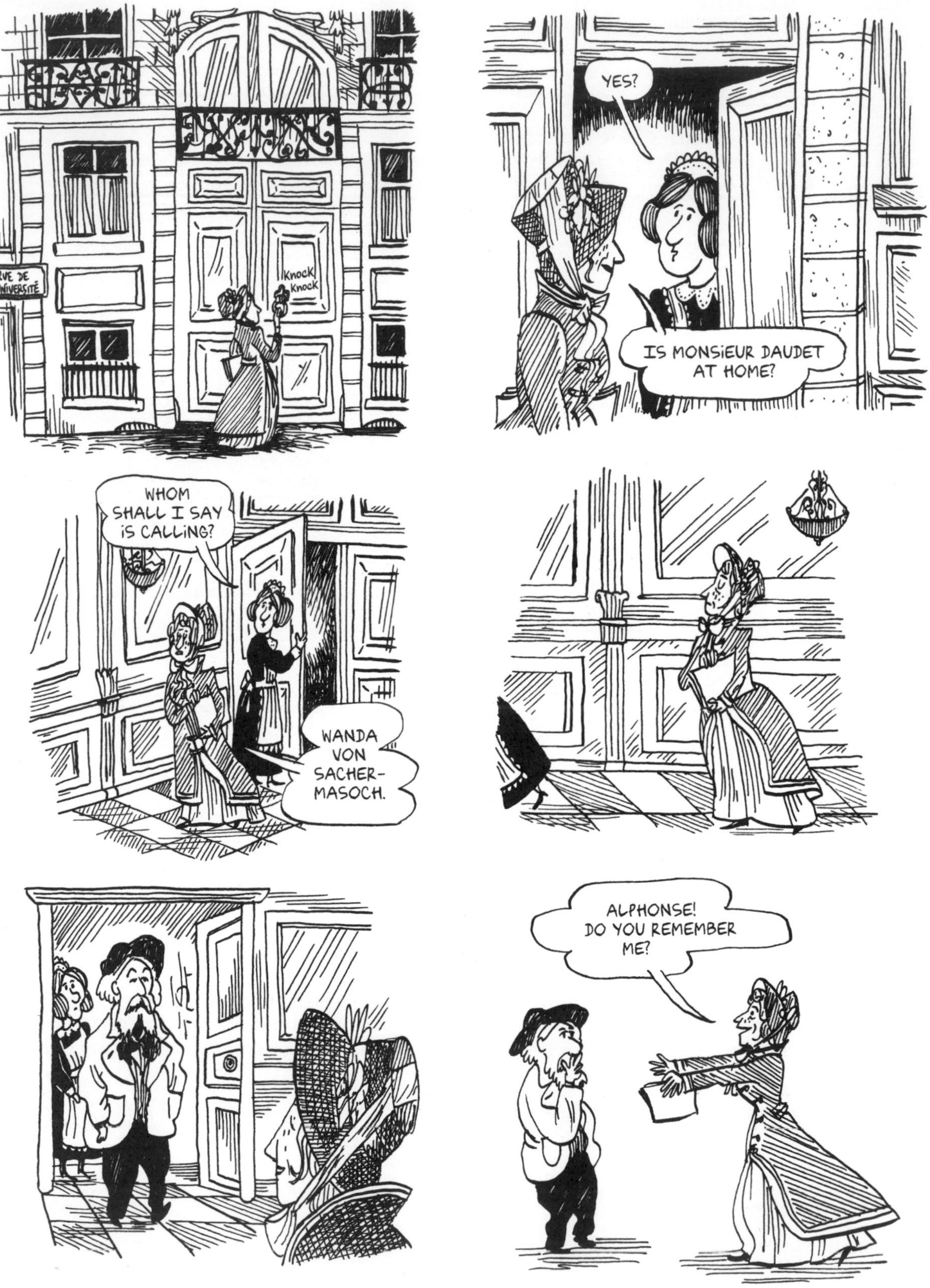
RVE DE L'UNIVERSITÉ
Knock Knock
YES?
IS MONSIEUR DAUDET AT HOME?
WHOM SHALL I SAY IS CALLING?
WANDA VON SACHER-MASOCH.
ALPHONSE! DO YOU REMEMBER ME?

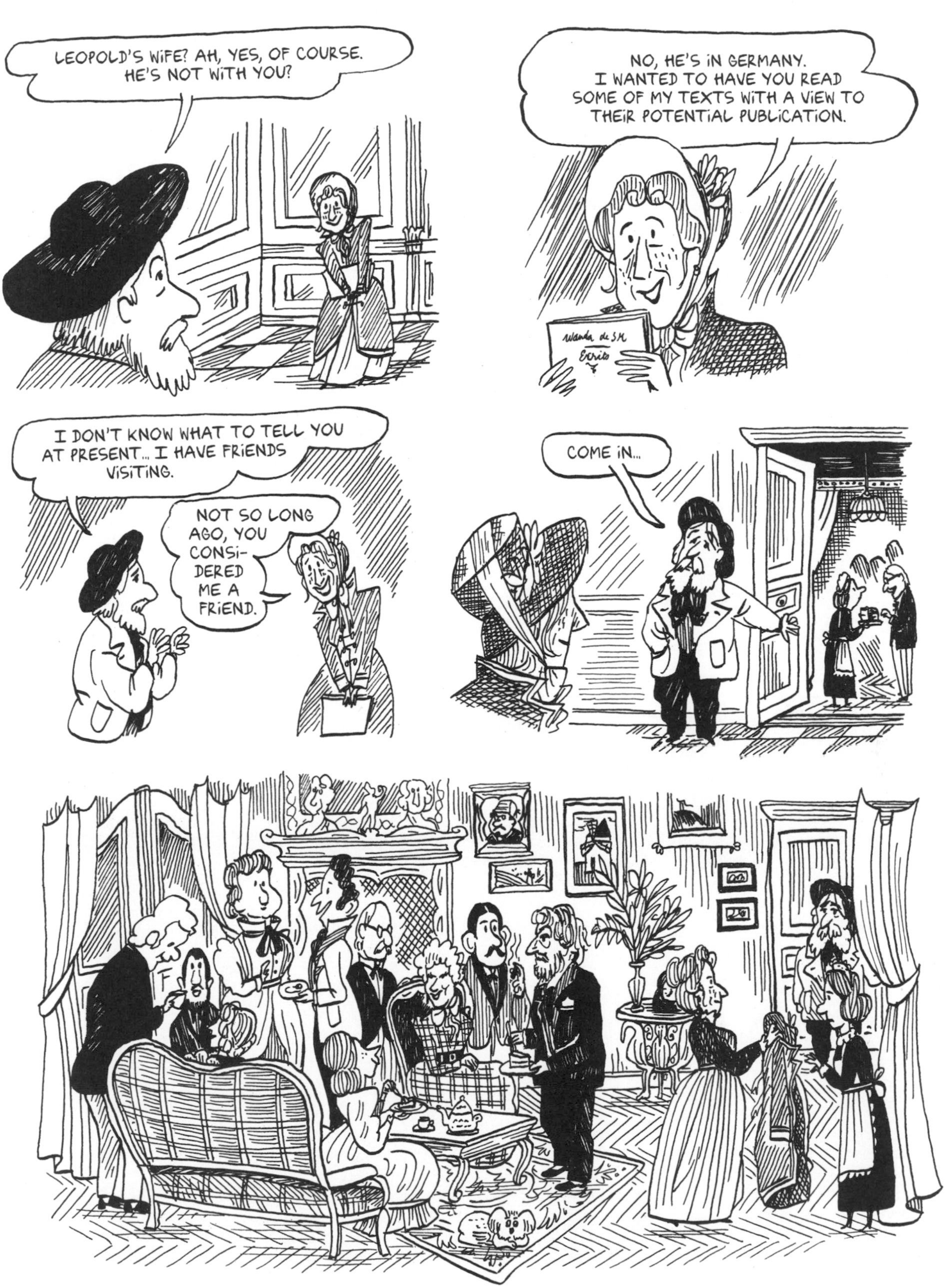
LEOPOLD'S WIFE? AH, YES, OF COURSE. HE'S NOT WITH YOU?
NO, HE'S IN GERMANY. I WANTED TO HAVE YOU READ SOME OF MY TEXTS WITH A VIEW TO THEIR POTENTIAL PUBLICATION.
I DON'T KNOW WHAT TO TELL YOU AT PRESENT... I HAVE FRIENDS VISITING.
NOT SO LONG AGO, YOU CONSI-DERED ME A FRIEND.
COME IN...

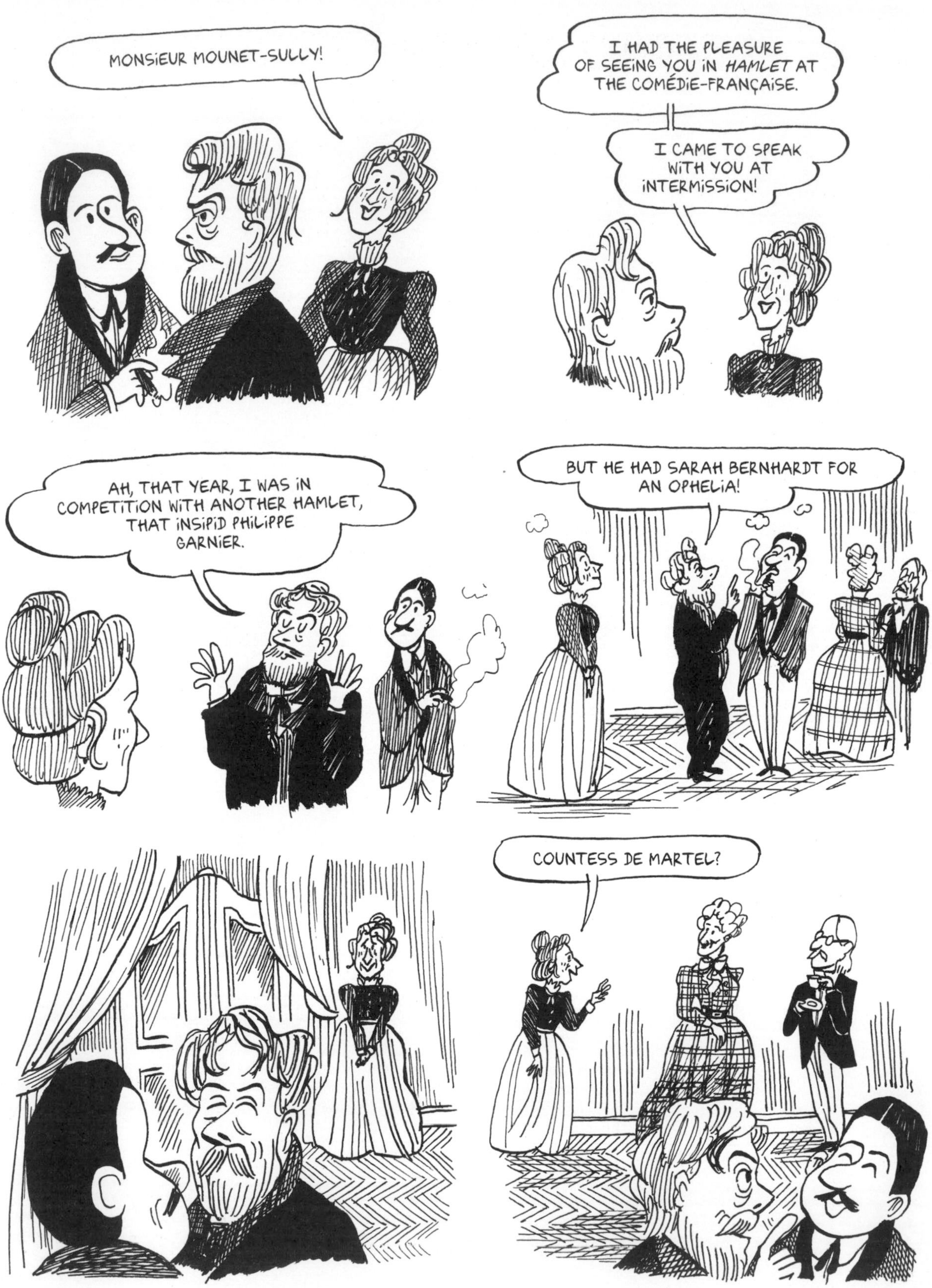
MONSIEUR MOUNET-SULLY!
I HAD THE PLEASURE OF SEEING YOU IN *HAMLET* AT THE COMÉDIE-FRANÇAISE.
I CAME TO SPEAK WITH YOU AT INTERMISSION!
AH, THAT YEAR, I WAS IN COMPETITION WITH ANOTHER HAMLET, THAT INSIPID PHILIPPE GARNIER.
BUT HE HAD SARAH BERNHARDT FOR AN OPHELIA!
COUNTESS DE MARTEL?

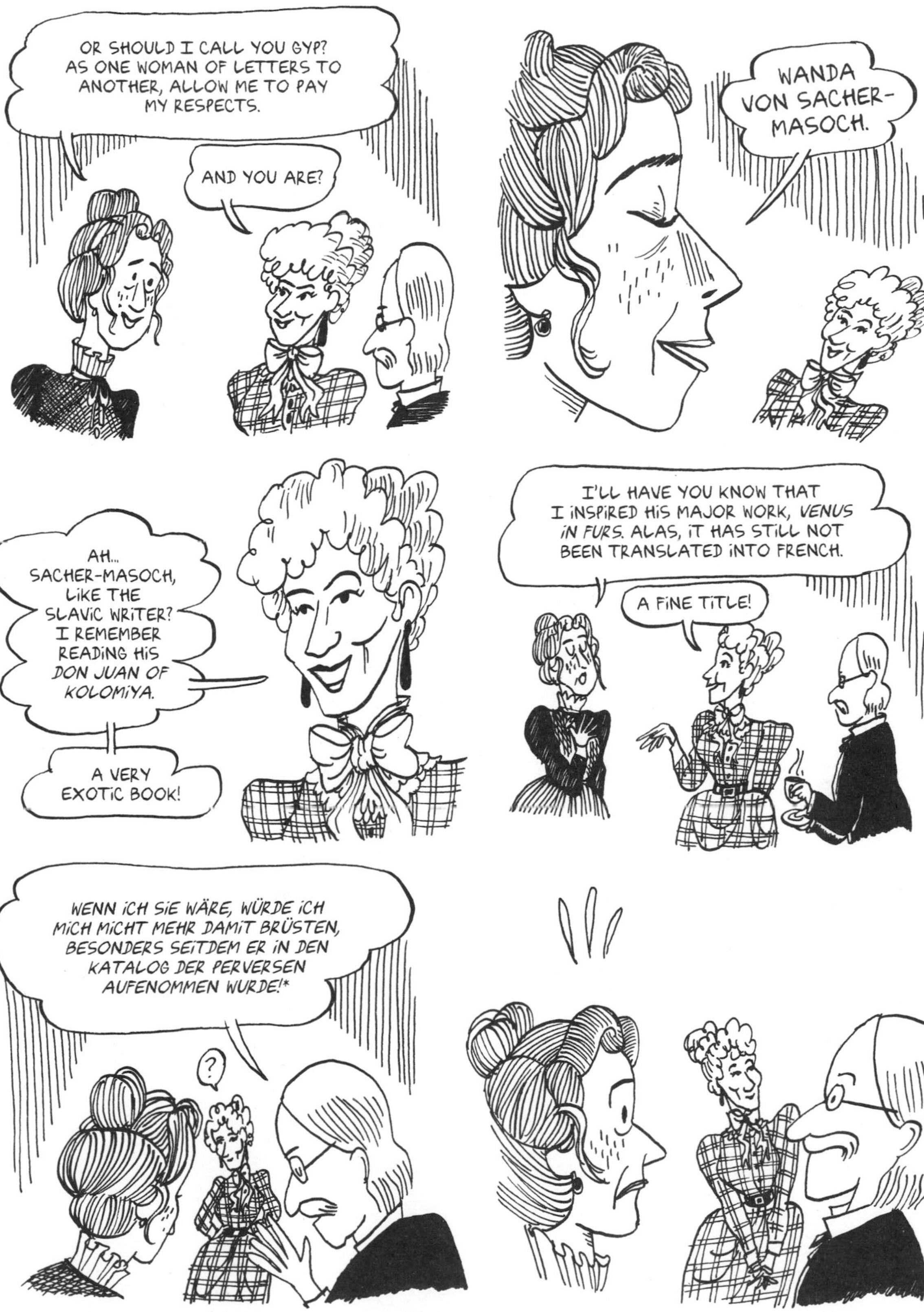
OR SHOULD I CALL YOU GYP? AS ONE WOMAN OF LETTERS TO ANOTHER, ALLOW ME TO PAY MY RESPECTS.
AND YOU ARE?
WANDA VON SACHER-MASOCH.
AH... SACHER-MASOCH, LIKE THE SLAVIC WRITER? I REMEMBER READING HIS *DON JUAN OF KOLOMIYA*.
A VERY EXOTIC BOOK!
I'LL HAVE YOU KNOW THAT I INSPIRED HIS MAJOR WORK, *VENUS IN FURS*. ALAS, IT HAS STILL NOT BEEN TRANSLATED INTO FRENCH.
A FINE TITLE!
*WENN ICH SIE WÄRE, WÜRDE ICH MICH MICHT MEHR DAMIT BRÜSTEN, BESONDERS SEITDEM ER IN DEN KATALOG DER PERVERSEN AUFENOMMEN WURDE!**
?

*If I were you, I wouldn't boast about that, especially since he now has an entry in the great catalogue of perverts.

MY POOR DARLING.

YOUR FATHER IS A MONSTER, AND NOW THE ENTIRE WORLD WILL KNOW.

DISGRACE HAS TARNISHED YOUR NAME, AND THAT OF YOUR FUTURE CHILDREN.

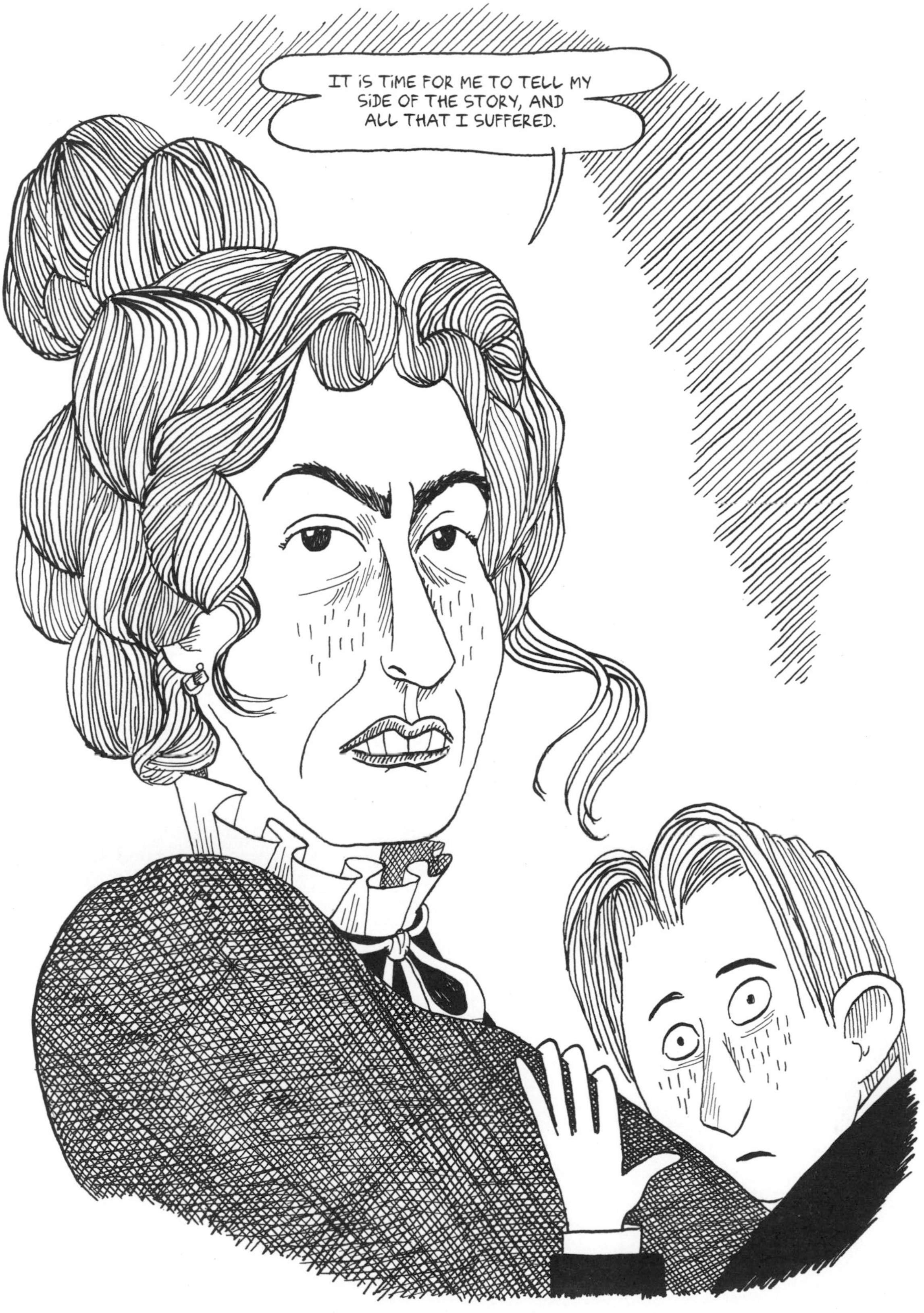
IT IS TIME FOR ME TO TELL MY SIDE OF THE STORY, AND ALL THAT I SUFFERED.

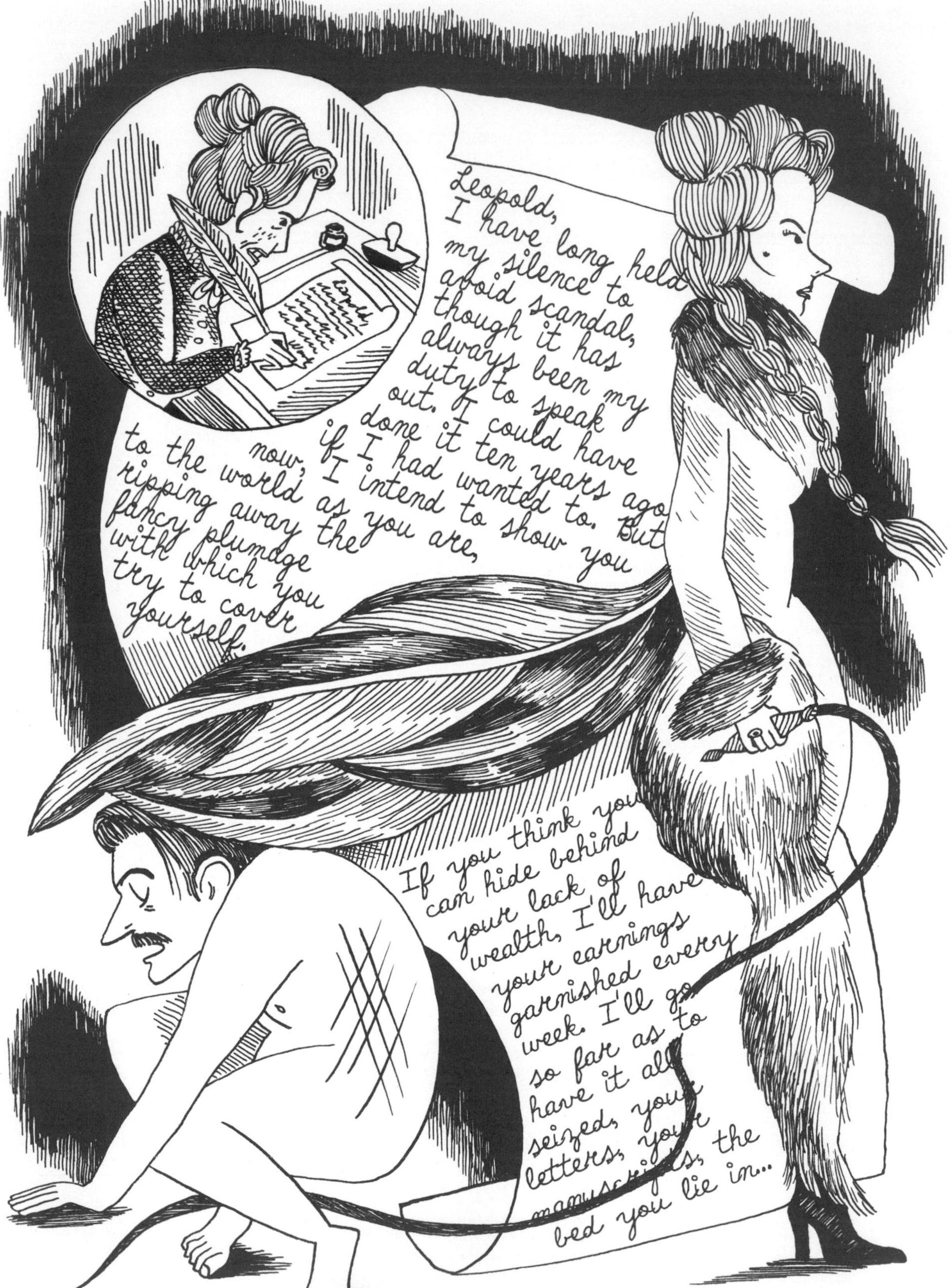
Leopold,
I have long held my silence to avoid scandal, though it has always been my duty to speak out. I could have done it ten years ago if I had wanted to. But now, I intend to show you to the world as you are, ripping away the fancy plumage with which you try to cover yourself.
If you think you can hide behind your lack of wealth, I'll have your earnings garnished every week. I'll go so far as to have it all seized, your letters, your manuscripts, the bed you lie in...

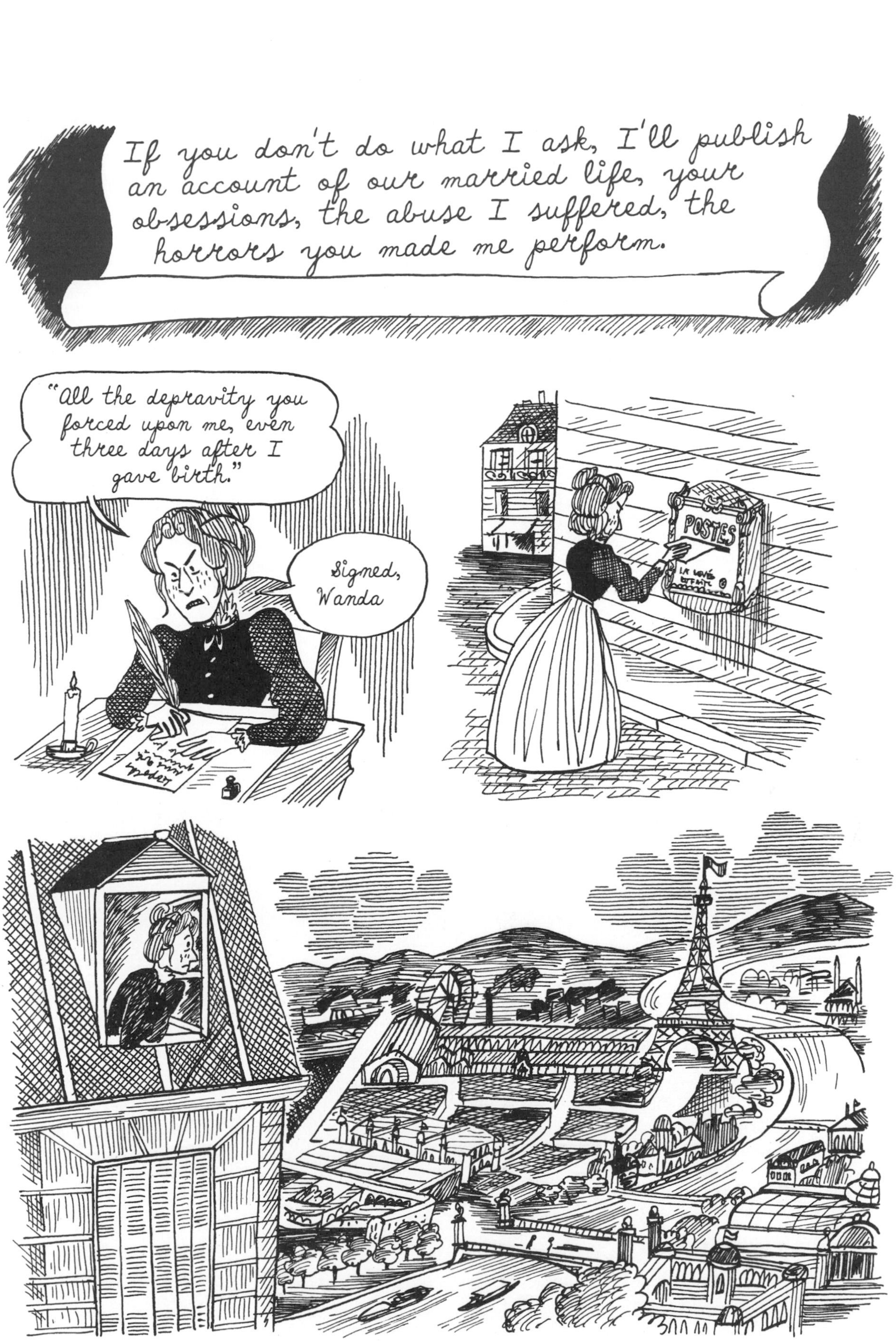
If you don't do what I ask, I'll publish an account of our married life, your obsessions, the abuse I suffered, the horrors you made me perform.
"All the depravity you forced upon me, even three days after I gave birth."
Signed, Wanda
POSTES

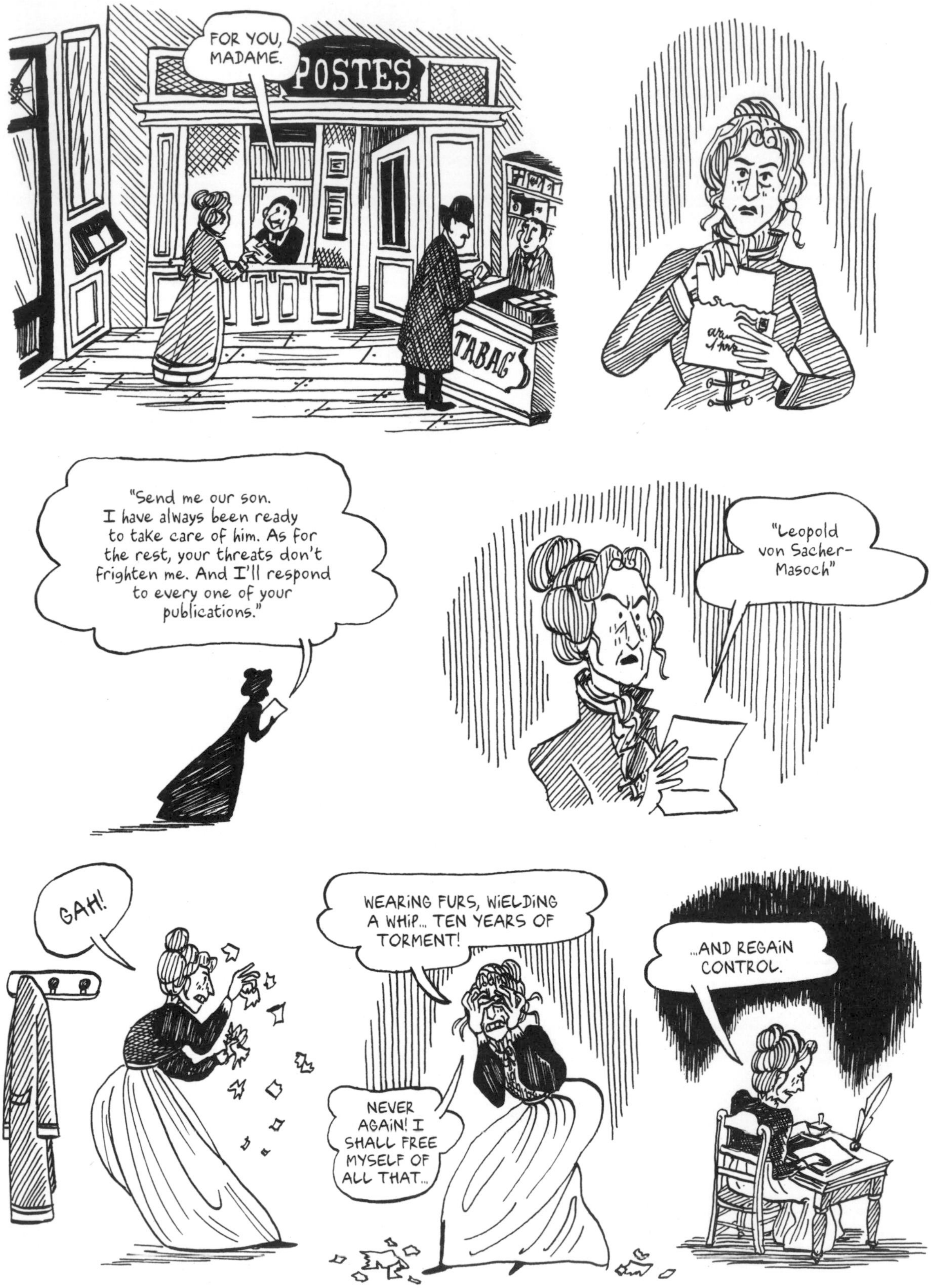
FOR YOU, MADAME.
POSTES
TABAC
"Send me our son. I have always been ready to take care of him. As for the rest, your threats don't frighten me. And I'll respond to every one of your publications."
"Leopold von Sacher-Masoch"
GAH!
WEARING FURS, WIELDING A WHIP... TEN YEARS OF TORMENT!
NEVER AGAIN! I SHALL FREE MYSELF OF ALL THAT...
...AND REGAIN CONTROL.

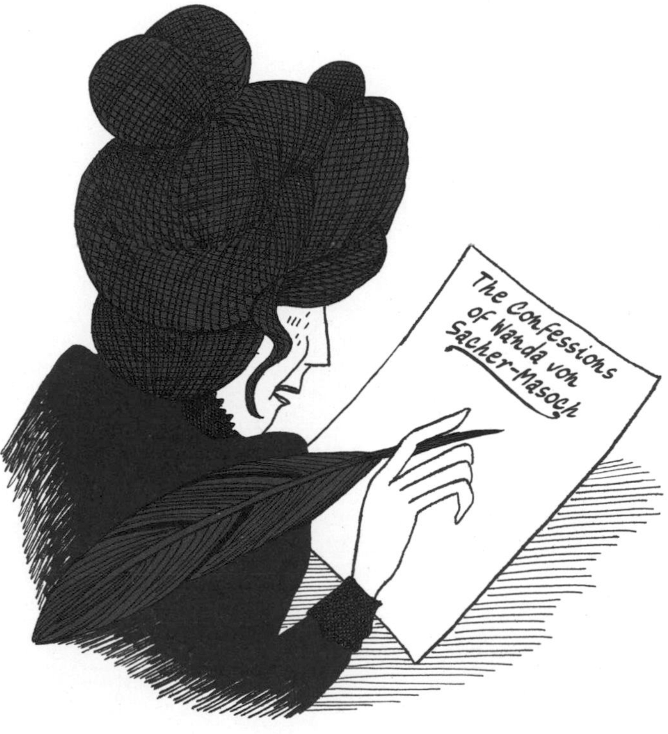
The Confessions
of Wanda von
Sacher-Masoch

Lindheim, 1892. The famous author of *Venus in Furs* is living out his final years with his faithful Hulda and their three children.

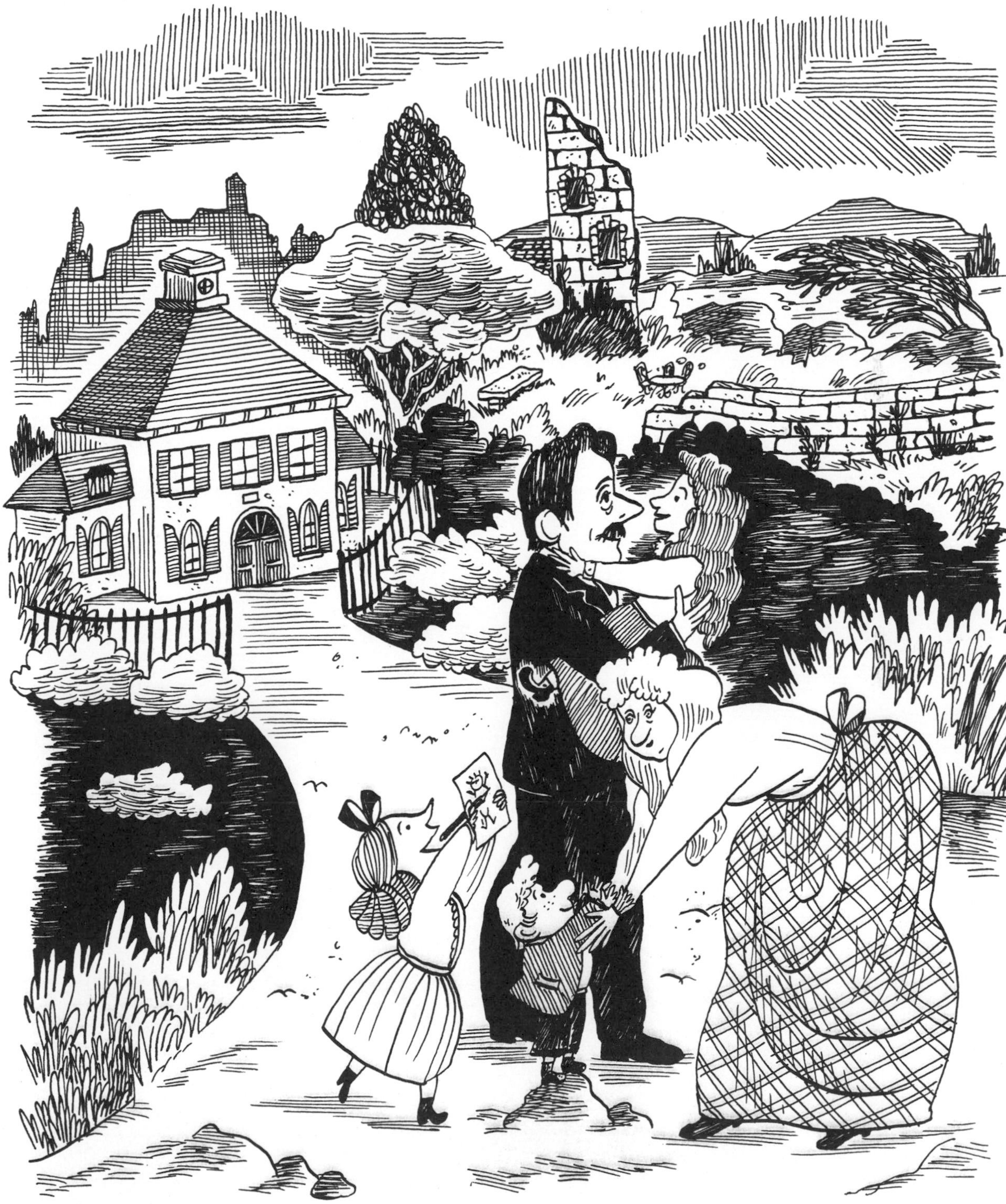

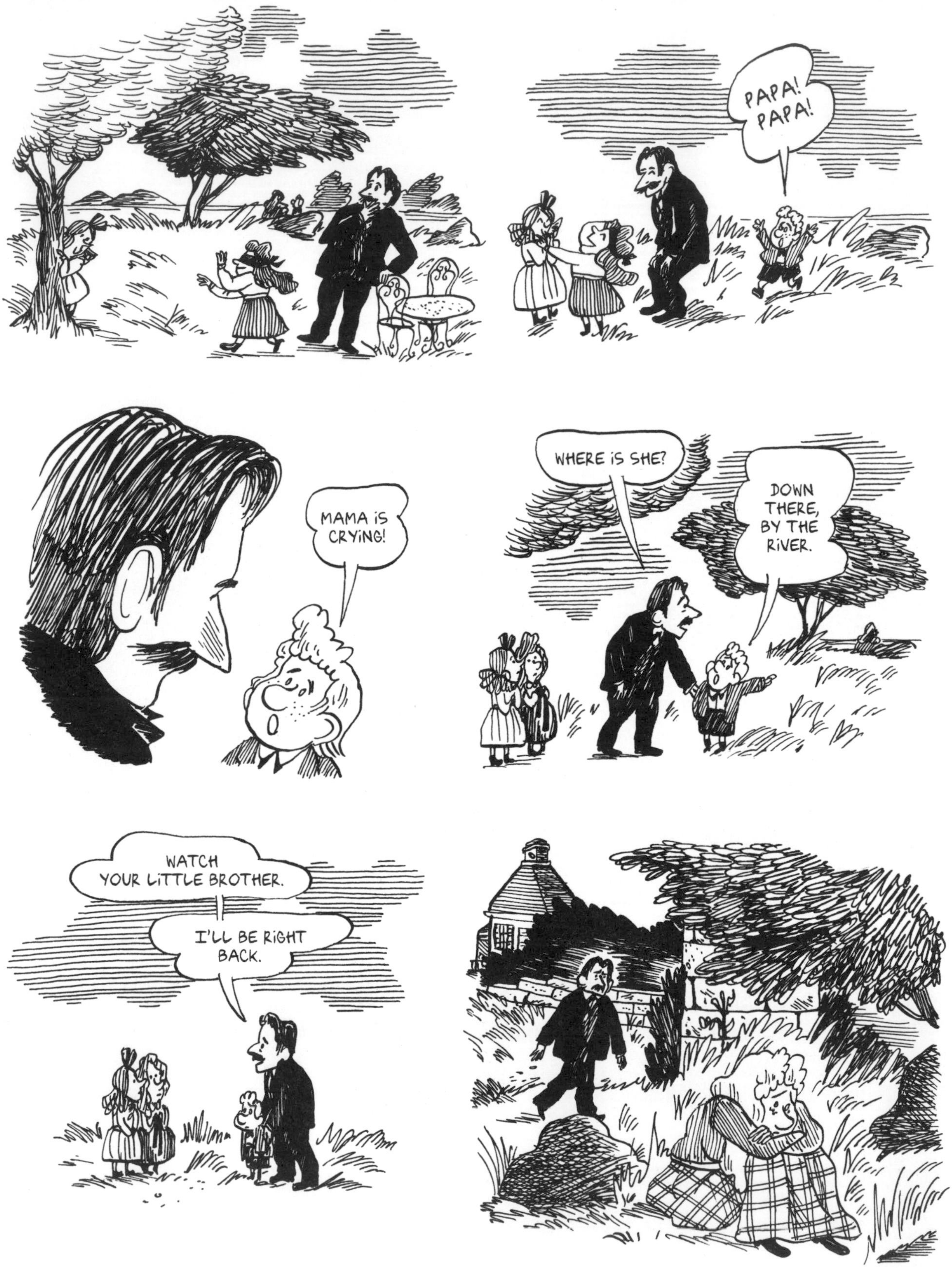
PAPA! PAPA!
MAMA iS CRYiNG!
WHERE iS SHE?
DOWN THERE, BY THE RiVER.
WATCH YOUR LiTTLE BROTHER.
I'LL BE RiGHT BACK.

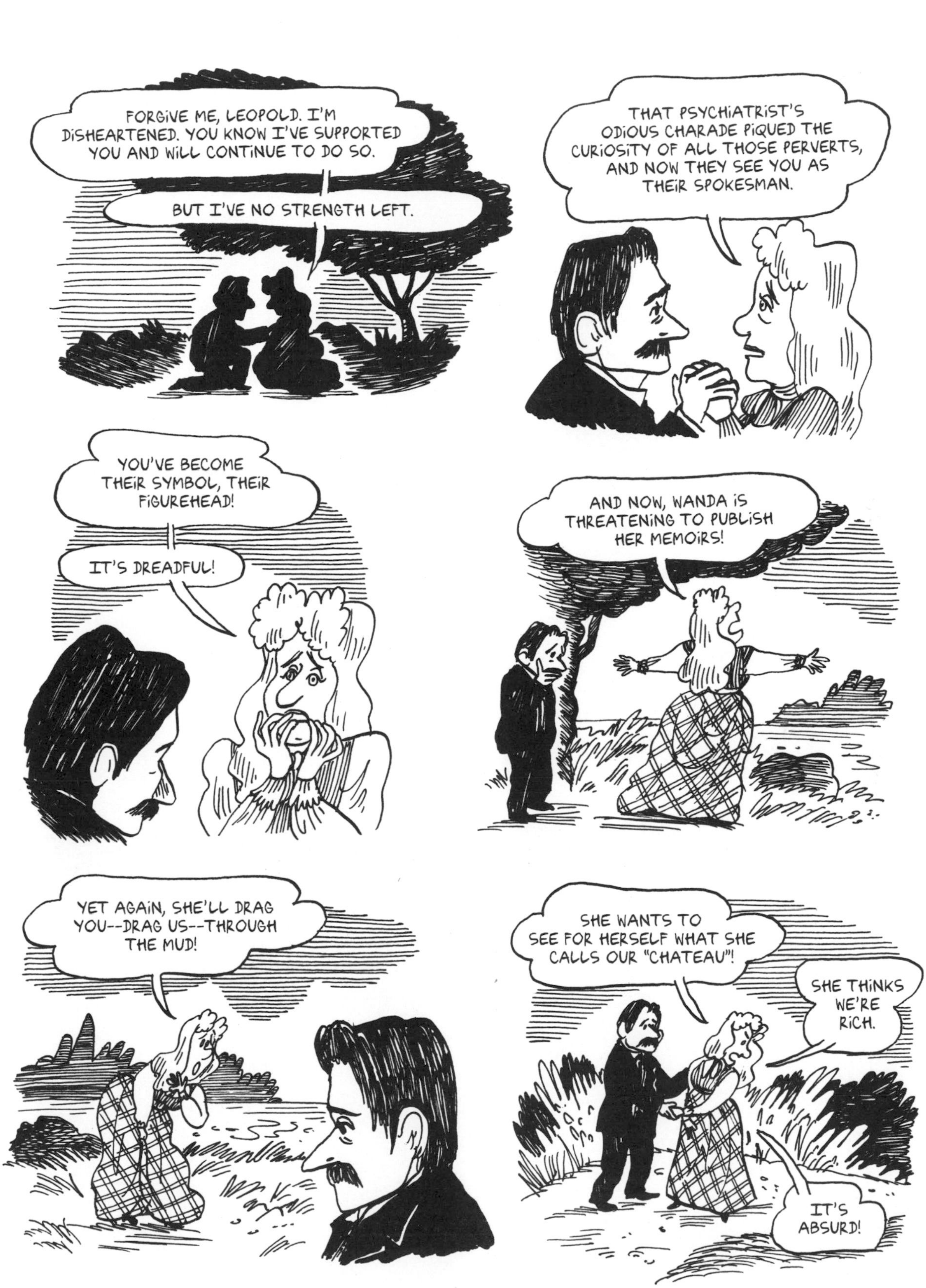
FORGIVE ME, LEOPOLD. I'M DISHEARTENED. YOU KNOW I'VE SUPPORTED YOU AND WILL CONTINUE TO DO SO.
BUT I'VE NO STRENGTH LEFT.
THAT PSYCHIATRIST'S ODIOUS CHARADE PIQUED THE CURIOSITY OF ALL THOSE PERVERTS, AND NOW THEY SEE YOU AS THEIR SPOKESMAN.
YOU'VE BECOME THEIR SYMBOL, THEIR FIGUREHEAD!
IT'S DREADFUL!
AND NOW, WANDA IS THREATENING TO PUBLISH HER MEMOIRS!
YET AGAIN, SHE'LL DRAG YOU--DRAG US--THROUGH THE MUD!
SHE WANTS TO SEE FOR HERSELF WHAT SHE CALLS OUR "CHATEAU"!
SHE THINKS WE'RE RICH.
IT'S ABSURD!

YOU WANTED HER TO GRIND YOU UNDER HER HEEL, AND SHE'S STILL DOING IT TEN YEARS LATER.
I'M SORRY.
WITHOUT YOU, I'D HAVE DIED A HUNDRED TIMES, OF RAGE AND DESPAIR.
IF WANDA THINKS SHE STILL HAS THE POWER TO MAKE MY LIFE DIFFICULT, SHE'S WRONG...
BUT HULDA, MY WORK--THE WORK OF A LIFETIME--WILL BE FORGOTTEN, REPLACED BY A SINGLE WORD!

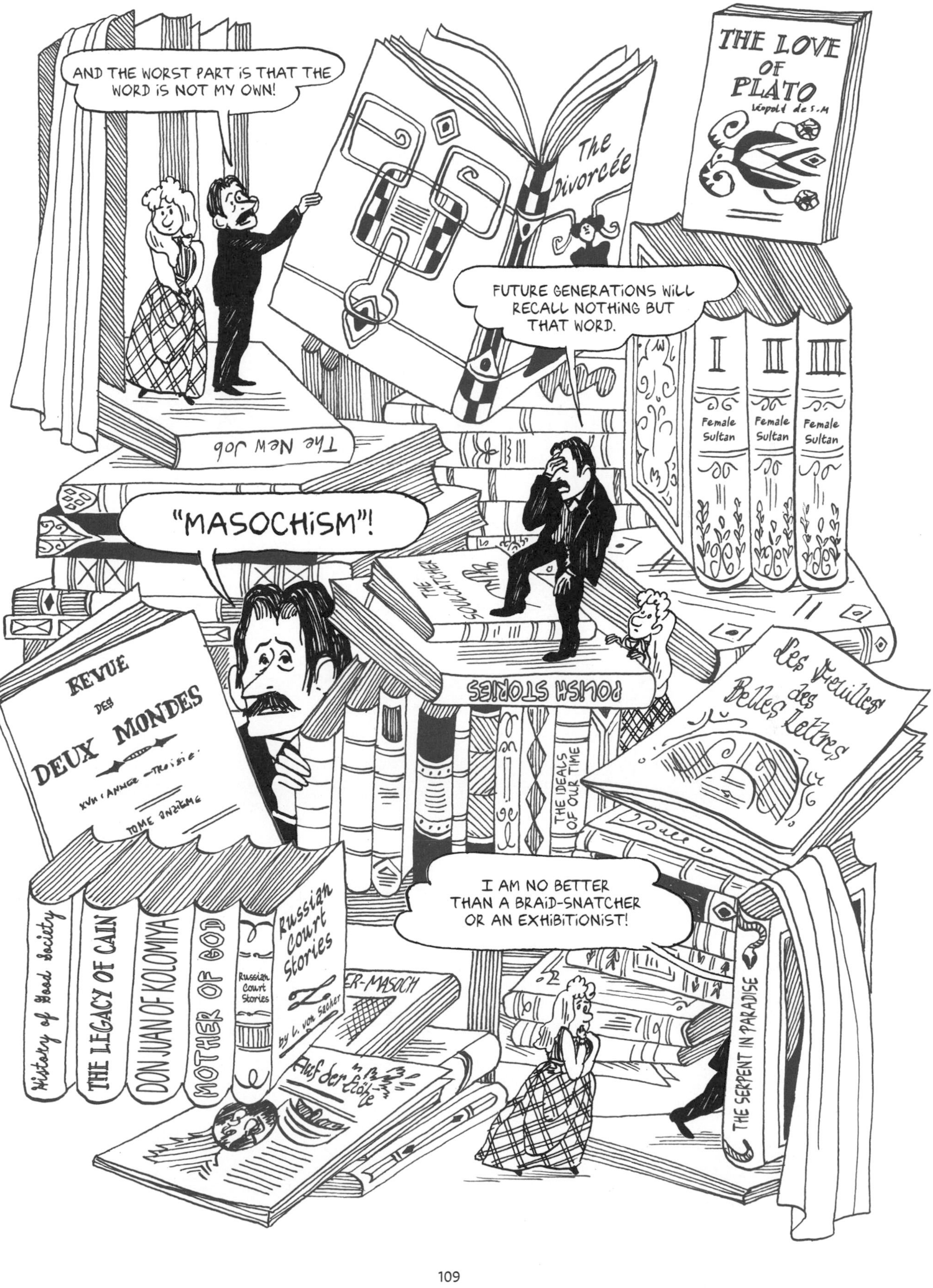
AND THE WORST PART IS THAT THE WORD IS NOT MY OWN!
FUTURE GENERATIONS WILL RECALL NOTHING BUT THAT WORD.
"MASOCHISM"!
I AM NO BETTER THAN A BRAID-SNATCHER OR AN EXHIBITIONIST!
THE LOVE OF PLATO
The Divorcée
The New Job
Female Sultan
THE SOULCATCHER
POLISH STORIES
REVUE DES DEUX MONDES
TOME ONZIÈME
THE IDEALS OF OUR TIME
Les Feuilles des Belles Lettres
History of Good Society
THE LEGACY OF CAIN
DON JUAN OF KOLOMIYA
MOTHER OF GOD
Russian Court Stories
Russian Court Stories
by L. von Sacher
ER-MASOCH
Auf der Höhe
THE SERPENT IN PARADISE

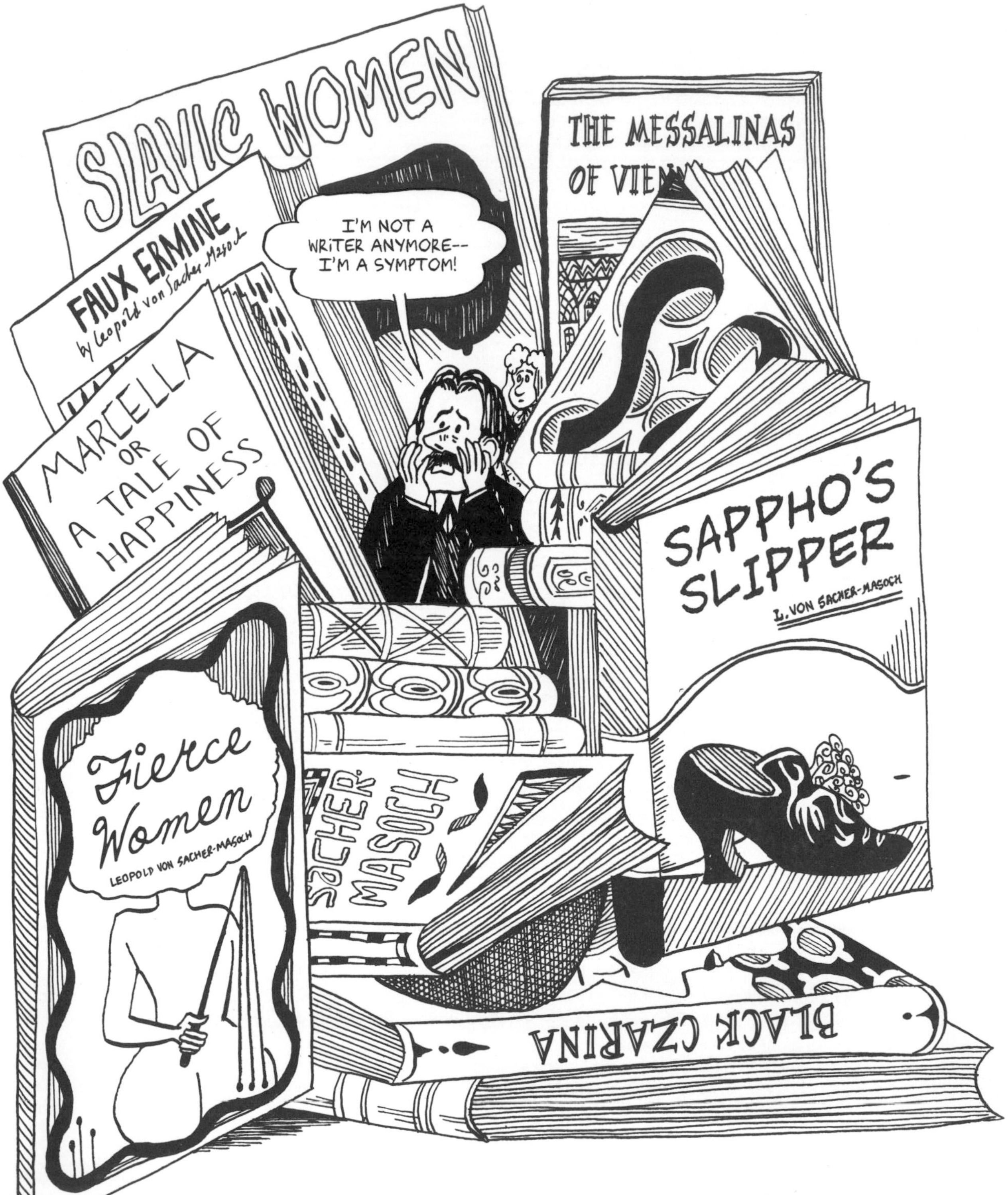
SLAVIC WOMEN
THE MESSALINAS OF VIENN
FAUX ERMINE by Leopold von Sacher-Masoch
I'M NOT A WRITER ANYMORE-- I'M A SYMPTOM!
MARCELLA OR A TALE OF HAPPINESS
SAPPHO'S SLIPPER
L. VON SACHER-MASOCH
Fierce Women
LEOPOLD VON SACHER-MASOCH
SACHER MASOCH
BLACK CZARINA

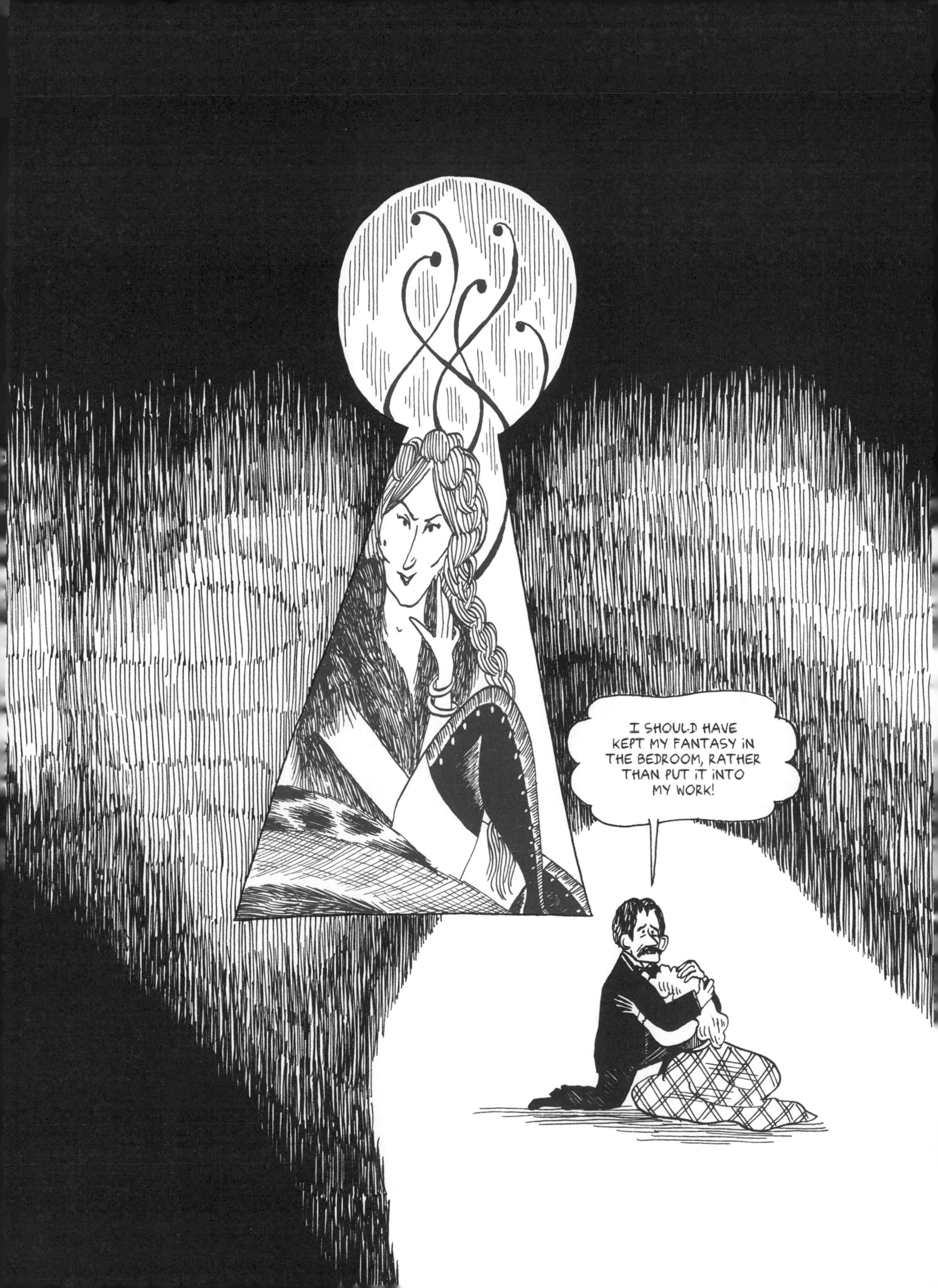
I SHOULD HAVE KEPT MY FANTASY iN THE BEDROOM, RATHER THAN PUT iT iNTO MY WORK!

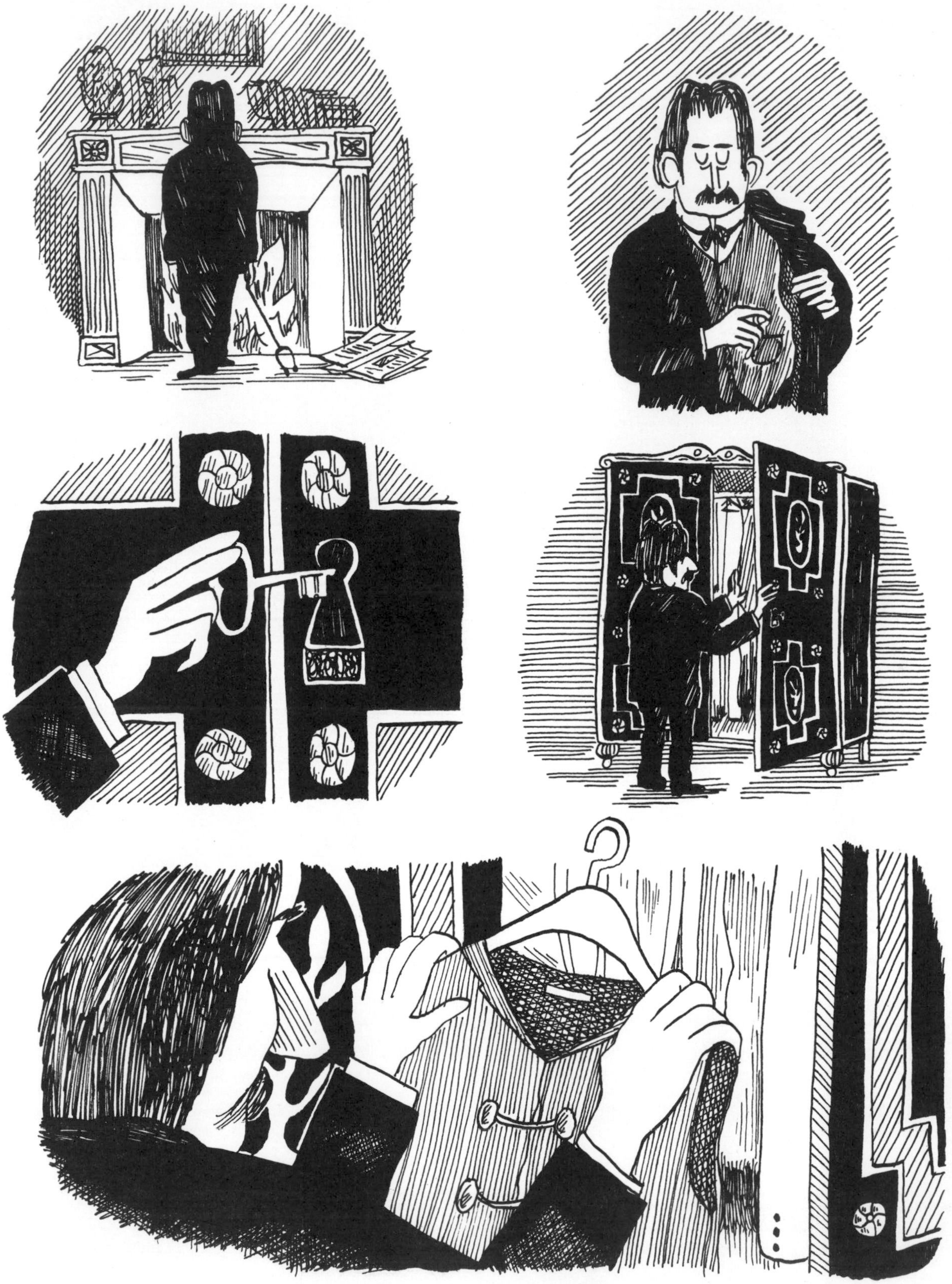

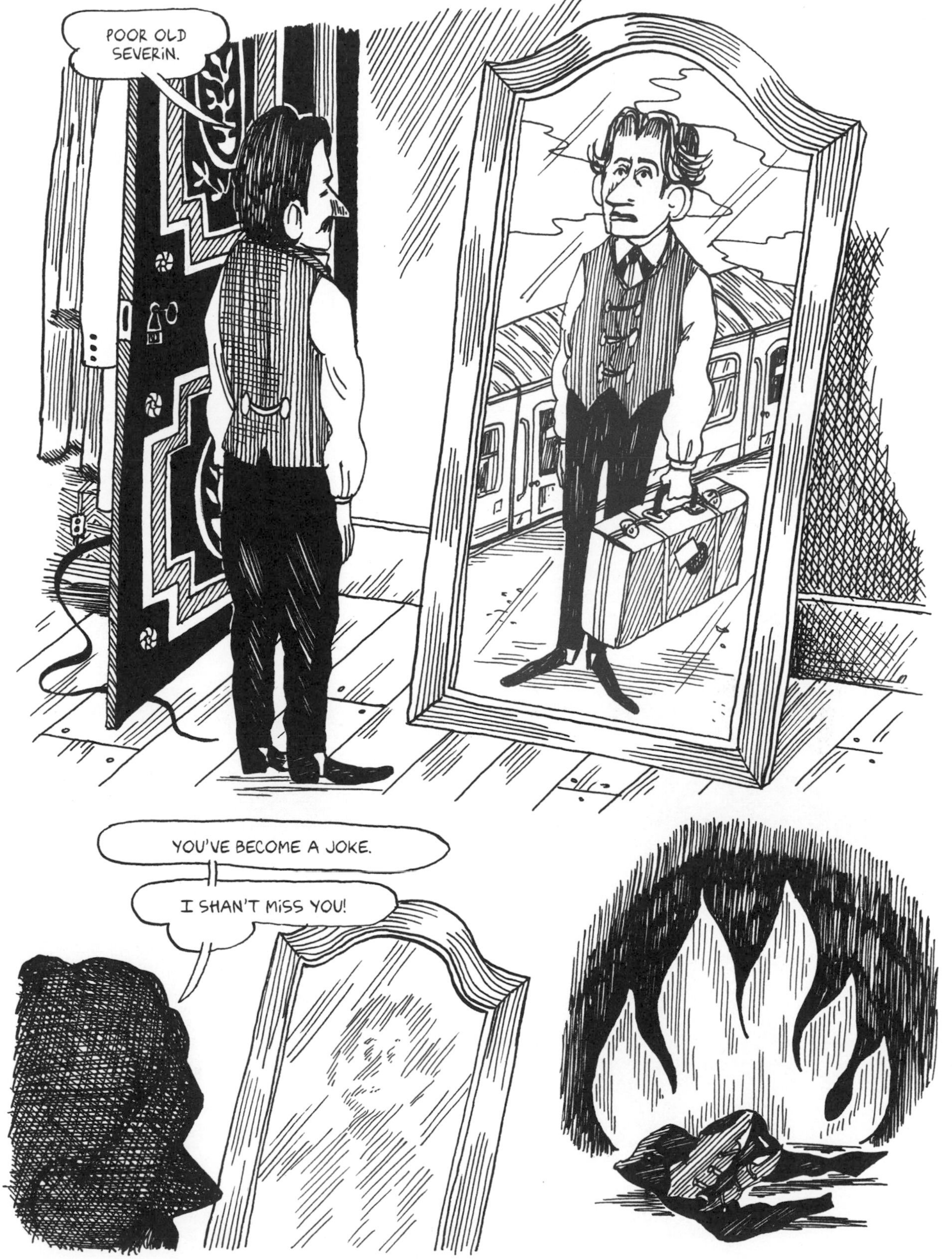
POOR OLD SEVERIN.
YOU'VE BECOME A JOKE.
I SHAN'T MISS YOU!

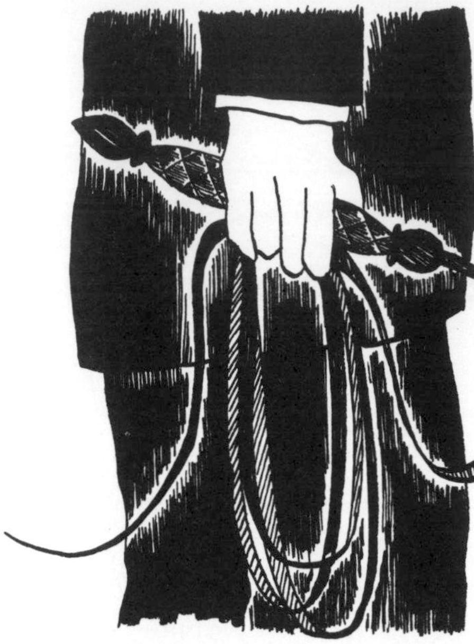

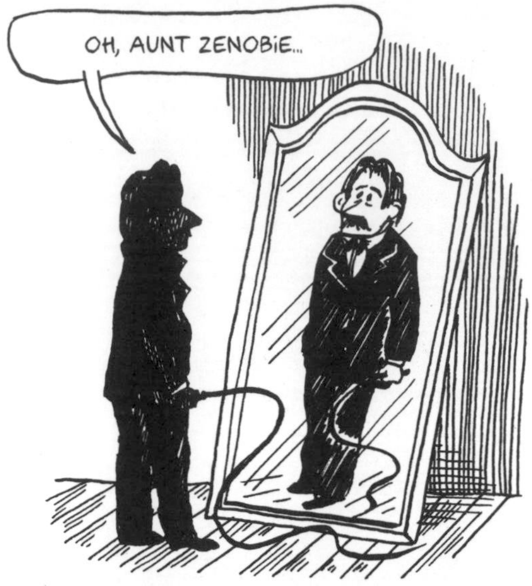
OH, AUNT ZENOBIE...

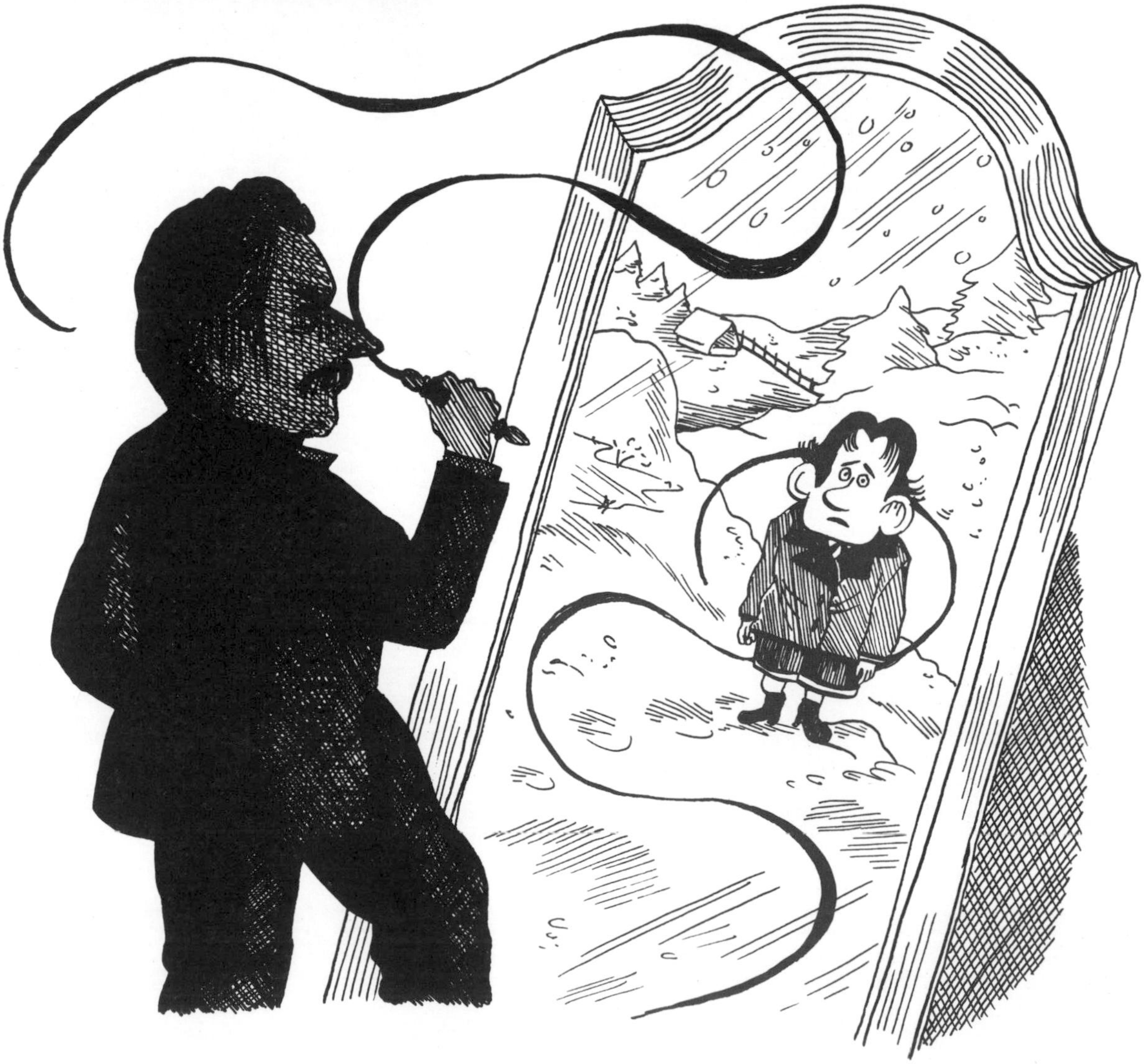

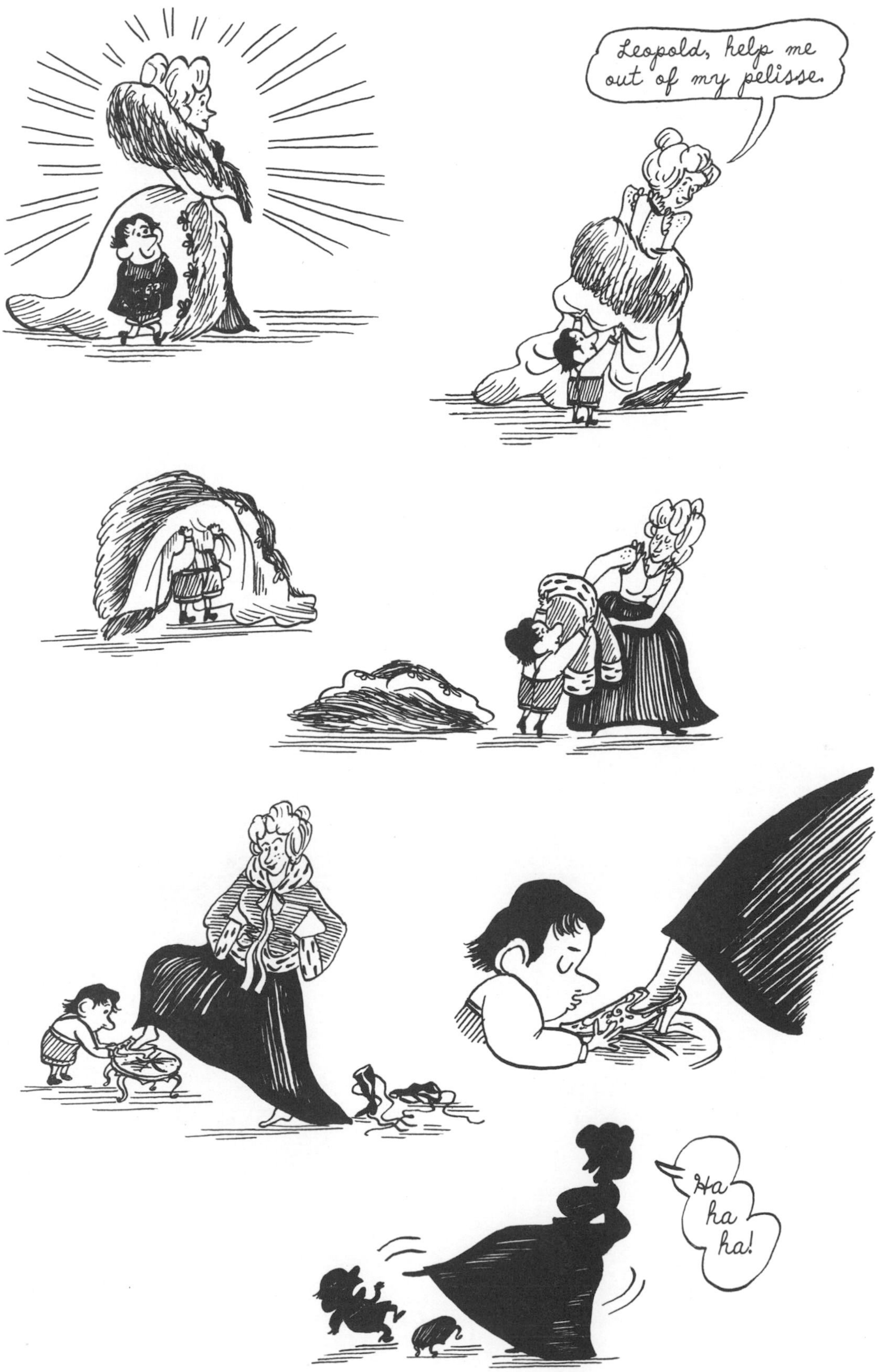
Leopold, help me out of my pelisse.
Ha ha ha!

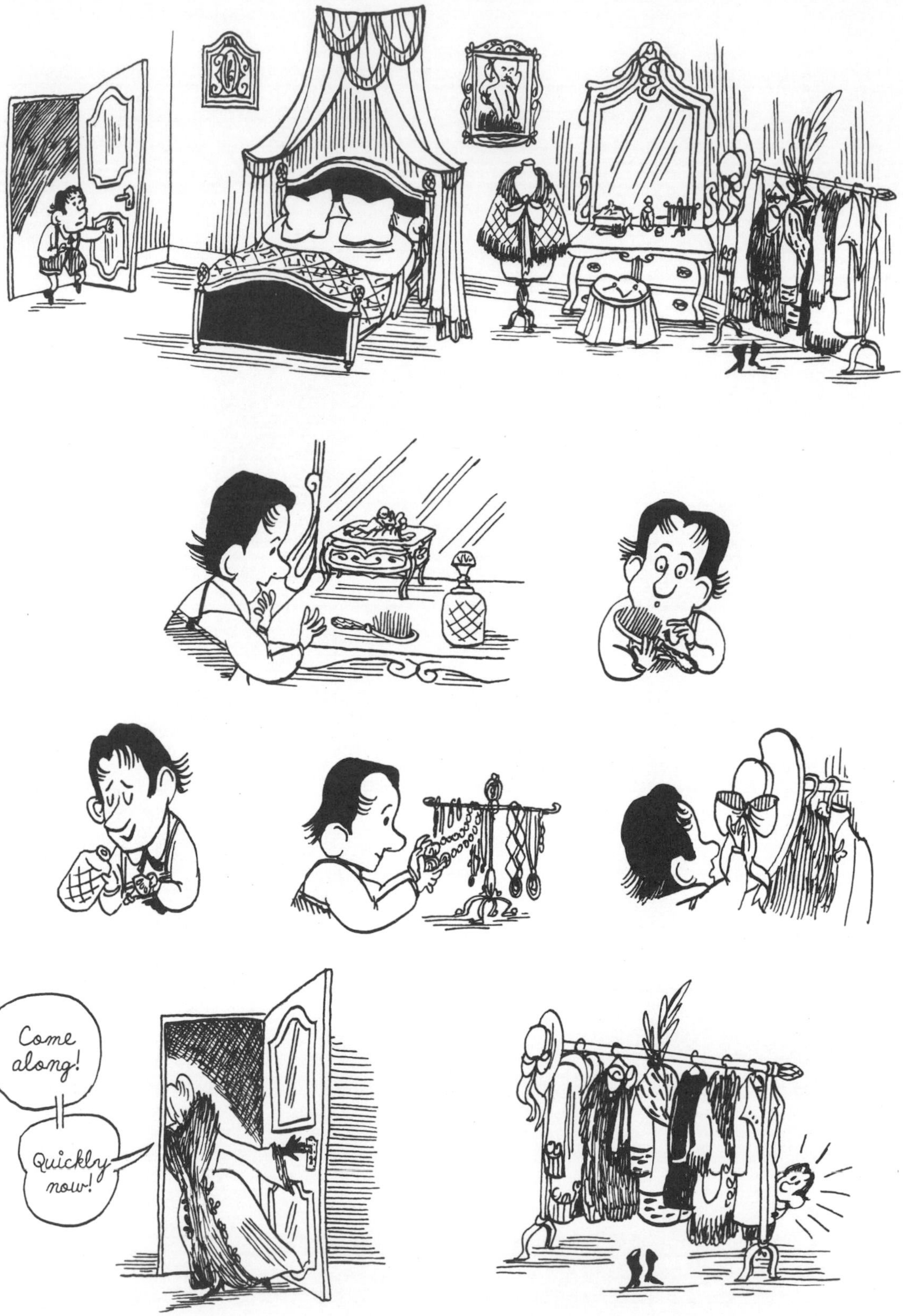
Come along!
Quickly now!

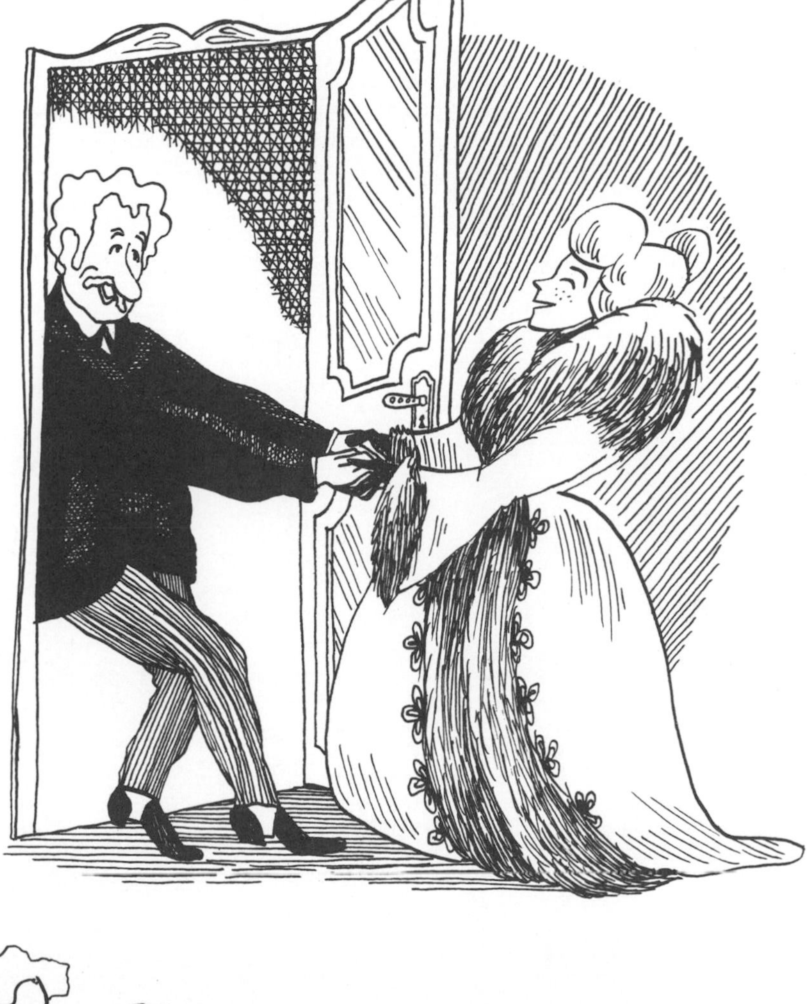

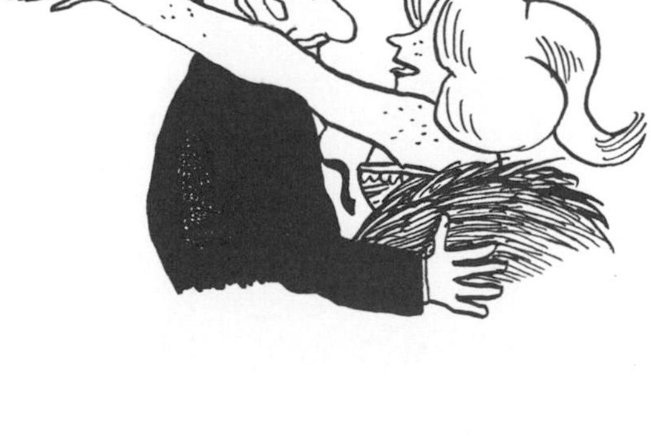

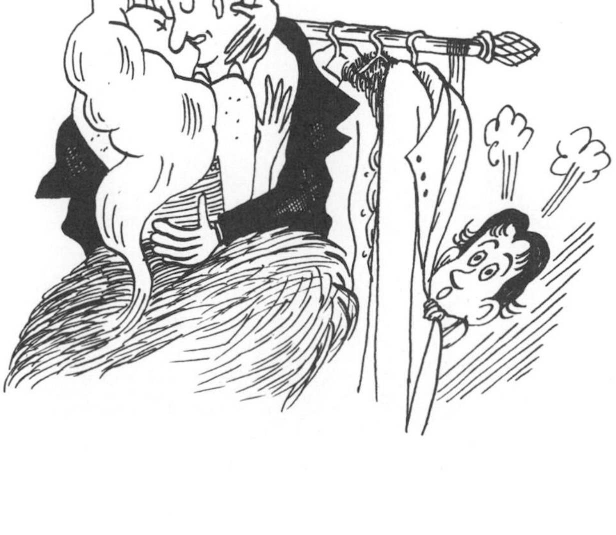

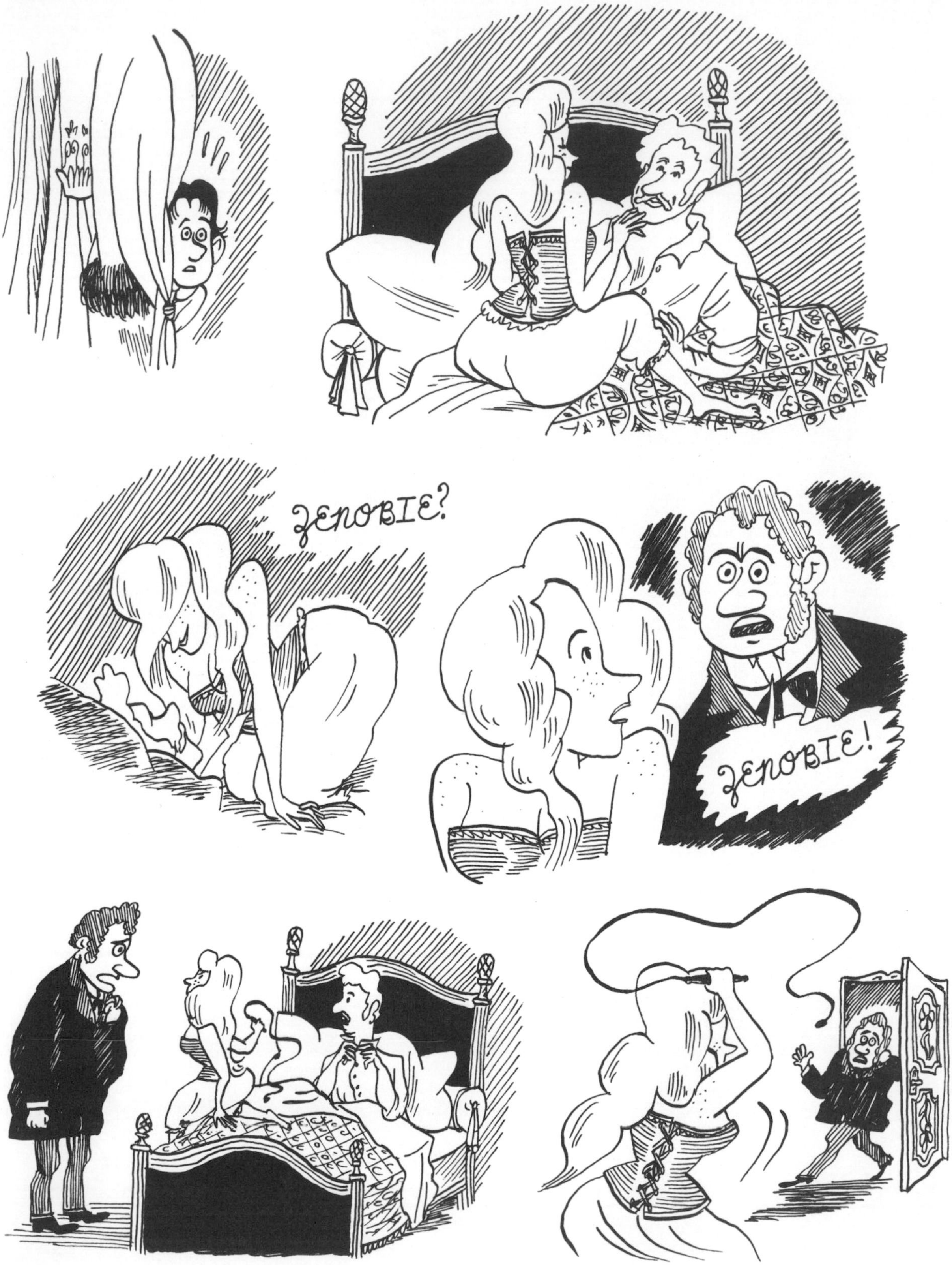
ZENOBIE?
ZENOBIE!

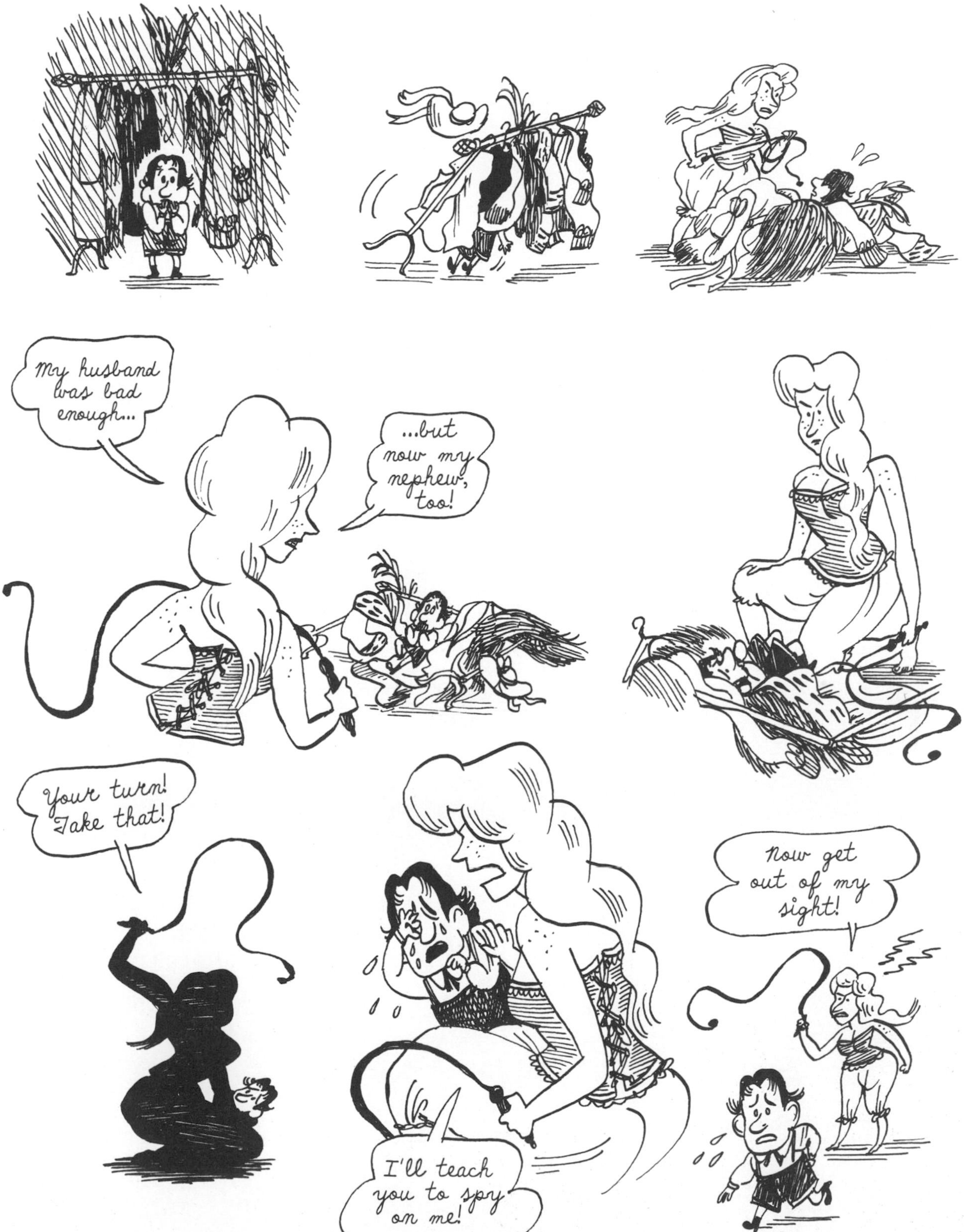
My husband was bad enough...
...but now my nephew, too!
Your turn! Take that!
I'll teach you to spy on me!
Now get out of my sight!

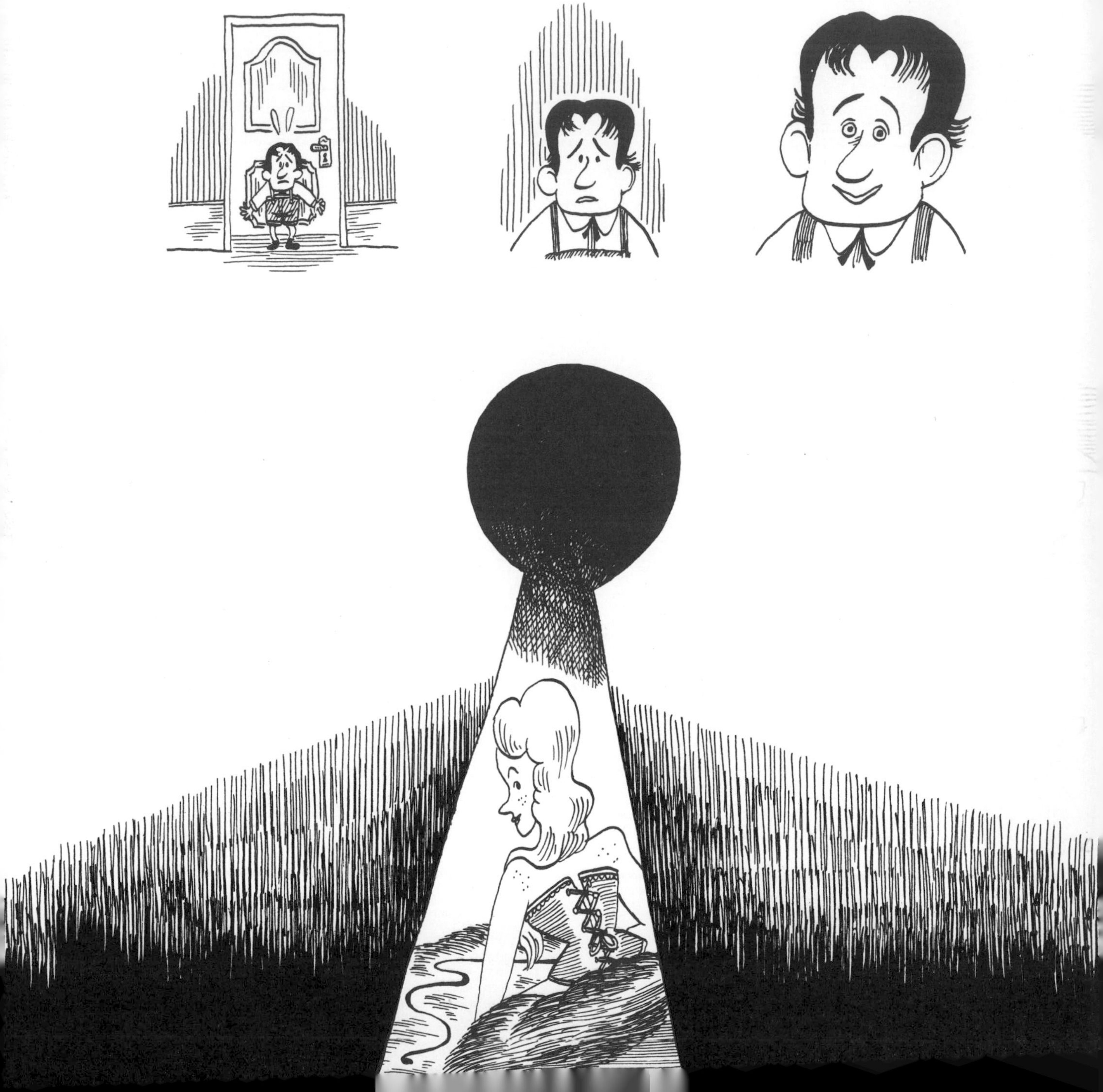

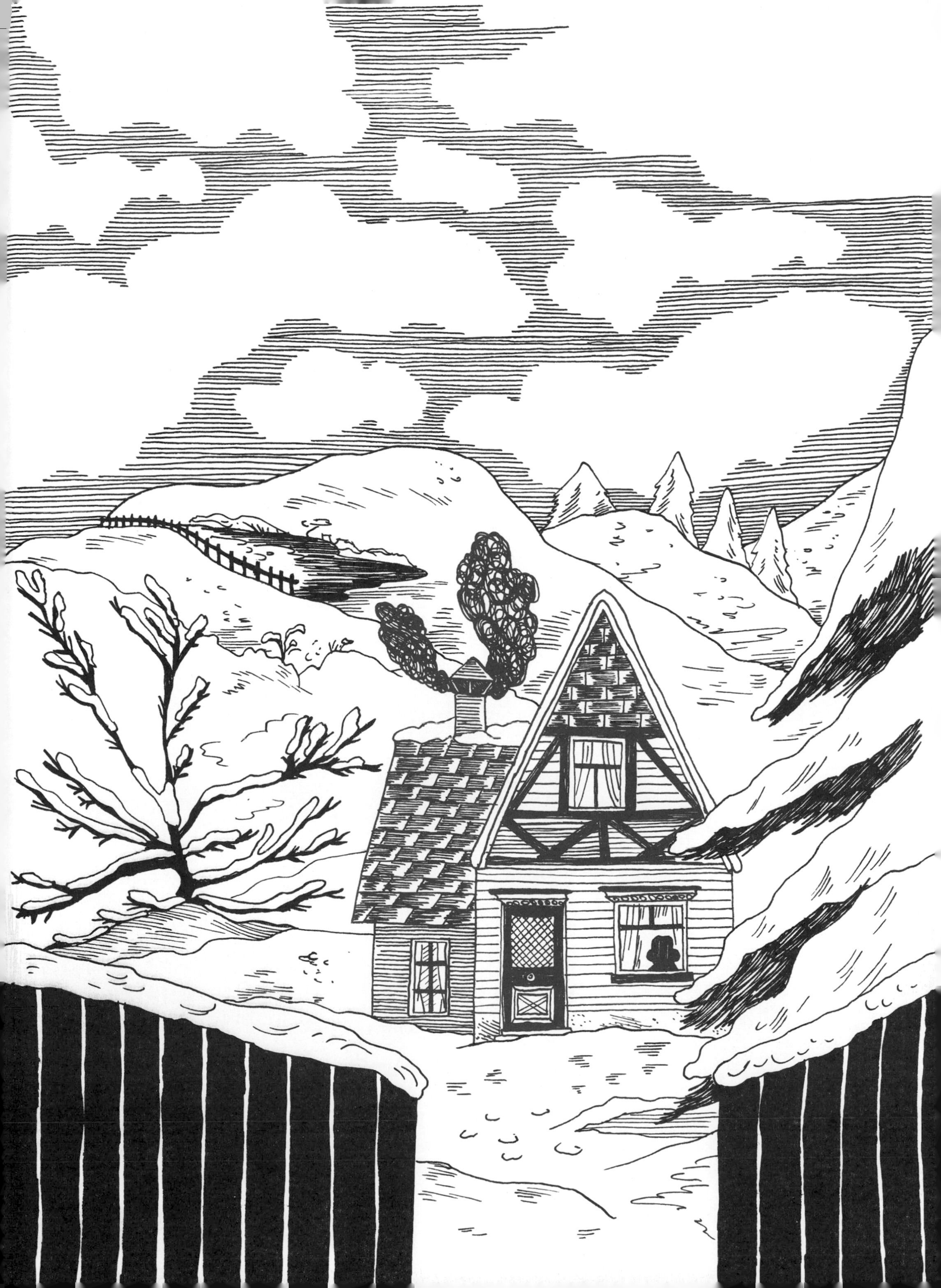

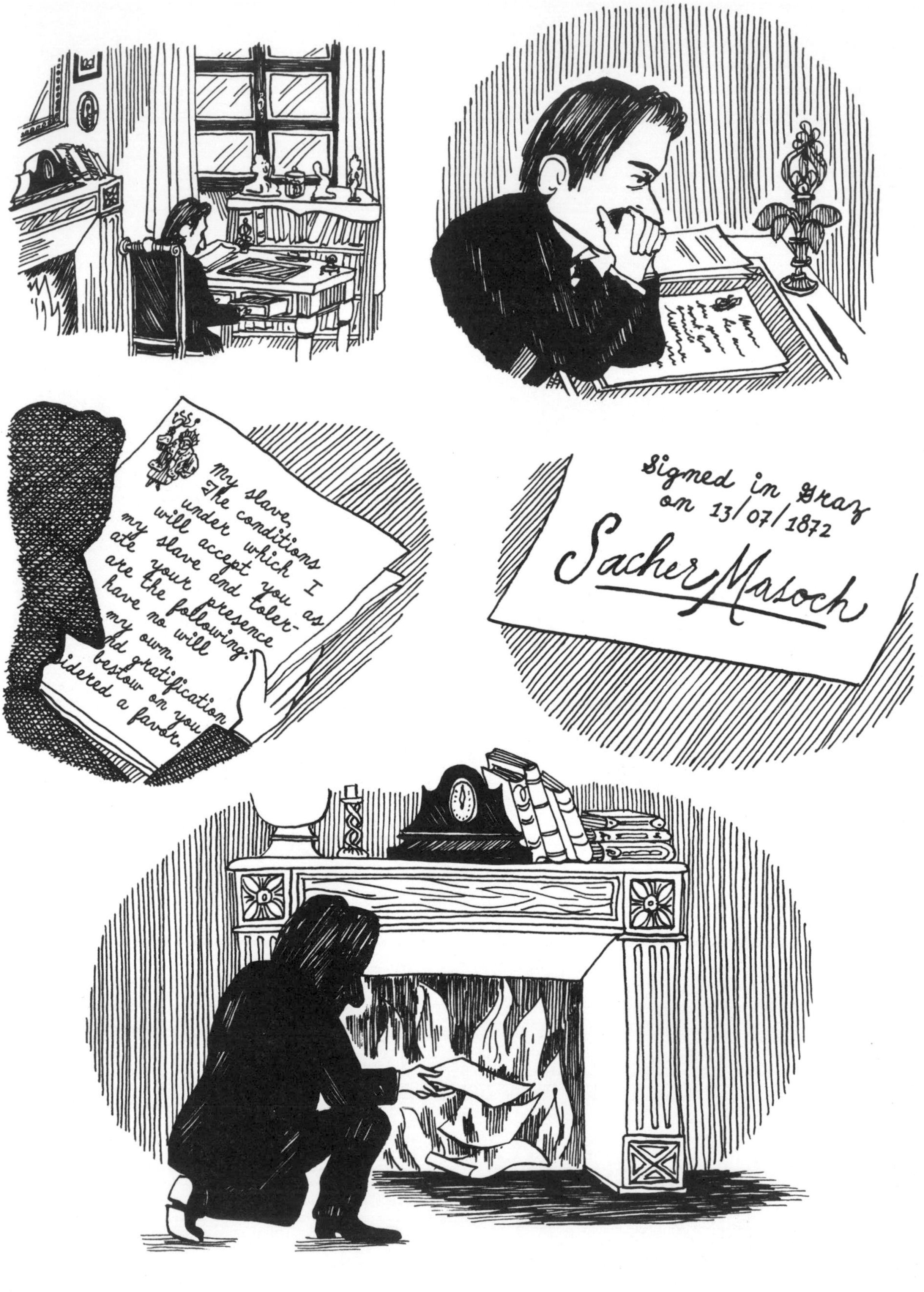
My slave,
The conditions
under which I
will accept you as
my slave and toler-
ate your presence
are the following:
have no will
my own.
nd gratification
bestow on you
idered a favor.
Signed in Graz
on 13/07/1872
Sacher Masoch

EPILOGUE

Two years later, the press erroneously report Leopold's death, describing him as "a great but poor man." As he read the article, Leopold burst out laughing and said, "What else can I do now but actually die?" He passed away on March 9, 1895. His last words were: "Love me." Just as he foresaw, his work was eclipsed by the neologism "masochism" derived from his name.

Eleven years later, Wanda von Sacher-Masoch publishes her *Confessions*, a book deeply critical of her husband's practices. The same year, a Carl Felix von Schlichtegroll brings out a spirited rebuttal, *Wanda Without Mask or Furs*, in which he defends the author using extracts from his journal. Wanda does not take long to respond with *The New Confessions of Wanda von Sacher-Masoch.*

TIMELINE

1836: Leopold von Sacher-Masoch is born in Lemberg (in present-day Ukraine) in the province of Galicia, part of the Austrian Empire. His father, Leopold von Sacher, is a police chief, and his mother, Caroline Masoch, is a doctor's daughter. The family's name is hyphenated two years after Leopold's birth.

1848: Leopold's father receives a job in Prague. The teenage Leopold witnesses the city's revolutionary uprising against Austrian rule.

1854: The family moves to Graz, in Styria. Leopold sits the examination to obtain a doctorate in Philosophy.

1857: Leopold publishes his thesis, entitled "The Revolt of Ghent Under Charles V," and begins teaching at the University of Graz.

1858: Publication of his first novel, *A Galician Story*.

1865: His first play, staged in Graz, is a success.

1868: Leopold leaves his position at the university.

1869: He meets Fanny von Pistor, the true inspiration for *Venus in Furs*. He becomes her slave for several months and they sign a contract.

1870: Publication of the first volume of what was intended to be a series of works entitled *The Legacy of Cain*. The volume comprises five short stories, including *Venus in Furs*.

1872: Aurore Rümelin enters his life and becomes his Wanda. They sign a contract.

1874: Alexander is born. Leopold and Wanda's marriage begins to suffer.

1875: Demetrius is born. The couple resume their erotic games and begin to look for their "Greek" using personal ads.

1876: Several of his short stories are translated into French for the *Revue des Deux Mondes*.

1881: After moving to Germany, Leopold takes over the cosmopolitan literary review *Auf der Höhe*.

1882: Wanda begins her relationship with Armand, whose theft of Leopold's money drives the author from the family home with his son, Alexander.

1883: Leopold is awarded France's Legion of Honor.

1884: Alexander dies of typhus.

1885: The literary review is sold off.

1887: Leopold obtains a divorce from Wanda. Despite her appeal, she is judged at fault.

1890: Leopold and Hulda are married. Professor Richard Krafft-Ebing publishes his *New Research in the Area of the Psychopathology of Sex*, in which the word "masochism" appears for the first time.

1893: Leopold founds an association devoted to adult education, in which he becomes very involved.

1895: Leopold dies in Lindheim.

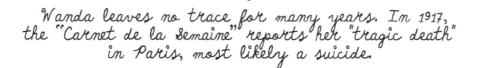

Wanda leaves no trace for many years. In 1917, the "Carnet de la Semaine" reports her "tragic death" in Paris, most likely a suicide.

FANTAGRAPHICS BOOKS INC.
7563 Lake City Way NE
Seattle, Washington, 98115
www.fantagraphics.com

Editor and Associate Publisher: Eric Reynolds
Translation: Mercedes Claire Gilliom (for Europe Comics)
Book Design: Keeli McCarthy
Production: Paul Baresh
Publisher: Gary Groth

ISBN 978-1-68396-480-3
Library of Congress Control Number 2021937419

First printing: November 2021
Printed in China

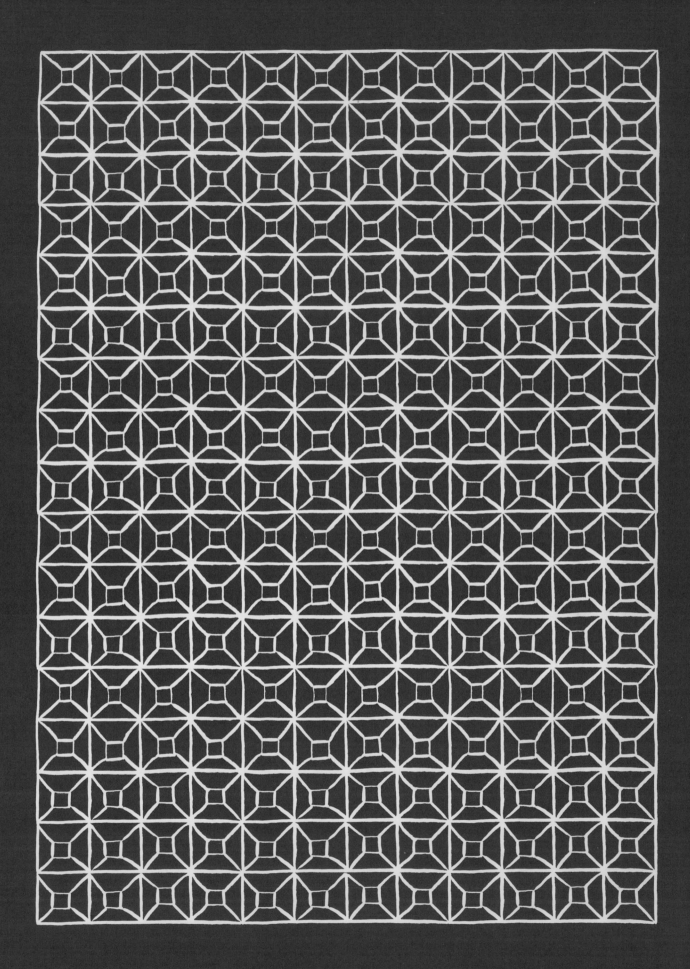